BK 649.1   C583T
TEACH YOUR CHILD DECISION MAKING : AN EFFECTIVE 8-
STEP PROGRAM FOR PA   /CLABBY, JO

W9-DFH-653

3000 697003 30017
St. Louis Community College

649.1 C583t   FV
CLABBY
TEACH YOUR CHILD DECISION MAK-
ING : AN EFFECTIVE 8-STEP PRO-
GRAM FOR ...   16.95

WITHDRAWN

**St. Louis Community
College**

Library

5801 Wilson Avenue
St. Louis, Missouri 63110

Teach Your Child
Decision Making

Teach Your Child Decision Making

AN EFFECTIVE 8-STEP PROGRAM FOR PARENTS TO TEACH CHILDREN TO SOLVE EVERYDAY PROBLEMS AND MAKE SOUND DECISIONS

John F. Clabby, Ph.D.
Maurice J. Elias, Ph.D.

Doubleday & Company, Inc.
Garden City, New York
1986

DESIGNED BY WILMA ROBIN

Library of Congress Cataloging in Publication Data

Clabby, John, 1950–
  Teach your child decision making.

  Includes index.
    1. Child rearing.   2. Decision-making in children—
Study and teaching.   I. Elias, Maurice.   II. Title.
HQ772.C53   1986   649'.1   85-10123
ISBN 0-385-19398-0

COPYRIGHT © 1986 BY JOHN F. CLABBY, PH.D. AND MAURICE J. ELIAS, PH.D.
ALL RIGHTS RESERVED
PRINTED IN THE UNITED STATES OF AMERICA
First Edition

For my wife, Wendy,
our children, Lauren, Jack, Sheila, and Patrick,
and my parents, John and Virginia

J.F.C.

For my wife, Ellen,
our children, Sara and Samara,
and my parents, Agnes and Sol

M.J.E.

Preface

With society as complex and demanding as it is today, it is more important than ever that children learn to deal with troublesome situations when their parents are not around. But the decisions facing children are growing more and more complicated—and parents will not always be beside them to provide assistance. How can parents help their children learn about "what to do" to make effective decisions and solve their *own* everyday problems?

An eight year old, upset about his parents' divorce; a fifth grader, anxious about a change to middle school; a twelve year old, never accepted for fun and games at recess—these are examples of children with problems many children face. When children do not know how to cope with these situations, it not only causes them a great deal of unhappiness but also affects their performance in school, their relationships with other people, and the way they feel about themselves. Research has found that children who do not learn how to get along with others when they are young are likely to continue to have problems in their later life. These problems arise in school and work settings as future impairments in psychological and physical health, and even relate to the likelihood that children will, at some point, break the law.

Clearly there is a need for children to learn how to solve problems while they are young. What can be done to help children learn to cope successfully with problems? There appears to be a growing recognition of the need to prepare children for their current and future social roles. An initial response to this concern, the "back to basics" movement in public schools, is facing a harsh realization: it is not enough to provide children with academic tools in a competitive world that places numerous pressures on individuals and families. Some mechanism must be found to help children establish a foundation of interpersonal and emotional coping skills that will not erode beneath the force of society's demands.

While many mental health professionals, educators, and parents find the present situation to be unacceptable, the enormity of the task has tended to stifle efforts to address it. A comprehensive response to this situation was begun in the fall of 1979 in the concerned community of Middlesex Borough, New Jersey. Realizing that the task at hand was too important to ignore, but too enormous for any one agency in the community, two psychologists joined forces and collaborated with the Middlesex schools in creating a model of partnership on behalf of children. John Clabby, Ph.D., working for the University of Medicine and Dentistry of New Jersey (UMDNJ)—Community Mental Health Center of Rutgers Medical School, and Maurice Elias, Ph.D., working at the Psychology Department of Rutgers University, met with Tom Schuyler, the principal of an elementary school in Middlesex Borough, and developed a plan for action.

A program was initiated in the school district involving elementary school teachers in the research and development of a method for teaching problem-solving and decision-making skills to children. The program was based on three ideas:

1. Children's capacity to make thoughtful decisions is related to their ability to cope with everyday problems.
2. These skills can be successfully taught.
3. Adults who are responsible for children, and come in contact with them most often, are in the best position to teach children these skills.

Elias and Clabby took a leadership role in designing a curriculum building on the work of many other educators and researchers, such as John Dewey, George Spivack, Myrna Shure, Steve Larcen, Phyllis Elardo, Ellis Gesten, Roger Weissberg, and Emory Cowen. The purpose was to help children establish a foundation of interpersonal and emotional coping skills. The lesson objectives are designed to

1. increase the children's expectation about their ability to positively influence problem situations.
2. increase their ability to perceive other people's feelings.
3. increase their ability to consider multiple and varied alternative solutions to a problem *and* consider the probable consequences of that solution before planning to do it.
4. teach them to plan ahead and prepare for any obstacles they might encounter.
5. encourage them to try out the best plan they can think of.

In this way, children learn a specific strategy for responding to problems in an active and constructive way. The emphasis is placed on thinking through problems, trying one's best, and using mistakes as important information for making better plans in the future. These themes have been organized into a strategy that teachers have been using since 1980 to teach children decision making and problem solving. This decision-making curriculum is now a regular component of the health curriculum in the Middlesex schools. It is viewed as a fourth R—an essential skill related to the goals of schooling. Students participate in decision-making lessons two times per week for two school years. Middlesex educators are also at work expanding the program to other grade levels. A number of other schools in the county and state have followed suit.

Since 1980 the success of this project has been documented in many ways, such as meaningful gains in children's problem-solving abilities, teachers' reports of improvements in the children's social behavior, and enthusiastic reports from the children that they enjoy the biweekly lessons. In addition, there has been a marked positive impact on the teachers' thinking about ways of handling classroom problem situations. Results such as these contributed to the decision of the National Institute of Mental Health and the William T. Grant Foundation in New York City to award what is now known as the Improving Social Awareness-Social Problem Solving Project (ISA-SPS) multi-year funding to develop and assess the effectiveness of this social problem-solving approach.

ISA-SPS project activities have now reached numerous school districts across the country. Through support of the Middlesex County Mental Health Board and the funding of the Middlesex County Board of Chosen Freeholders, the project is now developing a countywide training unit to offer social problem-solving training and program development consultation to other interested school districts. The ISA-SPS project has also trained professionals in New York, New Jersey, Pennsylvania, Illinois, and Virginia to use the decision-making approach in schools, clinics, and elsewhere to help children grow in a sound, healthy manner. To date, however, the success of the project has been published primarily in scientific journals and presented at professional conferences. The time has now come to make information about this strategy more available to children's first teachers: the parents.

In fact, the need to communicate with *parents* of the children in the ISA-SPS project, so that both teachers and parents can complement each others' efforts, has been strongly recognized. Both sets of adults are needed because with twenty or thirty other students in the classroom, there is not enough time for teachers to give the personal attention it takes to develop each child's individual coping strategies to the fullest. In addition, parents are often in a position to work with children at the moment a real problem is occurring. When parents have the skills to help children apply problem solving to their real-life situations, it enhances learning and increases the chances that their children will apply the ideas they learn to real-life problems.

In this book we have attempted to describe for parents and other interested adults the strategy we have developed and researched for teaching children decision making for everyday living. The strategy is based around a series of thought-provoking steps that provides a framework for parents to help children learn to think effectively and cope with life's daily challenges. Rather than offer a wide variety of procedures, we have endeavored to present activities and examples that describe one basic procedure for teaching children a step-by-step decision-making strategy. We have attempted to take parents through each step of the procedure as if they were being led through the dark by an encouraging and instructive guide. This guide is called *Teach Your Child Decision Making*.

Acknowledgments

Without doubt this book represents the work and experiences of many, many people. Indeed, we consider ourselves fortunate to have been able to collaborate with numerous caring and talented people over the past seven years. There are several who have made very special contributions to this book, which we would like to specifically acknowledge.

Charlotte Hett is a specialist in the area of school-home partnerships and in particular on how parents can fully become involved in their child's education. She is a certified teacher, has been involved in the administration of a variety of social service agencies, and is a tireless advocate for parents. Ms. Hett was a constant source of encouragement during the preparation of this book and was invaluable during the final stages of editing. She was a principal consultant in the writing of Chapter 13, concerning decision making and children's education, and we are privileged to have benefited from her sensitivity and insights.

Peggy Rothbaum, Ph.D., is a developmental psychologist, who has specialized in understanding expectable emotional stresses which accompany chronic pediatric conditions. In that latter capacity, she has served as a consultant to the Department of Pediatrics at the University of Medicine and Dentistry of New Jersey's primary teaching hospital, Middlesex General University Hospital. She is presently a postdoctoral fellow in the Rutgers-Princeton Program in mental health research which is supported by the National Institute of Mental Health. Within this program Dr.

Rothbaum is pursuing her work on psychological aspects of long-term pediatric conditions and public policy concerning mental health. Dr. Rothbaum has also served as a principal statistical consultant to our research team, and she was instrumental in motivating us to write this book. Her belief in the value of our work has been energizing. In addition to assisting in the preparation of the prospectus for this book, Dr. Rothbaum was the primary contributor to the preparation of Chapter 12, for which we are grateful. She acknowledges Drs. Edward Krisiloff and Max Salas for reviewing her contribution, as we also do.

There are many individuals who have contributed greatly to our understanding of how to teach decision making. Tom Schuyler, first as the principal of Hazelwood Elementary School and later as principal of Von E. Mauger Middle School both in Middlesex Borough, New Jersey, has been a primary mentor to us in understanding how to bring innovation into the schools. We have also learned much from teachers in Middlesex and other districts. Among those are master teachers of problem solving and decision making, with whom we have worked most closely: Eileen Eichner, Jo Feder, Regina Forgash, Helene Goodwin, Jackie Lutman, and Karen Welland. Both their work and ours has been made possible through the encouragement of school administrators, particularly Virginia Brinson, Ron Campbell, Robert Conway, David Ottoviano, Phil Sidotti, Bud Van Hise, and Gene Vescia. In the South Plainfield, New Jersey, public schools, a similar array of professional educators have been contributors to our thinking and have allowed us to work with children and parents in their community. They include Mario Barbiere, Sol Heckelman, Len Tobias, Sue Grimes, Lillian Kaiser, Rich Flamini, Anne Kaczorowski, and Joe Kovaleski. And parents in both school districts have shown openness and caring for their children by working with us in a spirit of striving for improvement in education.

The financial and consultative support of the William T. Grant Foundation of New York City and the National Institute of Mental Health has allowed us to planfully explore and research the benefits of teaching decision making to children and parents. Robert Haggerty, Robert Rapoport, and Linda Pickett of the Grant Foundation have especially encouraged our action-research work in this area.

There have also been numerous professional colleagues who have served as mentors or guides. We especially note with appreciation Gary Lamson, George Spivack, Myrna Shure, Steve Larcen, Bruce Blakeslee, Steve Gordon, Stefani Sheppa, Neil Geminder, Karen Marcus, Lucille Carr-

Kaffashan, Linda Sabo, and the marvelous office staff at the Northern Community Focus Team of the UMDNJ-Community Mental Health Center.

To bring this book to fruition, we were fortunate to work with four other people. Linda Bruene, research coordinator for our research team, helped organize the development of our prospectus and, through her buoyant spirit and leadership, taught us a great deal about decision making and problem solving. Denise Marcil believed in the value of our work and took the time to visit the schools and see our approaches in action. Without her we would simply have a set of ideas. As our literary agent, she helped shape our work into a coherent whole. Susan Schwartz, our editor at Doubleday, shared our enthusiasm about the importance of parents' teaching decision making to their children. She is a remarkable editor— insightful, caring, supportive, and meticulous. Finally, Annette Martini bore the brunt of manuscript preparation. She worked cheerfully, helped us meet our deadlines, and did so in her usual, excellent manner.

Our thanks also to our many talented undergraduate and graduate students and the children and parents with whom we have been fortunate to work. We hope we have returned some small part of what we have learned from them.

The word "acknowledgment" seems so inadequate to describe the contribution of our wives and children, and other family members to our efforts. This book is enriched because of the love, support, and patience you have shown.

Contents

Preface   vii

PART ONE
Giving Your Children the Tools They Need

1: Parenting: Using All That You Know   3
2: Preparing Your Child to Cope in the Real World   26

PART TWO
A Step-by-Step Approach for Decision Making

3: Getting Ready for Decision Making   47
4: Look for Signs of Different Feelings   67
5: Tell Yourself What the Problem Is   91
6: Decide on Your Goal   116
7: Think of As Many Solutions and Consequences As You Can   141
8: Choose Your Best Solution   168
9: Plan It and Make a Final Check   192
10: Try It and Rethink It   219

PART THREE
*Special Applications of
the Decision-Making Strategy*

11: Keeping the Channels Open:
Being a Decision-Making Parent with Your Teenager   251
12: Decision Making with Children Needing Special,
Long-Term Care   270
13: Decision Making and Your Child's Education   291
14: Not for Children's Problems Only: Practicing
What You Teach   313

Index   333

I

Giving
Your Children
the Tools They Need

Getting teased, being dared to do something risky, and feeling left out of a school activity are all examples of everyday problems that confront children. How are children prepared to handle situations such as these? What tools do they need to cope with problems and make decisions? And how do parents try to guide their youngsters toward sound, sensible growth and independent functioning in an increasingly complex world?

In Part One, we help parents identify the approaches they use to help children deal with everyday problems. We also explore the origins of these parenting "styles" by guiding parents through the completion of a "Parenting Family Tree." These active ways of learning allow the major points of Part One to be made. We examine what parents already use and value in their own parenting styles and help parents become aware of how these approaches have been learned. Next, parents are introduced to an eight-step decision-making strategy that children can learn to use when they are faced with difficulties, stress, or decisions that have to be made. By using specific examples, we show parents our approach to teaching their children decision making for everyday living.

1

Parenting:
Using All That You Know

"Mommy, what should I wear today?"
"Dad, the kids are picking on me. I don't know what to do."
"Mrs. Smith, should we do our math now or later?"
"Mom, I won't know anybody there. Do you think I should still go?"

These are the voices of some of our children. When they ask us these kinds of questions, they can sound a bit uncertain and even underconfident. What steps can we take to help our children handle problematic situations? One of our tasks may be to prepare our children to handle problematic situations with good judgment and some confidence, because we know that as our children grow, they'll develop more and more independence. Our children go to school, play away from home, and visit friends in their homes. If we can prepare our children for those times when we or another adult will not be there, then we have done something important for them. That is what this book is all about—to try to help you in your efforts to raise confident children who can think for themselves. Decision-making and problem-solving skills are our focus as we show you what a step-by-step approach can help you accomplish.

It may seem surprising, but choosing to read this means that you have probably done some decision making. You've balanced a number of options and selected one of them. In the process (and you may not have even been aware of having done it), you may have chosen not to talk to someone, take a rest, or plan some other activity. At almost the same time, you made a decision about whether to sit or lie down, or listen to music or not as you read. You've done a lot of quick thinking. Unfortunately too many children grow up to be adults who have difficulty at work, with their families, or with their friends because they have never learned how to think effectively before they act. Consider those adults you know who seem to feel especially helpless and upset when they have to make a choice about whether to stay with or leave a job or a relationship, or even what to order for dinner. Why is it that some people know the importance of planning their actions? What is it about some people that allows them to make choices with competence and confidence? At an early age these individuals were taught how to make decisions. Most of us, as adults, don't recall our parents' teaching us decision making in a straightforward or deliberate way. Mostly we recall picking up ideas as we went along, learning from painful mistakes, paying attention and changing our styles as a result. For many of us, it is hard to remember how we learned decision-making skills.

Fortunately for us and our children things are much different and more structured today. Due to what is now known about decision making, children don't have to learn decision making in a haphazard and casual way. Certainly, if left on their own, they will learn something about decision making. We now know that children do much better if they have been exposed to some deliberate training in decision-making skills. For the past seven years, in our Improving Social Awareness-Social Problem Solving Project (ISA-SPS) we've been teaching decision making to many children in the schools. Specifically, we developed a comprehensive two-year, classroom-based decision-making curriculum. Then using the curriculum, we taught children directly ourselves. We next trained teachers and school administrators to teach decision making to youngsters. As practicing psychotherapists, we have also used decision making to help particularly troubled families. This book contains activities for families that were inspired by our practice and research in helping children learn decision making at school. Our efforts have been guided by action-research; that is, we have tried, every step of the way, to examine systematically how well the children have learned. Here are some of the things we've discovered.

> Children *can be taught* a series of decision-making steps.
> They *enjoy learning it.*
> They *put these steps to use* in their everyday lives.
> They handle the stresses of the real world better than children who have not yet been taught decision making.

> Adults who teach decision making to children, themselves improve as decision makers.

It seems that everyone benefits!

This book is our effort to respond to the many requests we have received from parents who want to use some of the decision-making teaching that their child's classroom teachers are now using. As your child's first and most important teacher, you are in a unique position to help your youngster use decision making to grow in happiness and confidence. You can help your child develop the ability to negotiate an ever more complex world.

It has been our experience that when children do not know how to think through problematic situations, it can cause them a great deal of unhappiness. A five year old may be upset about taking a bus to school, a nine year old may feel helpless about how to deal with a school buddy, and a thirteen year old can feel confused about how to handle peer pressure to smoke or abuse alcohol. Feeling distressed or helpless about such difficulties can also affect their performance at school, their relationships with others, and the way they feel about themselves. In fact, research over the past ten years tells us that the more skilled a person is at decision making, the less likely he or she will become delinquent, abuse drugs or alcohol, or have serious psychological problems.

Parenting Styles

As parents ourselves, we feel that it is helpful to start by getting to know our own individual parenting style. What is the most frequent way I respond to a problem that my child might have? The Parenting Styles Activity which follows is a quick way to get you thinking about your approach. Once you know a bit more about your style, consider what has influenced you to be the kind of parent you are today. Am I imitating some part of my mother's behavior or am I actually reacting to a feature of hers that I did not like? The Parenting Family Tree will help you in that regard. When we better understand our parenting approach and where it comes from, we will be better able to consciously use our parenting skills in a controlled fashion to teach decision making to our children.

Now take a moment to get a pen or pencil. We would like you to take some time to look at some situations where you as a parent will be making decisions.

Think about your child for a moment. Consider how he or she plays and interacts with you, family members, or friends. Think about yourself, too. As you read this section, remember the approaches that you have taken when you have encountered your child in the kind of situations that we will present. We have chosen to provide only a minimum of detail so that you can fill in the plots and make them more personally significant for you. Circle the letter of the response that you think you would make. Some patterns will appear as you move along from situation to situation. Just give your first impression and move on. At the end, we will discuss your responses.

Parenting Styles Activity (PSA)

1. One rainy day your child has a group of friends over whom she hasn't seen in a long time. You are glad that she is still able to be friendly with these other children. As they play, some of them are making more and more noise, talking loudly and excitedly with each other about what they are doing. You are beginning to get mildly annoyed.
   A. You say, "It sounds like you all are pretty excited. Sometimes I get a little bit bothered though when it gets too noisy."
   B. You decide, for the time being, to move away from the noise to another room. You feel that because your child is enjoying what is going on, you will let her play with the friends and then gradually quiet down.
   C. You say, "Why don't you try a game where you don't have to talk so loudly?"
   D. You approach the children and say, "What are some ideas that you have about playing together without making as much noise?"
2. Your child has just come home from school. She has finished eating her snack and has gone outside without cleaning up after herself.
   A. You say, "I feel frustrated when I have to keep after you about cleaning up. I know you must be tired of it too."
   B. You decide to let her dish and glass stay where they are. You don't clean them up for her but leave them for her to take care of when she comes back. She doesn't get anything else until these items are put away.

    C. You remark, "It will take you two minutes to clean up your dish and glass. Why don't you just come in now and get it over with."

    D. You approach her and say, "What will happen if you don't clean your plate up?"

3. You are at a picnic with other families whom you know. You notice that your child is sitting away from groups of other children who are playing kickball and softball. Your youngster, not participating, looks sad to you.

    A. You move alongside your child and say, "It looks like you're feeling a little sad because you're not playing with the others. I've felt that way too sometimes."

    B. You realize that being "left out" sometimes happens to both children and to adults. Because your child is going to have to handle these situations on his own when you are not there, you decide to watch and not get involved at this time.

    C. You quietly move over to your child and suggest, "If you would like to play, maybe you could ask one of the children if you could join in."

    D. You sit down next to your youngster and say, "I wonder what ideas you can think of that will help you get the other children to include you."

4. You have gone to the playground with your child. You watch as your youngster walks up to a group of children he does not know, asks to join, and then is refused. Your child looks hurt and upset.

    A. You say, "It can sure make you feel sad when the others won't let you play with them."

    B. You decide not to talk to your child at this moment, feeling that he can probably work it out on his own.

    C. You observe, "Why don't you wait for a better time and ask again?"

    D. You say, "I wonder what ideas you have that might help you out."

5. Your child has a friend visiting. This friend is using a red pencil. You see your child walk over, grab the pencil, and say, "You've had that long enough. It's my turn now."

    A. You say, "It's hard to wait for something that you really want."

    B. You comment, "Look, here is an idea. Why don't you apologize and use the black pencil for now and then switch in a few minutes."

C. You decide to wait and not say something at this time because you feel that your child will learn more by this friend's reaction than from your interference right now.

D. You say, "How else could you have gotten that pencil?"

6. You are at your mother's house for a holiday gathering of family and friends. It is a busy, happy time. You look into the basement where the children from the various families have been playing together. You see a youngster, irritated, push your child away from a toy.

A. You approach your child and the other youngster and comment, "It is hard when two people want the same thing. Sometimes that can get you into a fight."

B. You feel a little sad and somewhat irritated yourself. But at this point, you decide not to get actively involved. You continue to keep a watchful eye and ear. You are acting this way because you realize that children learn from other children how to be in a group.

C. You crouch next to both of the children and suggest, "Why don't you just take turns? Each of you can play with it for a while."

D. You move alongside your youngster and the other child with your arms supportively on your child's shoulder and remark, "I wonder what ideas you might have about how to be able to use that toy that you want."

7. The family is having dinner together. Your son does not like his dinner and is ignoring it, talking instead.

A. You turn toward him and say, "It's hard when you don't like what's being served. Try your best though."

B. You feel that it is fruitless to try to persuade him to eat something he doesn't like. You might end up in an argument that ruins your own and the others' dinner. Therefore, you ignore his disinterest and plan on giving him no dessert or snack after dinner.

C. Since you know that he likes some moderate seasoning on his food, you suggest, "Why don't you try a little butter on it to make it taste better?"

D. When he has quieted down a bit, you say, "How can you make your dinner taste better?"

8. Your child has recently got a haircut. You overhear one of the children in the neighborhood tease your youngster about it. Your child silently enters the house.

A. You approach your child and observe, "It can really make you feel sad when you get teased."

B. Uncomfortable as it is for you, you decide to let things go for the time being because you feel that your child can learn from this experience by sorting it out on her own.

C. You go over to your youngster and say, "You know, maybe it would be a good idea to try to ignore remarks like that or try as hard as you can to not let it get to you."

D. You wait a few moments and remark, "What are some things you could do when you get teased?"

9. It is a Saturday afternoon. You are inside and you happen to glance out the window at your child playing ball with some friends. A ball that your youngster throws accidently breaks a neighbor's window. You see your neighbor begin to irritatedly talk to your child.

A. You say to your youngster, "It can be pretty upsetting when you accidently hurt someone's property or feelings."

B. You don't go outside at this point. Rather, you let your neighbor's words have their impact, feeling that this exchange is what your child and his friends need in order to be more cautious next time.

C. You go over to your child and say, "Maybe you could apologize and offer to do some work to make up for the broken window."

D. You go outside and comment to your child, "What are some ideas that you have that might make the situation better?"

10. Dinner is over and you are at the table going through your mail, paying the bills, and so on. Your child comes over to you, says that she is having some trouble with math homework, and asks, "Could you please help?" You say that you are "busy now, but will be able to help in a couple of minutes." But your child keeps coming back every few moments, demanding that you stop what you are doing.

A. You remark, "I am beginning to get angry because you keep asking me over and over to do something when I have asked you to wait until I am done. You are probably getting a little bit upset too."

B. You become irritated now. Because you feel that people should know about the impact that their behavior has on others, you raise your voice somewhat and say, "Stop it! This is impolite and I don't want you to interrupt me again! Understood?"

C. You suggest, "Why don't you put your math down for now 'til I

am done here. If you can, start on your spelling or take a break
until I am done."

D. You say, "What are some of the things that you can do until I get
a chance to help you?"

We're sure that if you were *actually* faced with these situations, the
particulars of how and when they took place would affect how you handle
them. Also, there are certainly many more ways to have handled these
situations. For example, giving a no-nonsense directive in some of those
situations may be another good approach. Too, recalling with your child a
way of handling the problem which he or she may have used successfully
in the past could help. But we want to call some particular techniques to
your attention. So let's take a look at one way of categorizing the responses
that you have chosen. Count the number of times you have chosen each
response, A, B, C, or D, and put that in the blank space next to the
corresponding letter.

____   A. *Verbalizer of Feelings*
____   B. *Real-Life Consequences*
____   C. *Giver of Advice*
____   D. *Elicitor of Ideas*

Verbalizer of Feelings. If you chose this category often, it may reflect
the value that you place in making sure that your own and your child's
feelings are understood in a problem situation. You may feel that before
any other sensible action can be taken, the parties involved should reduce
their confusion, identify what is going on, and then feel understood.

Real-Life Consequences. Those situations prompting you to select B
responses reflect the belief that oftentimes children learn the most when
they experience the impact of their actions upon other people. We are
referring to those situations where your child won't listen to you anyway
and then you feel frustrated and rejected because your ideas are ignored.
Sometimes parents needlessly and fruitlessly get involved and no one wins.

Giver of Advice. When you choose C responses, it means you are gently
trying to educate your child by pointing out a sensible course of action.
Later we'll refer to this approach as *suggesting* a way for your child to
think or act. It comes from a part of us that wants to give some reassuring,
educative answer to the complex problems that our children encounter, or
to start the ball rolling when a child is hesitating about what to plan or do.

Elicitor of Ideas. Those who chose D responses are seeing this encounter as an opportunity to help a child practice thinking independently. To elicit ideas, you must *ask* your children open-ended, thought-provoking questions. *Asking* signifies the awareness that you will not always "be there" when your children are stuck, and you want your children to get in the practice of generating their own ideas . . . to eventually *ask themselves the questions* that you are asking now.

Take a look, for a moment, at how your pattern emerged. When categorizing responses to the Parenting Styles Activity, some parents may strongly identify with one type of response. Others have two predominant responses, others have three favorites, and so on. It's as varied as the number of parents and their individual preferences. In fact, it may be advantageous for each of us to have a variety of parenting styles, which we can use flexibly, based upon different circumstances. You will see that you can use a technique in conjunction with whatever beliefs you have about how to raise children.

We don't believe that there are correct answers to be given to specific problems that parents and children have. Each situation is unique. We respect this uniqueness and therefore encourage "decision-making"—an approach that will allow each parent and child to select the best of several of his or her own solutions to the problem. So, when you are very busy and your child asks repeatedly for help with math homework, you may have chosen any one of the four parental responses. It depends upon the point you are trying to make with your youngster or the value that you are trying to teach at the time.

Exploring the Roots of Your Parenting Style

You've made the first move in learning about decision making. You've taken a brief look at your own style and values. Once you know your parenting style, you might find it helpful to discover where that style came from. One influence, certainly, is one's own parents. In our work we've looked at the influence parents have on how their children develop as parents. How much of what you do as a parent is a duplication of, or reaction to, one's parents' style? To answer this question, we can diagram a Parenting Family Tree, representing the important parenting influences in a family.

Let's look at four families and what may have led four different sets of parents to carry out four different solutions to the same problem. In this case let's re-examine problem situation 10. Take a moment to think about why you chose the answer that you did. Imagine your youngster repeatedly trying to ask for your help with homework while you are busy doing something else.

The Russell Family. Jan Russell is thirty-two years old. She is divorced and works outside the home as a teacher. She is the mother of ten-year-old David and eight-year-old Erica. Her ex-husband Mike is an aloof, quiet man. In fact, Jan often felt she had to "read his mind" to find out what he was thinking. It certainly caused problems with the marriage. Jan's parents are still living. She remembers her father, Gregory, as a shy but affectionate person. Her mother, Barbara, was always able to state her mind about how she felt, sometimes a bit *too* harshly, as Jan recalls. David, Jan's son, repeatedly asked Jan for homework help while she was trying to balance the checkbook. She responded by saying, "Dave, I am getting angry because you keep asking me over and over again to do something when I have asked you to wait until I am done. You are probably upset too."

Here is the Russell Parenting Family Tree. In making the diagram you will see that the circles represent females and the squares represent the males. We offer a brief description of the various important influencing personalities.

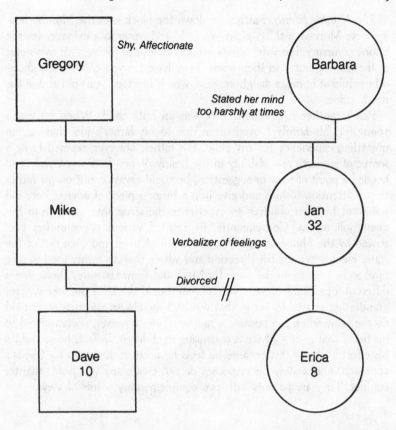

Jan, aware or not of it, adopted her mother's Verbalizer of Feelings parenting approach. Why? First, she on some level felt that Dave should never have to "read her mind" about her feelings as she had to do with her ex-husband. Second, she tried to combine the best qualities of her mother and father as an alternative. She liked her mother's emotional honesty but her mother's bluntness was a bit too hard to take. So Jan modeled a bit of her father's affection by being able to add "You are probably upset too." This addition seemed to soften things up somewhat and Jan liked that. In this encounter with Dave, Jan Russell was demonstrating her uniqueness. This approach may work very well for her. We think she will be more effective as a mother if she becomes aware of this particular style that she has and why she chose it.

The Monroe Family. Farther on down the block lives the Monroe family. Pete Monroe is thirty-eight years old and works as a manager for the phone company. His wife, Sheila, works the four-to-twelve shift as a nurse at the nursing home in their town. They have ten-year-old Mark and one other child at home, a daughter, Kim, who is fourteen years old and in the ninth grade.

Pete's mother is a widow. Pete was an only child. When he was a youngster, his family moved often due to his father's job changes, an unsettling experience for any child. His father, however, seemed to be a source of strength and stability in the family. When Pete was a child and needed a point of view or suggestion, he could always count on his father to pay attention to him and give him a tip or a piece of advice. Pete did not want his own children to experience the stress that came from frequent job moves. Consequently, he resisted various opportunities presented by the phone company to move out of town and even out of the state. He appreciated the direction and advice that his father used to give him, so he tries to do the same for Mark and Kim. His wife, Sheila, has a different idea. She believes that children should think for themselves. Her grandfather related to her in that way and she always said that she would do the same when she became a mother. Pete, however, is committed to his belief that giving advice is reassuring to children. In fact, he redoubles his effort at doing this because he feels he needs to make up for Sheila's approach. Fortunately his responses do not create any significant marital conflict. They are parents with two complementary points of view.

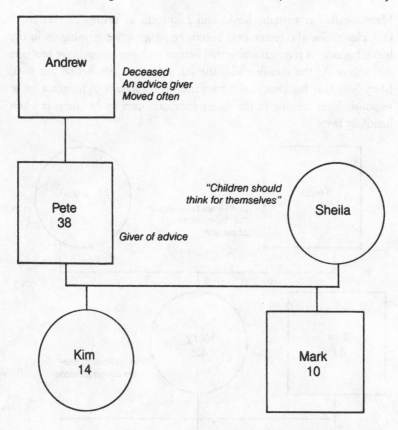

It is not surprising that when Pete is using his calculator to figure out his income tax form and Mark approaches him for the third time, he gives a *specific suggestion:* "Why don't you put your math down until I am done here. If you can, start on your spelling . . . or else take a break until I am done."

The Ryan Family. Across the street live the Ryans. Mary Ryan is forty-two years old and her husband, Tom, is forty-four. They have three children: Robert who is fifteen, Michael who is ten, and Patricia who is now seven. Two years ago Mary began working outside the home in real estate. Tom teaches physical education and coaches at the high school. Mary comes from a large Irish-American family. She was the third of five children in a busy household where both her parents worked out of the home.

Mary recalls her parents, Kevin and Maureen, as being "no-nonsense" individuals. She also remembers becoming tough while growing up in the house because of physical and verbal battles with her competitive brothers and sisters. As the middle child, she felt she was often left on her own. Mary feels that her present-day toughness and capacity to handle a lot of responsibilities are due to the direct approach used by her parents when handling her.

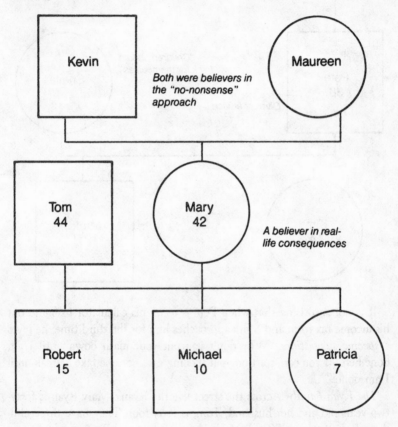

Mary has always been direct with her children and unafraid to give them a command she expects them to obey. Her husband Tom agrees. She believes that children learn social skills best by getting immediate feedback from others.

When Mary is working at home and Michael repeatedly approaches her for help she replies, "Stop it! This is impolite and I don't want you to interrupt me again. I will help you when I am done. Understood?"

The Salerno Family. One of Michael's classmates, Jennifer Salerno, lives with her father, Carl, who is thirty-one, and her mother, Marie, who is also thirty-one. Jennifer has a younger sister, Rachel, who just turned six. Marie works as a computer programmer, having gone back to school at nights when her children were younger. Carl is an electrician. Marie recalls her parents, Vincent and Anne, as loving and caring. However, she also remembers a subtle message that boys were more capable than girls. Her parents, who were second generation Italian-American, were overly protective of her. In fact, her brother Al, although one year younger, was able to stay out later on weekend nights and seemed able to do more than she could and at an earlier age. Al was able to get summer jobs at a local factory whereas Marie had to fight to be allowed to do more than baby-sit.

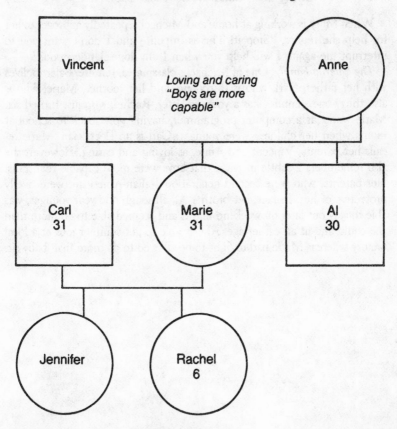

Marie still experiences subtle messages at work that men are more capable than women. She sees that men are paid more than women for the same work. Her irritation produces some lively discussion with Carl. It has affected her parenting approach too. She wants both of her daughters to feel competent and skilled. She talks to them about foreign countries, teaches them new words, and encourages their reading. Most important, she wants them to know that she values the ideas that they come up with on their own. She feels that Jennifer and Rachel, as girls, will need to feel independent since they may encounter some of the same negative subtle messages that she did. So, when Jennifer repeatedly interrupts her mother's efforts at working out a program, Marie turns to her and says, "What are some other things you can do until I get a chance to help you?"

Which family sounded most like yours? What is fascinating is that the same kind of family background can lead one parent to choose one style and another, a different style. For example, Marie Salerno was clearly committed to encouraging her two daughters' independence. Why? She felt that her parents' loving but protective approach did not give her the tough-mindedness she needed to compete in the world. She therefore chose a style of parenting in which she lets her daughters know that they have good ideas, that they can verbalize them, and that they should be willing to speak their minds. But . . . Marie Salerno could have also chosen a different approach to develop assertiveness in her children. Perhaps she could have chosen to do what Mary Ryan did, the no-nonsense approach. It all depends on how you as a parent have interpreted your experiences and what you set as your goal in parenting your children.

There are other influences that may also be important to consider:

> If your parents were immigrants or second generation, how do their
> struggles relate to your parenting approach?
> How secure were your parents financially?
> Were your parents separated or divorced?
> Were your parents healthy?
> Were they achievement oriented?
> How influential were teachers, neighbors, friends, brothers, or sisters?

Let's now think about the influences that have played a part in your life as a parent. The Parenting Family Trees that are presented in this chapter are experiences that have helped move many parents along in this process. First let's take a look at how one parent filled out her Parenting Family Tree. Jan Russell chose to be a verbalizer of feelings when her son, Dave, kept interrupting her work with his homework requests. If you remember, Jan had replied, "Dave, I am getting angry because you keep asking me over and over again to do something when I have asked you to wait until I am done. You are probably upset too."

You may want to see Jan's completed tree as a guide for how you can fill out your own Parenting Family Tree.

PARENTING FAMILY TREE of _Jan Russell_
                              Your Name

Barbara
Your Mother's Name

Gregory
Your Father's Name
my step father

Ethnic background (i.e. Polish American)
Hispanic

Ethnic background
English – I think!

How did your mother discipline you?
mostly she yelled at me

How did your father discipline you?
He never really did – mom usually was the one

Describe her approach with you when you had problems.
Even though she yelled – she could always understand my feelings

Describe his approach with you when you had problems.
He'd wait for things to calm down and then he'd listen

How did your parents get along with each other?
O.K. They got along as well as most couples I know

Were you first, only born, etc?

I'm the first;
one brother (younger)

Other influences:

I don't want my kids to have
to "read" my mind like I had
to do with my ex-husband

Jan
Child's Mother

_____
Age

Mike
Child's Father

_____
Age

divorced
11

Your Child/Children's Names and Ages

Dave (10)
Erica (8)

What parenting style of your mother would you be proud to see in yourself?

that she could tell
how I was feeling

What parenting style of your father would you be proud to see in yourself?

his affection for
his kids

Not want to see in yourself?

her bluntness

Not want to see in yourself?

too quiet!

We learned a few more things about Jan that we didn't know before. Her parents seemed to get along "okay." Her mother, Barbara, seems to have taken on a leadership role in the family. Perhaps some of her mother's ease with feelings is due to a family environment that allowed others to know how she felt. There may also have been some similarity between her father's personality and her ex-husband's. Both seem to have been quiet men. Jan gets frustrated when she has to guess how someone else feels. Perhaps she feels like she's "pulling teeth" and this feeling solidifies her need to be expressive with her kids. Jan is also the older of two children. Sometimes older children are "expected" to be achievers and win the approval of parent figures and do so by behaving "responsibly." In fact, being the oldest may have been a real factor that helped Jan handle in a "grown-up" way the responsibilities of being a working single parent.

Take a few moments to complete your own Parenting Family Tree. To do so, imagine that you are a child again at home with your parents. Think about what you might be wearing and what they are wearing. Try to picture it as clearly as you can. What do your parents' faces look like as you gaze up at them? When you get a clear picture, begin to fill in your Parenting Family Tree. Look again at how Jan completed her Parenting Family Tree. Note that she was fairly brief in her remarks. That's fine. We'd like for you now to do your own Tree with the form that we have provided. Some of the questions ask for facts such as your mother's ethnicity. Other questions seek your impressions such as "How did your mother discipline you?"

PARENTING FAMILY TREE of _____

Your Name

_____
Your Mother's Name

_____
Your Father's Name

Ethnic background (i.e. Polish American)

_____

_____

Ethnic background

_____

_____

How did your mother discipline you?

_____

_____

_____

_____

How did your father discipline you?

_____

_____

_____

_____

Describe her approach with you when you had problems.

_____

_____

_____

_____

Describe his approach with you when you had problems.

_____

_____

_____

_____

How did your parents get along with each other?

_____

_____

_____

_____

_____

Were you first, only born, etc?

_____

_____

_____

Other influences:

_____

_____

_____

Child's Mother
_____
Age

Child's Father
_____
Age

Your Child/Children's Names and Ages

_____

_____

_____

_____

What parenting style of your mother would you be proud to see in yourself?

_____

_____

_____

_____

Not want to see in yourself?

_____

_____

_____

_____

What parenting style of your father would you be proud to see in yourself?

_____

_____

_____

_____

Not want to see in yourself?

_____

_____

_____

_____

Now that you've done a Parenting Family Tree (and before that, the Parenting Styles Activity), you know more clearly who you are and where your parenting style came from. The challenge now is to realize that we don't have to be locked into the approaches that we've picked up from our past or use them just because we're accustomed to them. Rather, our challenge is to increase our repertoire of parenting skills. The decision-making steps we will present in the next chapter are ways of organizing our own thinking for a purpose: confidently preparing our children for a complex, uncertain, and exciting future.

2

Preparing Your Child to Cope in the Real World

Congratulations! You've taken a closer look at yourself as a parent! By combining the best ideas of your parents and others with your own, you've created your own unique parenting style. The decision-making strategy is another tool to add to approaches that already may be working well for you.

A major *step* in this chapter is to identify some common problems that your children might encounter. It is important to be able to imagine yourself at your child's age and experience what that might be like. Then we'll show you how to comfortably encourage problem-solving conversations with your youngster, and thereby give your child a strategy for solving them.

When we present problems at a particular age, keep in mind that those same difficulties could appear at other ages. For example, not being "first" in line at school may upset a six year old but it can also be disturbing for an eight year old.

Decision making is presented as a way parents can prepare their children (and themselves) to cope effectively in the real world.

Growing Up Is Not Easy

Beginning at five (and sometimes even earlier), children move into a world that will occupy much of their time and thoughts for at least eleven years: the school. Five and six year olds must adjust to new schedules, new adults who make rules for them, and a lot of other children who want the same attention, space, materials, and other things that they do. By age seven, many children develop a certain confidence that often blossoms at age eight. Nine year olds become a bit more aware of their feelings about themselves; there is more comparing with other children and more concern about standards of right and wrong. For ten and eleven year olds, the world is ever-widening. Children think more about doing well academically, about their parents, and about their best friends. One can say that this is a time of intensifying feelings that continues into age twelve and the teenage years. Twelve year olds are entering the period of puberty, with the many physical and emotional changes that result. Also, this is a time of transition for many youngsters as they leave (or prepare to leave) elementary school.

For children during these years, growth occurs through problem solving, through meeting new challenges and situations and mastering them. When our children cannot master new challenges, when they avoid new situations, or passively conform to others' demands or give in to things that are "too hard," growth can be slowed. As our children face more and more complex situations and as pressures on adults in the family mount, it is clear that everyone can benefit from a strategy to help make decisions and resolve problems. Don't you feel more confident, and generally turn out to be more successful, when you use a road map in an unfamiliar place? For children, growing up takes them to *many* unfamiliar places. Rather than have them rely on good fortune, a fortuitous road sign, or lots of trial and error, we have learned that children gain confidence and competence from their own road map—a decision-making strategy they can use most anywhere they go.

Here are some examples of different children, at different ages, and the kinds of problems they regularly encounter. Note that the children, while simultaneously negotiating the difficulties that we will describe, *also* accumulate an astonishing list of accomplishments.

THE EARLY ELEMENTARY SCHOOL YEARS

Tony is five years old. It's a Tuesday morning in October. Between cereal bites, Tony announces, "Mom, I don't want to go to school today. It's no fun." Tony's announcement is a fairly common statement that five year olds can make about kindergarten. Other situations for five year olds could be: monopolizing dinner conversations, hitting others, fearing thunder or a parent's temporary departure ("Mommy, do you *have* to go to the movies?"), ganging up with a buddy on another child, telling parents only the negatives about school, and blaming the nearest person for their own problems: "Look what you made me do!"

Anne is six years old. She's now in school all day. Her mother is standing in the kitchen on a sunny June morning. Anne is holding the back door ajar. Her mother says, "C'mon, Anne, are you going to go out or come in?" Anne looks at her mother, anxiously twists her fingers, and says teary-eyed, "I don't know. I'm all mixed up!" This kind of indecision is not unusual for a six-year-old youngster who at this age can see more options than five year olds can.

Like most six year olds, Anne is spending a lot of time adjusting to a full day at school. She may express that adjustment by dawdling through her breakfast, which can cause difficulties for a busy family's tight schedule. A six year old can also arrive home from school and angrily react to Mom's directive that she change her clothes. Not being chosen for a recess game, always wanting to be "first," getting teased on the school bus by the eight to ten year olds, and getting overly excited in front of company can all be problems for a six year old.

Joey is more confident of himself now that he is seven. He shows this by his casual ignoring of his parents' expectations of neatness and orderliness. His coat is in the hall, his socks are under the kitchen table, and his baseball and comics are thrown about in his room. It's bedtime now. Joey approaches his mother as she's watching television and says, "Mom, where's my language arts book? I need it for tomorrow."

Other common problems that seven-year-old Joey might encounter could be: setting too high a goal for himself, quietly sulking if he doesn't get his way, throwing objects if a project does not work out right, wanting "to stay up as late as Chuckie does, Mom!" blaming a loss on the other team's use of unfair tactics, fearing new situations, and insisting on a regular space in the car.

Mary Jane at eight years old is beginning to feel more self-confident. Often these feelings are expressed as those of superiority over her five-year-old brother and his friends. For example, as a school veteran, she enjoyably gathers the younger children on the steps at home and assumes the role of teacher. The younger children are enjoying the attention that she is giving to them. One Saturday afternoon her father overhears Mary Jane telling the younger children about how troublesome school is, asking them difficult questions and then strongly correcting their mistakes. Mary

Jane is also now selecting "best" friends and feels hurt if she is rejected by them. She is also more willing to confront her older brother or other older children in the neighborhood. It would also not be an unusual activity for an eight year old to offer embarrassingly frank observations of adult behavior, "Grandma, your hair looks weird today."

THE LATER ELEMENTARY SCHOOL YEARS

At age nine, many children grow increasingly sensitive to "being a boy" and "being a girl." Boys and girls spend less playtime together and stay with members of their own sex. The nine year old accepts his growing independence. He wants respect for himself, creates high standards and rules, and becomes quite self-absorbed. For example, Peter, at age nine, comes home one day and unhappily announces, "Ricky and I and some of the other guys were playing kickball. We all said that none of the stupid girls could play. And then . . . Ricky goes and gets his dumb sister Anita and her friends to play . . . and they're not as good as we are!" Other situations common to nine year olds might include being so absorbed in talking to a friend that Mom's call to dinner is not heard, getting irritated when Peter's dad interrupts his project to offer help, feeling ashamed about an academic failure, and making statements like, "That's not fair, Mom."

As her horizons continually widen, ten-year-old Patricia is learning new approaches in math, listening to her friends' descriptions of their parents' ideas and ways, going on more sophisticated class trips, and learning about other cultures in school. Patricia is also in the process of making the difficult discovery that her parents do not indeed know everything. She also has a best friend, Kathy. Theirs is an intense relationship, full of intrigue and possessiveness. Patricia arrives home from school Wednesday afternoon looking very sorrowful and saying, "I'm never going to be friends with Kathy again. She told Linda a secret she wasn't supposed to. And Linda isn't even a part of our group!"

Other difficulties for Patricia and her age-mates include telling their parents that they don't want to be kissed good-night anymore, being angry at Mom and Dad for treating them like little kids, not wanting a lot of parental supervision of their hobby activities, and wanting to quit things like Little League because the coach gives them an "unimportant" position.

At eleven years old, Mike not only realizes that his parents aren't perfect, but he may actively reject and criticize them and older members of his family. He feels abandoned by older children who may now be dating and rejects the younger children. Instead, he invests more and more in his hard-won position with kids his own age. At times it seems that Mike is more interested in the feelings and plight of almost anyone other than his own family members. His mother, for example, will ask him to take out an overflowing pail of garbage and it will still be sitting there two hours later! Other dilemmas for an eleven year old may include a girl getting edgy prior to the onset of menstruation, a boy embarrassing an older sister in front of her friends, appearing thoughtless to his parents, and (depending on the nature of the school system) adjusting to the transition to sixth grade and middle school.

In school districts with the junior high/senior high system, age twelve may be the time for transition to junior high. It is also an age when cliques may be forming with a number of social problems arising when the youngsters feel included in or excluded from a particular group. What was an acceptable standard a few years back is less acceptable now. For example, when Sharon was eleven, she was liked by her classmates for her quietness and calmness. Now that she's twelve, some of the girls who are more talkative and active are moving into a position of popularity. Sharon feels somewhat confused and hurt, and her parents feel her helplessness too.

Other difficulties for twelve year olds might include: being confused by the first onset of clear sexual thoughts and feelings, handling "crushes" on other students, taking to leaving the house without telling their parents where they are going, being inattentive or bored at school because of poor sleeping patterns, and dealing with dares.

There are other problem situations that children may be called upon to handle and these can also occur at any age. These include such family stressors as adjusting to parents who are not getting along very well with each other or who are divorced, sharing household responsibilities when both parents work outside the home, or feeling overly competitive with a brother or sister. There are many "first-time" challenges that can provide stress as well: going to a first dance, baby-sitting for the first time, or sleeping over at a friend's house for the first time. Peer pressure calls to mind a variety of situations: being teased for being overweight, being dared to do something dangerous, or feeling pressured to please too many people.

What we have been describing are normal kinds of everyday social experiences that children have. Many of us can remember encountering such situations. Certainly most of us were able to resolve our difficulties in some way, slip on by, muddle through satisfactorily, or handle it competently. We, in our own individual ways, over the years, pulled together information, such as a tip we heard our parents give us or a friend's idea, and figured out our own solutions. How much better we would have felt as children, though, if we had had a reliable problem-solving and decision-making strategy to use. Children can be taught a step-by-step problem-solving strategy so they won't feel absolutely "stuck" when they're at a decision-making point. Using the following method, you can prepare your child to successfully handle everyday problems. This one approach can be used as a guide for parents and children *at any age*.

The Eight-Step Decision-Making Approach

Picture this: it's 8 P.M., early November, and you're at home. The phone rings and it's your mother. She's inviting you to Thanksgiving dinner at her house. You say, "That sounds really nice, Mom. I'll let you know soon if I can make it." The conversation is pleasantly over and you sit down to watch television. The telephone rings again! This time it's your mother-in-law. She invites you, your spouse, and the kids to her house for Thanksgiving also. She sounds excited. "I'm really looking forward to seeing you all on the holiday," she says. You feel a slight tension in your stomach, pause a moment, and say, "You know, seeing the whole family sounds great. It's been too long. In fact, we'd like to have you and my parents join us at our house for Thanksgiving. What do you say?" You talk for a few moments about arrangements and your mother-in-law agrees. Your own mother also agrees when you call her back.

Now, in a flash, you've gone through a kind of decision-making approach in your own mind. It happened so fast that you probably were unaware of the specific steps you used. We would bet that if we reviewed your thinking in slow motion, we would have seen you use something like our eight decision-making steps.

1. Look for signs of different feelings.
2. Tell yourself what the problem is.
3. Decide on your goal.
4. Stop and think of as many solutions to the problem as you can.

5. For each solution, think of all the things that might happen next.
6. Choose your best solution.
7. Plan it and make a final check.
8. Try it and rethink it.

In the chapters that follow, these steps will be discussed at greater length. First, though, an overview of how the whole process works will be presented.

Turn back the clock momentarily and imagine you've just heard your mother-in-law invite you over.

1. *Look for signs of different feelings.*

   "I feel tense in my stomach and that usually means I'm nervous about something."

2. *Tell yourself what the problem is.*

   "I feel nervous because my mother wants us to go to her house for Thanksgiving and my mother-in-law wants us to go to *her* house too."

3. *Decide on your goal.*

   "I want to enjoy Thanksgiving day and not feel guilty or tense."

4. *Think of as many solutions as you can.*

   We could spend part of the day at my mother's and part of the day at my mother-in-law's.

   We could go to my mother's since she asked us first.

   We could invite all of them to our place.

   We could go to my mother-in-law's because we really haven't been there in a long time.

5. *For each solution think of all the consequences.*

   It would be too tiring to visit both of them in one day. They might be somewhat happy though.

   My mother-in-law rarely invites us over. If we didn't see her at all she might feel hurt and not extend an invitation to us again.

   If we did not see my mother on Thanksgiving Day at all, she'd really feel sad because we're really the only family she has.

   If we had Thanksgiving at our house it would mean a lot of work for me, but at least I wouldn't have to deal with feeling guilty or upset about leaving somebody out.

6. *Choose your best solution.*
We'll have Thanksgiving at home because I'd be happier doing the extra work in the kitchen and knowing that no one's been left out.

7. *Plan it and make a final check.*
Well, if I can, I'd better try to get both of them to accept my invitation tonight. That way I can put my mind into planning dinner and not into worrying about getting them on the phone later this week.

8. *Try it and rethink it.*
It's good to be watching TV and have that settled. But, this experience makes me think that I might be trying too hard to please everyone. I'm going to have to work on that.

When we are at our best . . . that kind of thinking occurs rapidly and works well for us. As mentioned earlier, most people learn a particular problem-solving strategy in a haphazard way over the years. Too many individuals took their psychological bruises in the process, too. Your child doesn't have to learn the hard way—on his own—and over many years. You can teach your child this kind of decision-making process in a comfortable, deliberate fashion.

Here are more examples of the entire process put into use.

PETER: PROBLEM SOLVING HIS WAY THROUGH A KICKBALL CRISIS

Consider nine-year-old Peter again. Remember what he said? "Ricky and I and some of the other guys were playing kickball. We said that none of the stupid girls could play. And then . . . Ricky goes and gets his dumb sister Anita and her friends to play."

Peter is the second of Ernie and Ann's two children. His older brother, Joe, is now thirteen. Because he does not have sisters, Peter has not had as much experience sharing his time with girls as Ricky has had. This will make the usual nine-year-old liking for boys playing with boys and girls with girls more touchy for Peter (see Peter's Parenting Family Tree).

Ricky is more comfortable playing with girls. His mother, Eileen, is divorced and works outside of the home. There are many times that she counts on Ricky to take care of Anita (see Ricky's Parenting Family Tree).

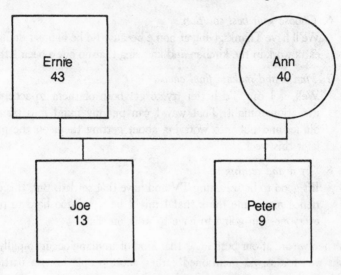

Let's take a look at how Peter's mother uses the decision-making steps to guide her son.

Peter: . . . and then . . . Ricky goes and gets his dumb sister Anita and her friends to play . . . and they're not as good as we are.

Mom: I wonder how that makes you *feel?*

Peter: Mad, and that's it. And that's the last time I'm playing with Ricky.

Mom: I'm not following you too well. What's the *problem?*

Peter: It gets boring when the girls play. Less fun.

Mom: Tell me what it is that *you want to have happen.*

Peter: You know . . . I want to play kickball and have a good time.

Mom: What ideas do you have?

Peter: What do you mean?

Mom: You know, some ways you could think of that could help you play kickball and have a good time.

Peter: I can't think of anything.

Mom: C'mon, try.

Peter: Okay . . . well, I could tell Ricky that I'll only play with him if the girls are out of the picture.

Mom: I wonder what else you could do.

Peter: Find some different guys to play with.

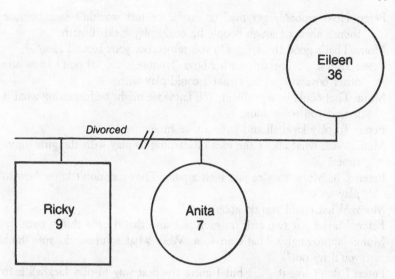

Mom: That's good . . . you already have two ideas . . . I'm thinking about another idea.

Peter: I know, I know, you're going to say I could learn to be more patient with the girls.

Mom: (laughing) How did you know I was thinking of that?

Peter: (smiling) Because you're a girl.

Mom: Yes, I suppose you're right. And we usually get along all right, don't we?

Peter: Yeah, I guess so.

Here, or at any earlier point, the conversation might end because Mom may have had to leave the house, Peter may have had to go to the bathroom, or there might have been some other interruption. No matter how far they got into this conversation, however, problem solving has begun and that's what's important. If there was no interruption and more time, here's how the conversation might have continued.

Mom: Anyway . . . let's see what would happen if you tried out some of these ideas.

Peter: Okay. But I already forgot what we thought of.

Mom: Well, first you said that you'd tell Ricky that you'd only play with him if the girls weren't part of it. What would happen if you said that?

Peter: He'd probably get mad or maybe he just wouldn't care because there's always enough people he could play kickball with.

Mom: That's good thinking. Do you remember your second idea?

Peter: Yeah . . . find some other boys. Trouble is . . . I don't know any other boys around here that I could play with.

Mom: That could be a problem. You know we might be forgetting what it is that you really want.

Peter: To play kickball and have a nice time.

Mom: Well, what about the idea of learning to play with the girls sometimes?

Peter: Oh, Mom, they're just such a pain. They just don't know how to play well.

Mom: What could you do about that?

Peter: Maybe put two girls on each side and that'd even things out.

Mom: (approvingly) That's an idea. Well, what solution do you think you'll try out?

Peter: I don't like it . . . but I guess the best way to play kickball is to play with Ricky *and* Anita and her friends.

Again, here's a spot where the conversation might end. Ricky could be at the door calling for Peter or the telephone might ring. That's fine. A significant amount of problem solving has gone on. If there's still time and interest, the conversation could continue like this.

Mom: How do you think you'll do this?

Peter: I think I'll just wait until tomorrow and not say anything to anyone. I'll just play after school like I always do. If the girls join in, I'll just keep on playing, like nothing's bothering me.

Mom: So you're going to try your idea out, huh?

Peter: Yeah, what's for supper, Mom?

Peter's mother was interested in teaching Peter how to think. She guided his thought processes along with subtle suggestions and avoided telling him what he was ultimately able to figure out for himself.

We'd like to show you how another family used the decision-making steps.

ROSEANNE:
LEARNING HOW TO HANDLE STARTING A NEW SCHOOL

We've all had to deal with transitions: moving to a new town, starting a new job, getting married, getting divorced, growing older, and so on. Transitions will always be confronting us and our children too. It's our feeling that adults who handle transitions well probably had some successful earlier experiences handling transitions. Adjusting to changes provides many opportunities for decision-making thinking. Leaving elementary school to go to middle school or junior high, where children have to deal with locker combinations, nervousness about being picked on by older children, organizing themselves to move from class to class, and remembering the diverse demands of a variety of teachers, can be a difficult change.

It's August. Roseanne, at age eleven, is entering West End Middle School in September. She'll be taking a bus and all of it will be a brand-new experience for her. She's spent all of her school years at Parkwood Elementary School in her own neighborhood.

Roseanne is the youngest of two girls. Her sister, Anne, is sixteen years old and will be a junior at Verona High School. Her father, Bob, is forty-five and her mother, Beverly, is forty-two (see their Parenting Family Tree).

Beverly has been reading about decision making. She's made some important strides in patiently helping her children think through their own difficulties. Roseanne and her mother talk just before Roseanne goes to bed.

Roseanne: Mom, I don't feel well.
Mom: What's the matter?
Roseanne: My stomach hurts. It's not like I'm really sick though . . .
Mom: Sometimes your stomach hurts when you're upset, just like Daddy always gets a headache when he worries too much.
Roseanne: Well, I am kinda nervous and worried about school.
Mom: What do you mean?
Roseanne: School starts in just two weeks and I just don't know how I'm going to fit in.
Mom: Well, what would you like to have happen?
Roseanne: I don't want to be so nervous about school anymore.
Mom: I wonder what you could do to help make things better.

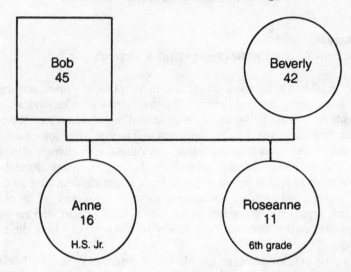

Roseanne: I don't know. I suppose I could talk to Anne about it. She went to West End.

Mom: (nodding) Mm Hm.

Roseanne: I could try to ignore it.

Mom: That's an idea. Anything else?

Roseanne: Maybe I could talk to Carol about riding together on the first day. She's a pretty good friend and I think she's nervous about school too.

Mom: Well, what do you think would work best for you?

Roseanne: Well, there's no way I can just ignore this, it just doesn't work.

Mom: Well, what about the other two ideas?

Roseanne: Well, forget about Anne, all we do is fight. I can't talk to her anymore.

Mom: Well . . .

Roseanne: Maybe, I'll just talk to Carol then and see if she wants to go together.

Mom: When will you see Carol?

Roseanne: I'll just call her. I'll call her tomorrow when we get back from the store.

The next step would be for Roseanne to try out her solution. If she's reassured and less nervous, fine. If not, we hope that she'll review what happened to learn how better to prepare for the next similar situation.

Creating a Problem-Solving Atmosphere

Engaging your youngster in a conversation about difficulties he or she may be having is a first step in problem solving. Your child may want to speak to you about only certain topics or he or she may be reluctant to discuss difficulties with you at all—this of course depends on a lot of things, including the child's age and sex, if it's been a good day, and so on. Regardless, we have some ideas about how you could increase the chances that your youngster will want to talk to you. A main goal should be that your child should perceive you as *approachable*. While still being able to set reasonable limits for your child's activity, you can also be someone he or she can go to with his or her ideas and feelings. We encourage you to keep and cultivate your natural conversational style and consider some of these ideas.

SHOWING OUR CHILDREN THAT WE'VE LISTENED AND HEARD

When your child seems troubled, your first duty as a parent is to communicate your availability to listen well. Before you start to talk, present yourself physically. Try to look at your child's eyes. If you can, leave your present activity for the time being and get and maintain eye contact. If there are other people present and you sense your child's need for privacy, you might go to an area where you can be alone. Certainly, we never know for sure when or where a child will present us with a need to talk. If you're driving in the car and sense that your child wants to discuss something, accept the opportunity and create an approachable atmosphere—turn the radio down or off and make your child aware of your willingness to have a discussion.

Try to keep in mind, too, that none of us can truthfully say, "I know exactly how you feel." Our children know this, too. The best that we, as parents, can do is to respect their feelings and convey to them that we care and are listening.

After a good amount of listening, it is important to give your child some message that you've heard what's been said. One of the best ways of doing that is to repeat back in some way the *content* of what's been told you. For example, recall six-year-old Anne standing indecisively in the doorway.

Mom: C'mon, Anne, are you going to go out or come in?
Anne: (teary-eyed) I don't know. I'm all mixed up!

If Anne's mother wanted to comment on the *content* of Anne's message to let Anne know that she was following, the conversation might have gone:

Anne: (teary-eyed) I don't know. I'm all mixed up!
Mom: It's hard to decide whether you want to play inside or outside.

With this possible result:

Anne: (relieved) Yeah.

Another way that Anne's mother could communicate that she was truly listening would be to comment on Anne's *feelings*.

Anne: (teary-eyed) I don't know. I'm all mixed up!
Mom: It looks like that can make you feel sad too.
Anne: (nods to her mother and walks over to her)

Responding to content and feelings are ways to invite your child to continue to talk to you. As your child shares more information with you, there's a much better chance that some problem-solving conversation will occur between the two of you.

QUESTIONS: POWERFUL TOOLS THAT MUST BE USED WITH CARE

We all have our own ways of encouraging our children to tell us what's going on with them. A natural for most of us is to ask questions. Sometimes, though, we can overuse questions. Here's an exaggeration.

Dad: What happened? Did someone hurt your feelings? Why are you upset? Why can't you tell me what the problem is? Who was involved?
Steve: (thinking, "Why doesn't he just calm down? I don't know the answers to all those questions.") C'mon, Dad, just let me talk.

In our eagerness to want to help our children feel better, we can sometimes bombard them with questions and come across very strongly—perhaps too much so. The children, in turn, can feel bewildered and "on the spot" or perceive us as anxious or pesty. Certainly those are not our intentions as parents, but it does happen and comes out of our interest in helping them. Unfortunately even dedicated parents can get discouraged when their children then lose interest in talking to them.

We suggest that you practice turning some of your questions into statements. With statements there is still the strong suggestion that you would like to get a response from your child. But it's more in the form of an *invitation* to respond, as opposed to a *demand* to respond. Here are some examples of how questions can be rephrased into statements.

Frank, what happened?	becomes	Frank, it looks like something happened to you.
Marcia, did someone hurt you?	becomes	Marcia, you look as if someone hurt your feelings.
Paul, why are you so upset?	becomes	Gee, you talk like you're really upset about something, Paul.
Why can't you tell me what the problem is, Mary?	becomes	Mary, sounds as if it's hard for you to tell me what's been going on.
Sharon, who was involved?	becomes	Sharon, I was wondering who the other children were.

Don't put all of your questions into statements—that would come across as uncomfortably as asking *all* questions. Rather, learn to combine questions, statements, and moments of silence together to give your child a variety of invitations to respond.

Regarding questions: try to ask ones that require more than a one-word answer. That's another way of encouraging more of an information exchange in a sincere supportive way. These are some instances where parents have changed their wording and have been rewarded by better conversations with their children.

Questions asking for one-word answers:		*Questions asking for more than one-word answers:*
"Did you have a nice day?"	becomes	"Tell me about your day."

Questions asking for one-word answers:		*Questions asking for more than one-word answers:*
"Is your new teacher nice?	becomes	"What's your new teacher like?"
"Did you play today?"	becomes	"Who did you play with today?"
"Did you finish your homework?	becomes	"What homework did you do?"

Even with the best of ideas, your child may just not feel like talking to you about something. Maybe your child feels that he or she would like to work it out independently for a while. When that happens, it's very natural to feel hurt, but remember your goal of being approachable. Even if your youngster is not talking to you about his or her problem, the fact that you have let him or her know that you are available is a great support. You may wind up spending a lot of silent time with your child in the car or you may end up talking about nonsense and not "really" what is bothering your child. Still, just being available to your youngster and not blanketing him or her with a series of questions can lead to some very important parent-child exchanges. When your child is ready to talk, and needs to talk to you, your child will probably find a way. If you pursue, and pursue, he or she will back away.

When your child does start to speak about some issues, provide some support. For example, you might consider holding back on giving advice prematurely. Let your child talk for a while. Sometimes when a child finally reveals something meaningful about what he or she did or feels, the parent gets excited and turns it into an opportunity to teach. Although well intended, the lesson can also discourage further revelation.

At times, and especially when your child is talking about doing something highly inappropriate, you need to provide guidance. But if every time a son tells his father a difficulty he's having—and then hears what Dad thinks he should do—the likelihood that Dad will get another chance to hear about such problems is lessened. It's a delicate balancing act for parents who need to learn how to listen, how to encourage good ideas, and to give direction only at appropriate times. Encourage your child's beginning efforts at successfully resolving his or her own difficulties alone. If you're pleased that your youngster has approached you to discuss something, consider letting him or her know that by a comment such as, "Jack,

I really liked having this talk with you," or "Sara, I'm glad you told me about all of this." At some point, consider asking your child if how you've listened or what you've said has been helpful.

Decision-Making Digest

You've seen several examples of decision-making thinking and conversing. Some parents react by saying how simple it looks, that they do this kind of thing all the time. If that is so, then you should be pleased. But the skills we are discussing are not simple. In fact, they elude far too many people—both adult *and* children. And the importance of ensuring that our children possess these skills cannot be overemphasized. To prepare our children to cope with the real world, we must acknowledge that we can't be sure exactly what their adult world will be like. So we must give them a decision-making strategy that they can apply to a wide variety of situations. In the next seven chapters we will show you how you can teach decision making and problem solving to your children in a step-by-step way.

II

A Step-by-Step Approach for Decision Making

Part Two illustrates how children can be taught a specific, step-by-step strategy for responding to problems in an active and constructive way. The chapters feature examples of children who use, or fail to use, the eight decision-making steps, guidelines for how parents can help children learn the steps, and family activities to build children's decision-making skills when the family is at home or away from the house. Among other things, parents learn how to read children's Feelings Fingerprints, how to help children think creatively and independently when they face problems, and how to help children be more careful to check their plans, anticipate obstacles to their good ideas, and learn from their experiences so they can become more thoughtful decision makers. Each chapter closes with an example of how different families can actually put the decision-making approach to work in the real world.

By the end of Part Two, parents will have the raw materials necessary to teach children decision making for everyday living and for making better plans in the future. These are the themes that have been organized into the decision-making strategy.

11

A Step-by-Step Process for Decision Making

3

Getting Ready for Decision Making

Is your child ready to have decision-making conversations with you? There are youngsters who are restless, or who hardly seem to listen to what others say or ask of them. Some withdraw from other children, jump from topic to topic without completing a thought, and so on. By age five, however, most children are able to listen carefully and accurately, follow directions, concentrate on an age-appropriate task, and feel comfortable spending time with friends their own age. These are skills that our children need to develop if they are to cope successfully with classroom and school routines. These are also the skills needed to *get ready* for decision making.

Let's take a closer look at the idea of "readiness" by thinking about preparing for a family vacation. Before leaving on a trip, we go through a process of getting ready. Where are we going? How long will it take to get there? Do we have directions? What do we need to bring with us? Who will we be seeing? What might we bring for them? The list of questions seems endless and, for most of us, there is always that one small thing we either forgot to consider or forgot to pack. But a good vacation is based on some preparation before embarking.

Good decision making is also based on preliminary activities, activities that we as adults sometimes take for granted. We know that children cannot make sound decisions if they lack information, an understanding of other people, or the patience to follow through a series of thinking steps. Sound decision making also requires the right balance of self-confidence and the ability to know when to ask for help. (Think of the times you've been out of town and wished you'd asked someone for help with directions, accommodations, restaurants, and the like.) Finally, we want good decision making to become a habit, not an occasional event. Our responsibility is to praise our children when we notice them using decision-making skills—and help them notice that praise and feel good about it. Following are examples of two children, one of whom is ready for decision making while the other needs a bit of work in this area.

CASE EXAMPLE: SHEILA IS READY FOR DECISION MAKING!

Sheila, a six year old in the first grade, is at the mall with her parents and her brother, Jerry, who is nine. Summer is coming and it's time to buy shorts, short-sleeved outfits, and other summer clothes. After about a half hour, Sheila and Jerry both complain about being tired and hungry. Their mom says, "Look, we have two more stores to go to. Then, we can stop for a snack." At the next store Sheila has just finished trying on three outfits without whining. Her mom praises her and reminds her that there is only one more store to go. Sheila smiles and starts thinking about what kind of snack she wants.

While standing in the middle of a long line, Sheila's mom notices a stain on one of the shirts. She really doesn't want to have to leave the line. So she says, "Sheila, look at this stain. I want you to take this back to the rack where we got it—right by the poster with the lions on it. Find another shirt that's the same color, the same size, and also the same brand. You know, Mr. B., with the little tennis racket on the pocket. Okay? Go ahead!" Mom carefully watches as Sheila walks back, finds the poster, and finds the rack. She looks for the blue one's, then the medium's, and then sees one with the Mr. B. label. With a big smile she takes it, checks for stains, and walks back to her mom, who is now next in line. Her mom says, "Terrific! This is just what we wanted. Now we can get to our snack much sooner!"

CASE EXAMPLE: JERRY IS NOT QUITE READY!

Jerry has to go to the bathroom, so his father takes him to find one. After successfully completing that task, Jerry once again asks for a snack. (His father repeats what has been said earlier: two more stores to go.) When they return to the store, Jerry and his dad pick two shirts and two pairs of shorts and go to the fitting room. His dad stands outside and says, "Just let me look at the ones that fit you. Put the rest on the hook by the door, okay?" "Okay," says Jerry. Jerry shows his dad one shirt. It fits, and they decide to buy it. "Okay, Jerry, just put back the clothes that don't fit. And be sure to bring all of your things, okay?" "Okay."

After they pay and meet the rest of the family, the parents see it's getting late and decide to go for a snack. As they enter the restaurant, Jerry's mother asks, "Where is your hat?" Jerry says he doesn't know. "Do you realize how many hats we have bought this year?" his mom says, not really wanting an answer. When they sit down at the table, Jerry takes off his jacket. "Whose shirt is that?" his mother asks in disbelief. Jerry looks down and looks at his father. Everyone sees the tag on the shirt. "We may as well wait until after we eat, in case they decide to arrest us," Jerry's dad says with a pained look on his face.

"CASETALK": A CLOSER LOOK AT THE TWO CHILDREN

Sheila and Jerry, children in the same family, have very different readiness skills. By listening carefully, following directions, and noticing when her parents praise her, Sheila is a big help to her family. But more important, her parents can begin to help her learn to make more mature, independent decisions. Jerry is often not quite focused enough to make thoughtful decisions. He is not using the information his parents give him. He is also not keeping track of his own possessions. In school Jerry is likely to forget assignments and to make careless errors. At home his parents get aggravated when he does not do his chores or when he strays from the backyard when he is not supposed to. And Jerry's friends are often annoyed with him for not concentrating during team activities and for borrowing things without returning them.

Any child is likely to be a mix of Sheila and Jerry. To help you get an idea of how ready *your* child is to learn about decision making, we have prepared a short checklist. The questions are ones you can ask yourself over a period of a few days and you should think about how they apply to different times during the day—morning, afternoon, and evening. If your answers are predominantly "not as often as I'd like them to," then the activities in this chapter will be important for you and your child to work on before moving ahead to Chapters 4 through 9. Otherwise, you can use your answers to focus on particular activities you might wish to repeat with your child regularly.

TABLE 1
HOW READY ARE YOUR CHILDREN?

A. How carefully and accurately do your children listen to what is said to them?
1. Very carefully—they quickly pick up on things that are said and they repeat things accurately
2. Pretty much—most of the time, I do not have to repeat things I say
3. Not as carefully as I'd like them to—I find myself repeating things or correcting them more than I'd like to
B. How often do your children follow directions?
1. Very often—most of the time, they follow directions well and without a lot of hassle
2. Pretty often—directions are followed some of the time, but at other times they are not
3. Not as often as I'd like them to—I find that my children do not follow directions as much as I'd like them to
C. How well do your children concentrate on tasks and follow through to try and complete them?
1. Very well—they concentrate well and usually follow through
2. Pretty well—sometimes there is a lapse, but usually they concentrate and try to follow through
3. Not as well as I'd like them to—I find myself asking them to stay on the task and finish what they start more often than I'd like to
D. How well do your children accept praise or approval when it is given to them?
1. Very well—they almost always smile or nod their heads or say "thanks" when praised
2. Pretty well—with most people they show that they heard or liked the praise
3. Not as well as I'd like them to—too often they seem to ignore approval or actually shy away from praise
E. How well do your children ask for help?

1. Very well—they don't hesitate to ask and they seem to usually find the right person to go to
2. Pretty well—on occasion they won't ask when they really need to, but most of the time they ask when they should
3. Not as well as I'd like them to—I find myself pushing them to get help more than I'd like to

F. How well do your children notice what other children are feeling?
1. Very well—they are really "tuned in" to what other kids say, and even how they look or sound
2. Pretty well—usually they'll pick up on how other children are feeling
3. Not as well as I'd like them to—I find that they're not as sensitive to other children's feelings as I'd like them to be

Family Activities

HOW TO USE THESE ACTIVITIES

A large part of each chapter in Part Two is devoted to family activities that will contribute to your child's development as a decision maker. These activities have been derived from our years of experience working with children and parents. We have studied the effects of these kinds of activities and find two important results: children can learn the lessons these activities teach, and parents can do the teaching. When we say "teaching," we mean that you can use the many natural opportunities provided to you by your daily routines to stimulate your child's thinking powers.

Some of the activities we present may seem familiar to you and may in fact already be part of your parenting repertoire. We hope to create a complete picture of all the skills that our research suggests children need for independent problem solving. You can then incorporate as much of the problem-solving picture into your household as you wish. You may emphasize different activities for different children and different situations. Of course, choices change as they grow. We are confident that if you attempt the activities presented in these chapters and then adapt them to your home environment, they will be helpful as you prepare your children to become thoughtful decision makers.

LEARNING TO LISTEN
CAREFULLY AND ACCURATELY

Ears Ready! A belief many of us share is that listening is done with one's ears. Not necessarily! "Listening" means understanding the meaning of the message that someone is trying to convey. It requires not only adequate hearing, but also mental attention and, especially for children, body position that assists the attending process. Think for a moment about what you actually do when you speak to a friend on the telephone. Perhaps you can picture the other person. Like many of us, you probably gesture to him or her during the conversation. Or think about conversations you have when you are driving. It's an effort not to look at, or lean toward, the person with whom you are conversing. And we all know drivers who turn fully toward their passengers when they speak to them! We mention this to highlight for you the need to *watch* how your children listen and compare what you see to our Ears Ready! activity.

Ears Ready! means that when listening to something important, your child should stand with both feet on the floor (if he or she is sitting, both knees or the child's bottom should be on the seat), face the speaker (or other source of sound), and look carefully. When the speaker is finished, the child should ask questions if something is not understood. Here is how Jerry's dad might help Jerry to avoid problems due to careless listening:

Dad: Okay, Jerry, just show me whatever fits you and put the rest on the hook.

Jerry: Okay.

Dad: Jerry, I don't think you really heard me, because you were not looking at me. Let's try Ears Ready! First, put both feet down. Good! Now face me and look at me while I speak. When I am finished, ask me a question if you don't understand. Okay, first tell me what you are going to do when I say, "Ears Ready!"

Jerry: I'm going to put both feet down and look at you.

Dad: What will you do when I finish speaking?

Jerry: I'm going to think about what you said and if I don't understand, I'll ask you a question.

Dad: Terrific! Okay, get your Ears Ready! Just show me whatever fits you and put the rest on the hook.

Jerry: What hook, Dad?

Dad: The one by the door.

Jerry: It's broken.

Dad: Well, what else can you do?

Jerry: I'll just leave them on the bench in a pile.

Dad: Sounds good to me. You know, Jerry, I'll bet there are lots of other times when you could use Ears Ready!

Jerry: Yeah, like when I talk to grandma on the phone, or when Mrs. Mabley gives us our homework assignments, or . . .

Jerry's dad has just been very supportive in trying to help Jerry listen more carefully. He has eased Jerry into Ears Ready! without a lot of explanation. He also had Jerry repeat how to do Ears Ready! and then showed Jerry how it could be used in the store to help him do something more easily. After a bit of practice, Jerry's dad and mom will usually only have to say, "Ears Ready!" and Jerry will put himself in a position to listen with a better likelihood of *hearing* what has been said. We use this activity with youngsters about twelve years and up, as well. We call it Listening Position and we find them to be highly motivated to learn this new skill, because they quickly understand how it helps them catch every last bit of gossip from their friends.

Instant Replay. We live in a world of many, and almost constant, sounds. However, we tend to be attracted by what our eyes can see. Often, when sight and sound are in competition, sound loses out. Try going to a movie and just concentrating on the sound track—it's quite a challenge! To help our children be more sensitive to things they hear, Instant Replay can be used. Basically, Instant Replay involves stopping the action and asking your child what he or she just heard. You can use television dialogue, radio news, commercials, records, and the like. In fact, prerecorded material is preferred, because then interactions like the following can be minimized.

Mom: What did the newsperson just say?

Billy: I don't know.

Mom: Was it something about a foreign country?

Billy: Nope, it was about a submarine.

Mom: No, that was two stories ago.

Billy: No it wasn't.

Mom: Yes it was.

You know how scenes like this end! With prerecorded information, you can do an Instant Replay and find out exactly what was said, by whom, and when. The idea is to engage your child in becoming a better listener, not to catch him or her in errors. Older children will be cooperative, especially if accurate listening reduces the number of disruptions in what they are doing. With younger children, we find it useful to make a little checklist or scorecard showing the number of Instant Replays tried and the number of times the child was listening accurately. Just posting such a scorecard on the refrigerator can be motivating; sometimes, tangible small rewards like stickers can help a child get used to Instant Replay.

Sound Detector, another variation of Instant Replay, some children find more enjoyable and some parents find easier to use when out of the house. In the car, for example, you can ask your child to clap to indicate when he or she hears a particular sound on the radio. Some examples include: a trumpet playing; a change in announcers' voices; every time the word "sun" is said in a weather forecast; every time a product name is mentioned during a commercial. When listening to the radio or television at home, you can ask your children to listen for certain words, such as happy or sad, or for certain tones of voice, such as happy or surprised. You can have your children clap or, as we often do, ask children to decide how to show what they heard. Snapping fingers, tapping something, and making beeping noises are favorites.

As children grow older, they generally become better at listening. However, some either get out of the habit of listening or allow their skills to remain untapped because they spend so much time with visual materials. You can make a useful application of Sound Detector by picking an area in which most older children *do* listen, such as popular music or sports. For example, you might ask your child to tell you the lyrics of one of his or her favorite songs and explain to you how he or she figures out the words. If you are convincing, you will get a fascinating guided tour through what probably has seemed like forbidden territory. You will also get a chance to praise your child's listening skills and in so doing, indirectly remind him or her of the benefits of careful listening.

Cereal Progression. Of all the places to teach careful listening to children from preschool age through third grade, the supermarket is difficult to beat. When Sheila goes shopping with her parents, her listening and thinking skills are given some exercise through Cereal Progression:

Mom: Sheila, please get me the third box from the bottom. It's below the Bran Flakes with Added Tree Bark—the one with the price label on the side.

Sheila: Uh, let's see . . . you mean this one, right?

Mom: Right! Wonderful! Now we'll go to the rear aisle. Okay, we need yogurt. Look for a strawberry one from this store, stacked four high and dated with a J for June.

Sheila: One, two, three, four . . . no date. One, two, three, four . . . M for May. One, two, three, four . . . J04. Is this it?

Mom: Yes, that's fine. J04 means June fourth—about twelve days away. If you hadn't been listening and you took one from May, it might have been spoiled and gotten us sick. I'm glad you're such a good listener!

Sheila's mother used Cereal Progression well. She named two or three or four (or more) characteristics of a product to be picked out. By listening carefully and accurately, Sheila was able to pick the correct item. By progressing gradually to include a larger number of characteristics (brand, location, date, price, location of price label, shape of container, and so on) for a given item, parents teach careful listening in a rewarding, confidence-building, and fun manner.

FOLLOWING DIRECTIONS

Following directions is a large part of what all of us do every day. In the morning our first encounter with following directions is probably turning off the alarm clock—provided we set it correctly the night before! There are directions for operating the shower, making toast, pouring cereal, making coffee, and transforming that frozen lump of citrus into tasty orange juice. At least as important are the informal directions members of a family must follow if the morning routine is to be completed successfully. Who showers first? Who gets breakfast on the table? Who cleans up? Most families have a set of rules, or directions, to help answer these questions, and most children learn to follow directions just through everyday family tasks. Others, however, can benefit from a little more practice. By learning to appreciate the good feelings and importance of being able to follow directions, children begin to develop the maturity they need for making thoughtful decisions.

Direction Following. The basic idea behind Direction Following is to cut complicated tasks down to size, into little, manageable pieces. Observe how the Fishman family prepares their dinner table for a visit from some cousins:

Mr. F: Let's see, there are four of us and we'll have eight guests. That means we'll need to send Debbie to get twelve dinner plates, twelve salad bowls, four large serving plates, knives, forks, spoons, the blue tablecloth and the matching napkins, the wood napkin rings, and both sets of bridge chairs from the basement.

Mrs. F: (laughing) Hold on a second! We can take this a step at a time. Try it this way. First, we'll give Debbie one thing to do. Then, two directions, then, three, and so on. As she shows us what she can do, we'll help her learn a little more. (calling the child in) Debbie, will you bring in twelve dinner plates?

Debbie: It's not my turn.

Mrs. F: We're having company. Paul is setting up the backyard and we'd like you to help with the table.

Debbie: Okay, I guess. Twelve plates, right?

Mrs. F: Right . . . Good! Now, we'll need twelve salad bowls and four large serving dishes . . . Fine. How about twelve small forks, twelve large forks, and twelve teaspoons? . . . Okay! Hmm. I think we'll need the blue tablecloth in the hall cabinet, twelve matching napkins, and the wood napkin rings. Can you remember all that?

Debbie: Sure I can.

Mrs. F: You sure can follow directions! I think I'll start the cooking, with your father's help.

Mrs. Fishman first gave Debbie one direction to follow. Then, she gave her two, and then three together. As long as Debbie is successful, Mrs. Fishman makes the next direction a *little* longer, or a *little* more complicated, thus expanding Debbie's ability to carry out what is needed. This kind of activity can also be done over a number of days at regular family meals. Another variation would be to sequence activities and use several family members. First, Paul could get the napkins; then Debbie could fold them while Paul gets the rings; Debbie could put the napkins in the rings while Paul gets the tablecloth, and so on. Children can also develop Direction Following by learning to use maps for trips and by using various kinds of building or construction sets. Games like Simon Says are fun and relevant, as well. And of course, the supermarket is an ideal place to build direction-following habits. The most important aspect of Direction Following, however, is that we break tasks into small pieces and help our children gradually learn how to follow increasingly longer and more complicated sets of directions . . . praising them as they go.

STAYING CALM AND KEEPING ON THE TASK

It's very hard to be a good problem solver and concentrate on a task when one is tense, upset, or anxious. Think for a moment about the last time you were *very* angry at your child. Where were you? What time was it? What was the situation? What did you do? Most important, how did you feel? Our guess is that if you were feeling upset, there is a good chance you didn't react in a calm, reasoned manner. Our children are no different —they usually do not act their *best* under stress.

Get Calm! Many adults and many children have learned how to calm down and keep focused on a task when they are upset. They have learned that keeping a normal rate of breathing and not exaggerating what is going on are helpful in staying calm and maintaining self-control. Call to mind that recent angry encounter you had with your child. You will probably find that when you were upset, your breathing was irregular, shallow, and tight. When you calmed down, your breathing was more regular, deeper, and easier, and you had put the event in a fuller perspective. Let's see how two parents prepare their upset children for problem solving.

Paula: That Michael is mean and nasty. He upset me and I will never, ever talk to him again. (She cries.)

Mrs. L: Paula, what happened?

Paula: Oooh, when I think about him, I get madder and madder. I'd like to get him back.

Mrs. L: I thought you were friends.

Paula: No way! Are you kidding? Never!

Mrs. L: Just calm down and tell me what happened.

Paula: (now screaming) I'm calm, I'm calm!

Mrs. L: So what happened?

Paula: He's just mean, that's all.

Mrs. L: Won't you just calm yourself?

Paula: I've had enough of this—I'm going to call Pam and tell her about Michael and about you, too.

Mrs. L tried to be helpful but probably needed calming herself by the time this encounter ended. Paula was not ready to be reasonable and she didn't know how to "calm down." When children are agitated or upset, parents can use an activity called Get Calm! to help restore the child's self-control and ability to stay on the task. Notice how Mrs. S introduces Get Calm! to her son:

Eli: That Sara—I hate her! I'm going to kill her! (He cries.)

Mrs. S: Eli, what happened?

Eli: I'll show her! I'm not her friend anymore!

Mrs. S: Eli, I can't understand you when you are crying. Come over here and take a deep breath. Here, watch me do it. (Mrs. S takes a deep breath.) It will help you calm down so I can listen to you . . . Good. Take another one. Good! Now, look around and tell me what you see —what is that over there?

Eli: No, I don't want to.

Mrs. S: Eli, if you do it, I'll be able to listen to you.

Eli: A refrigerator.

Mrs. S: And what's that?

Eli: My magazine.

Mrs. S: Good—you seem a lot calmer now. Okay, tell me where you were with Sara.

Eli: In the back.

Mrs. S: What happened?

Eli: She's mean, I hate her.

Mrs. S: What did she do?

Eli: She didn't want to get off the swing so I could have a turn . . .

Mrs. S realized that she could not hold a reasonable conversation with Eli until he calmed down—so *she taught him how.* She *showed* him how to take a deep breath. She had him look around and tell her what he saw to distract him from his anger and buy a bit of time. Later that evening she would sit down with Eli and explain what she taught him. When a similar problem occurs again, Mrs. S can ask Eli to Get Calm! as soon as he gets upset. Once Eli is about nine years old, Mrs. S can ask him to tell himself to Get Calm! before he starts to take a deep breath. Eventually this exercise will help him begin to Get Calm! on his own. Some parents find it easiest to introduce Get Calm! when children come indoors out of breath from some sports activity, when they are acting rowdy from being overtired, or when they seem anxious about studying or doing an assignment. After some practice, Get Calm! can be extended to times when children are upset over some conflict with peers or adults.

LEARNING TO RECEIVE PRAISE AND APPROVAL

The next time your family is involved in some activity together—cleaning the house, gardening, eating at a restaurant, washing the car—try this little experiment. Praise or compliment everyone in the family for something he or she is doing. Say something specific like, "I think it's wonderful when you ask politely like that," or "You're being very careful with the flowers—great!" Then praise yourself, "I think the car is spotless—I did a good job!" How did each person react? Are they beamers (people who clearly show they heard and enjoyed the praise), dreamers (seemingly oblivious to your comments), or steamers (seemingly annoyed or uncomfortable with praise)? Your beamers are easy to handle—just keep praising them. They appreciate hearing good things and they show their appreciation. This attitude will lead people to praise them even more. Your dreamers must be brought out of their own thoughts a bit: "Billy, did you hear me? No? Well, c'mon, get your Ears Ready!, young man . . ."

Steamers pose a bit of a challenge. Some people do not feel praiseworthy and do not allow compliments to stick. You can administer some adhesive in several ways. First, try praising your child when he or she is calm, perhaps just before bedtime. Ask what was the best thing he or she did during the day or that evening and then ask for some details. It may take several weeks before you detect some beaming, so don't be discouraged. The next step is to teach your child how to respond positively to praise, so that others will be more likely to praise him or her again. Often this may be best accomplished at a quiet moment. Praise your child and then indicate that you would like to know if your words were heard:

Mrs. Jackson: You know, your singing is getting better and better. I just love to listen to you.
Michael: (silence—he looks down in discomfort)
Mrs. Jackson: I would feel so much better if I knew you heard me when I praised you. Smiling or saying thanks or something like that encourages people to want to continue saying nice things to you.
Michael: (hesitating) Okay. Thanks, Mom. I have been practicing a lot.
Mrs. Jackson: Michael, you did that very well.
Michael: (smiling) Thanks!

In addition to using quiet diplomacy, you should show children how to respond to praise. When one member of the family praises a child and gets no response, it is useful to ask if the child heard the words. If the child does not respond to a repetition, you can ask directly for a response. We're emphasizing this point because we have seen many instances of young children who turn off sources of praise because they did not know how to receive compliments. In school situations and as they get older, children who learn to recognize praise and respond to it are more likely to have self-confidence. As noted earlier, sound decision making requires self-confidence. Being in tune with praise helps ensure that decision making is sound. By teaching children to receive praise, you set up a cycle of positive behavior that will make the children's family, school, and peer activities more rewarding.

KNOWING WHEN AND HOW TO GET HELP

For many of us, it is important that our children learn to be self-reliant and good problem solvers. But they must learn that there are times when it is appropriate to ask for help. When we ask for help, we can learn new things, or learn to do familiar things in different ways. Sometimes children seem to have the idea that they must do everything themselves, without help. Perhaps they think they are expected to be perfect, or perhaps they are simply too shy to approach someone for help. To be a "complete" decision maker, a child should recognize when help is needed and be comfortable with the idea of seeking help. In a rapidly changing society, help is often needed to obtain information, as well as assistance for particular tasks. Here are some ways to improve your child's ability to seek out help.

Helping in the Media. While watching television with your family, ask about examples of help that different people notice: "Did anyone notice how the detective found that clue?" "What is an 'assist' in basketball (or baseball or hockey)?" "How many examples of helping did you see? How did you know help was needed—what were some signs you picked up on? How did it turn out?"

These questions begin to alert family members to how common helping really is. After talking about television situations, your children will be better prepared to talk about their own helping activities.

Helping in Everyday Situations. Parents can accomplish a great deal by engaging in a Helping Exchange with their child. Let's listen to Mrs. Pawelk and her son Wally.

Mrs. P: I had a wonderful day today. I got a lot done and I even helped a few different people with problems they had. How was your day?

Wally: It was okay.

Mrs. P: What made your day okay?

Wally: Oh, I don't know. I had fun, played ball, and I hardly have any homework.

Mrs. P: Were you helpful to anyone today?

Wally: Hmm. Yeah. I showed Billy how to do a math problem. He sure was happy.

Mrs. P: And how did you feel when you did that?

Wally: Good.

Mrs. P: Did you need help with anything today?

Wally: Well, I asked Lenny if he would help me with my report on fish.

Mrs. P: Why ask Lenny?

Wally: He knows all about fish. His father is a tuna fisherman. And he really helped me. He was happy to do it and I sure needed it.

Mrs. P: That's nice to hear about. I'd like to see the report—I once did one on fish . . .

Mrs. Pawelk *modeled* the fact that helping was something that made her feel wonderful. She then *asked about helping* (which is easier for children to discuss than to talk about *their* needing help) and then, after hearing Wally talk about helping others, she *asked about his needing help.* Once conversations like this become occasional parts of a family routine, children will accept help more easily.

The Helping Hand. Sometimes we want help but we are unsure how to get it. We've suggested parents make a Helping Hand. Draw and cut out a hand. Then on each finger you can write a way to get help. Our favorites are

1. ask your family.
2. ask a friend.
3. look it up.
4. watch someone else.
5. take some lessons.

Posted on the refrigerator or elsewhere in the house, the Helping Hand is something you can point your children toward when they are "stuck" with a problem. Then they can make a decision about which method they will choose.

Using Readiness Skills to Handle an Everyday Problem: The Little League Outburst

The activities you have started teaching your children—Ears Ready!, Direction Following, Get Calm!, accepting praise, and seeking help, among others—can build their readiness skills in a number of ways. First, they raise awareness of the importance of these actions in the family. Second, they provide practice in learning how to carry them out. Third, they provide a label, a kind of shorthand, to remind children to use what they have learned. For example, for young children, you can say, "Okay, it's time to use Get Calm!" For older children (age nine or ten), you can remind them to use the activity by saying, "Think to yourself how you might calm down (follow directions, get help, and so on)."

The Allen family uses these skills as they go to watch twelve-year-old Brandon play in a Little League championship game. Mark is thirty-three years old and works as a teacher in a public school. His wife, Leslie, age thirty-one, works in a bank as an assistant branch manager. Brandon is the oldest child. His sister, Lynn, is nine and his brother, George, is eight.

The Allens get along well, although Leslie feels more strongly than her husband that the children should excel when it comes to school, sports, and extracurricular activities. Little League has been a sore point at times because Brandon, though a good player, is not a star. He has had problems concentrating when at bat, in the field, or on the bases. However, both his parents have been working with him to build his readiness skills so that he can improve his self-control, concentration, and team play, and seek help when he needs it.

It is now the middle of the game. Brandon's team is down by one run. There's a time out on the field. Brandon is coming up to bat with one out and a runner at third base. Here is my big chance to tie the score, he thinks, and am I ever nervous! Before he steps to the plate, his parents take him aside for a word.

Mark: (putting his arm on Brandon's shoulder) Okay, son, you'll be up in a minute. What did the coach tell you?
Brandon: Uhh, he, uhh, said I should, ummm.

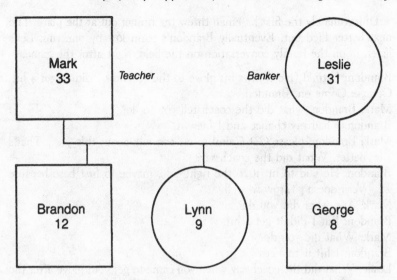

Leslie: Brandon, I think it's time to try to Get Calm! You know what to do. (Brandon takes several deep breaths and looks around and names objects and people to himself. His parents see his shoulders and face muscles loosen—a bit.)

Mark: Good! Maybe you should go over to the coach, get your Ears Ready!, and find out what to do. Good luck! We're rooting for you! (Brandon goes to the coach, faces him, and asks what he should do. The coach, who knew the Allens used Direction Following with Brandon, broke the instructions down into steps, steps that *this time* Brandon was ready to hear.)

Brandon: (now at the plate, to himself) I've got to hit it to the right side, the right side.

Umpire: Strike one!

Leslie: Get Calm!, Brandon. Get Calm!

Brandon: (to himself) Billy's pitching. He's not so tough—he can hardly run in gym. There's the ball. He's winding up . . .

Umpire: Ball one!

Brandon: (to himself) I got a hit last week off Tom, and Tom's a better pitcher. I can do it. Coach helped me to learn how. Here it comes . . . (He swings and hits a ground ball to first.)

Mark: Run, Brandon!

Unfortunately the first baseman threw the runner out at the plate. The next batter flied out. Eventually Brandon's team lost by one run. Let's listen in on the family conversation on the field, right after the game.

Brandon: I stink! (He throws his glove to the ground.) I didn't get a hit.
George: Come on, Brandon.
Mark: Brandon, what did the coach tell you to do?
Brandon: I had my chance and I blew it.
Mark: Brandon, please Get Calm! so we can talk about this . . . That's better. What did the coach say?
Brandon: He said to hit it to the right side, maybe to first base because Vern doesn't throw so well.
Mark: And what did you do?
Brandon: But I didn't get a hit.
Mark: What did you do?
Brandon: I hit it to Vern.
Leslie: What did the coach say when you came to get your glove after the inning?
Brandon: (mumbles, looking down)
Leslie: What was that? I can hear you better when you face me.
Brandon: Nice job. Vern made a lucky throw.
Mark: Nice job. Vern made a lucky throw. What does it mean when someone says something like that?
Brandon: I guess I followed directions. That Vern, he's so lucky. I've seen him throw the ball in the stands, on a bounce, I've even seen the ball go through his legs . . .

Brandon had some pretty intense feelings to deal with. First, he was nervous about batting. His parents and coach helped him listen, stay calm, and be clear about what to do. Brandon was able to follow through because his parents and coach had practiced readiness activities with him during less stressful times. When his actions didn't work out, the competitor in Brandon was ready to take the blame. Again, the readiness activities were available to Mark and Leslie to use as signals, as prompts to help Brandon sort out his intense reactions. By getting calm and being sensitive to the coach's praise, Brandon was able to shift much of his frustration and disappointment away from himself and place it on events, a once-in-a-lifetime throw by Vern, and so on. The child avoided a failure experience, and he can actually feel good about his accomplishments, especially how he stayed calm and followed directions in the clutch. It took the Allens a while to reach this point, but times like this make the activities and practice pay off.

Decision-Making Digest

Before children can be expected to make sound decisions, they must be *ready*. Being ready is like leaving for work dressed, with your car keys, and with gas in the car. Forget any of these, and you won't get far. To help our children get ready for decision making and problem solving, we can help them learn to *listen carefully and accurately, follow directions, stay calm and keep their self-control, and stay on task* when they are in a stressful or upsetting situation. We also want them to learn *how to seek out help* when it's needed and *how to receive praise*, so that they can recognize when their actions are getting approval. With these skills our children are more ready to venture forth with confidence into the more challenging and difficult world of responsibly solving problems and making decisions.

Before we move on and share with you the basic building blocks of preparing your child for decision making, we would like you to review the chart that summarizes the main family activities in this chapter and what each activity teaches. The following chart can be a handy reference to keep available as family teaching situations arise.

Decision-Making Digest:
Getting Ready for Decision Making

If you'd like your children to	*Then try these activities:*
1. learn to listen carefully and accurately	1. Ears Ready! Listening Position Instant Replay Sound Detector Cereal Progression
2. improve at following directions	2. Direction Following
3. learn to stay calmer and have better self-control	3. Get Calm!
4. feel more comfortable accepting praise and compliments	4. Learning to Receive Praise and Approval
5. learn when it's acceptable to ask for help and to feel comfortable with needing help, at times	5. Helping in the Media Helping Exchange
6. learn how to get help when it's needed	6. The Helping Hand

4

Look for Signs of Different Feelings

"Hi, how are you?"

"How are you feeling?"

How many times during a typical day do you or others use these greetings? Sometimes these greetings are used so often that the answer is an automatic "okay" or "fine." But the ability to get answers to these questions, to find out how another person is really feeling, is quite important. That's because feelings are like a compass or a gyroscope. They help us navigate through the sometimes choppy waters of having to get along with others. Feelings are signals—to approach someone or something, or to avoid doing something; to hug someone or to ask to be hugged; to resolve a problem or to make a decision. Many of us know that sometimes when people say they are "fine," they don't mean it. We figure out when we can believe the words, and when we cannot. And we know people who lack this skill, who seem to be somewhat insensitive to how others are really feeling.

For our children to get along well with teachers, friends, neighbors, siblings, relatives, and, of course, their parents, they need to be sensitive to signs of how people are feeling. They also must learn how to sort out strong and confused feelings they have, so that they can know what signals to send and what actions to take. Feelings provide information that is essential for sound decision making. *Looking for signs of different feelings* is the first decision-making step, the one that sets our course through the following seven other decision-making steps. In this chapter we introduce a new format, one that will help you teach the decision-making steps in a flexible, comfortable, and enjoyable manner.

"Steptalk":
Where We've Been and Where We're Going

We have taken a look at what children must do to cope in the real world. We have also examined how parents are "prepared" for the task of teaching children to cope successfully. It all amounts to quite a challenge, but one that can be uniquely rewarding! In the last chapter we took a look at some skills our children require to be ready for decision making. By staying calm, listening, following directions, receiving praise, and getting help when needed, our children give themselves the time and information needed to avoid hasty decisions and actions. Now we want to move toward the positive, to teach our children decision making that will prepare them for everyday living.

This chapter and the six that follow begin with "Steptalk," a review of the problem-solving steps already learned and a preview of what is to come. Our first problem-solving step is

1. Look for signs of different feelings.

You probably do this quite well without even knowing it. Think about that last family gathering, when you took one look at Aunt Mary and Uncle Oscar and *knew* they were having a rough time with each other. Perhaps you stayed away; perhaps you asked your cousin Shirley, who always knows what's going on, for some details; or maybe you went right up to Mary and Oscar and tried to find out what the problem was. Regardless, you used the *signs of different feelings* to give you *information* that influenced your *decision making*. Of course, we remember those friends or relatives who *miss* these signs and go on to cause discomfort, embarrassment, or hurt to others, and perhaps to themselves. We prefer that our children learn to recognize signs of different feelings. Our work and the work of colleagues has convinced us that children are happier for it and grow up to be better accepted and more able to cope. Let's look at one such child.

CASE EXAMPLE: DAVID KNOWS THE SIGNS

When David, a twelve year old, sat down in his seventh grade social studies class, he knew that today would be a quiz day. He recognized that familiar feeling in his stomach—a "jumpy, squeeshy" feeling, he calls it.

Actually, this feeling used to be worse. As he sat there, he thought back to a time when he felt worse—had a "flashback."

The feeling would start when he first heard there would be a test and then it would bother him when he tried to study. He failed a quiz once, because he couldn't sit still to review his book. *That's* a feeling he won't forget. When he got home that day, his mom had asked, "How are you, David?" He kind of smiled and said, "Okay." Mom said, "David, your eyes look very narrow and serious and your voice seems shaky." David gulped and told her he failed the quiz. She asked how he *really* felt, and he said, "Lousy." Then she asked him a funny kind of question: "Show me *where* you feel lousy." David said, "I feel lousy in the kitchen, in the living room, on the porch." "No, that's not what I mean. Where *in your body* do you feel lousy. Our body sends us signals, David. When we're upset or nervous, our body lets us know. What does Daddy do when I show him the credit card bill?" "Uh, well, oh yeah, he sits down kind of slouchy and grabs the back of his neck and rubs it. Then he says . . ." "That's enough, David. Daddy's neck is sending a message to him that there's a problem or something he has to deal with. What message are *you* getting?"

David learned that his stomach was very, very tight and that he felt uncomfortable after he failed the quiz. His mother helped him realize that it was hard to sit still and study because he didn't understand the "jumpy, squeeshy" feeling he had. He couldn't run away from it. The feeling seemed to get less and less intense as he studied better and learned his work. And he'd rather deal with *that* feeling than with the way his stomach felt after he failed.

David ends his flashback because the quiz papers are coming out. The jumpy feeling he had been remembering is there, but it doesn't bother him. He knows why it's there and that it will be gone by the time the quiz is over. After the quiz he sees Gerry slumped in his chair, tapping his hands more than usual. "That sure was a hard quiz, huh, Gerry?" "Yeah. I don't think I did too well. If you're going to lunch next, can I sit with you?" "Sure."

When David came home, his mother saw a smiling face and a bouncy walk. "How was your day today?" "Fine!" David then went into his room to get changed. His mother probably won't hear how David handled the quiz or how he helped Gerry to feel more comfortable. But she smiled as she heard David humming in his room.

CASE EXAMPLE:
BARBARA NEEDS HELP WITH THE SIGNS

Barbara began high school just last month. What a huge building! So many kids and teachers! It sure seems tough to manage. Today is a history quiz and, as Barbara sits in her seat, she's kind of fidgety. She just doesn't feel comfortable. Her teacher, Mr. Chasin, decides to review some of the material before the quiz. He asks Albert about the Queen of England and Albert gets it right, as always. Then he asks Barbara about Parliament. She starts feeling so uncomfortable that she doesn't hear his entire question. She gives a wrong answer that Mr. Chasin corrects. Barbara now feels like crying, yelling at Albert, and running away—all at once. When the quiz is given out, she has a lot of trouble. The rest of the day, most of the other kids just seem to stay away from her and that makes her feel worse.

When she gets home, her mother asks, "How are you, Barbara?" "Okay," she says through clenched teeth. "I've got a wash to do, so I'll be up in a little while." "Okay," says Barbara, even though it really isn't. Barbara goes into her room and just can't sit in one place. She remembers one time when she felt like this before. It was last year and she was up at the blackboard. She got a math problem wrong and one boy laughed at her. She threw the chalk at him and the teacher sent her to the office and the principal spoke to her and made her apologize to the teacher. And there was the time she talked and talked about her trip to the mall with her mother while Sally's mother was in the hospital. Barbara didn't know Sally could cry so loud! After these flashbacks, Barbara feels more and more upset.

Her mother calls, "Barbara, please help me hang up these clothes to dry." She goes to the yard and starts. "Barbara, I do wish you'd get rid of these jeans—look at those holes." "I like them, so tough on you," she says angrily. Her mother now realizes something is wrong. "What's the matter? Are you upset?" But Barbara doesn't "read" her mother's concern. "No, I'm not upset," she says louder and louder, "I'm not upset. Take the stupid wash. I don't care about it." She throws some clothes and storms into the house.

"CASETALK":
A CLOSER LOOK AT THE TWO CHILDREN

David and Barbara differ not only in their ability to read signs of different feelings, but also in their *willingness* to look for signs of different feelings. David knows when he feels stress and has a label for it—"jumpy, squeeshy." His mom, using his dad as a model, also helped him find a *location* for it—his stomach. And she helped him differentiate it from the much worse "tight" feelings of failure. Because he could read his own signs, David could study more easily, setting up a nice, positive pattern—as he studies and doesn't fail, he will feel less and less "squeeshy." Because David is learning how to label and locate his unpleasant feelings, the feelings are easier to control.

David also knew that Gerry was feeling troubled because he noticed Gerry's posture and hand movements. These observations are becoming "automatic" for David because he's in the habit of looking for signs of different feelings. Shortly we'll help you build that habit in your children, too. When that skill is missing in people, the results can be painful. Barbara hurt Sally's feelings because she didn't tune into Sally's signals—either at the start of their conversation or as it went along. It also seems as if Barbara's mother was not as sensitive as she could have been to *Barbara's* signals. If you reread the example you'll see that Barbara was sending out messages. Her flashback was as jumbled to her as were her present feelings; she had no labels to sort things out, no guidelines as to what to look for in the past situations. Words such as "angry," "frustrated," or "embarrassed" could have helped Barbara a great deal. When Barbara's mother finally caught on to the problem, she inadvertently escalated it by asking a closed-ended question to which she knew the answer: "Are you upset?" When Barbara heard that, she figured her mom was going to be of no help. However, if she had watched her mom's eyes and the concerned look on her face and in her voice, Barbara might have gotten *past* the words. She might have seen the signs of caring feelings and followed up those signs. But her own distress and not being in the habit of *looking for signs of different feelings* exacerbated the situation.

Your children may be very good at looking for signs of different feelings. You observe that they have a knack for saying the right things, not pushing you *too* far *too* often, and for being liked by friends, relatives, and others. If your child is not as sensitive to feelings as you would like, the activities we will discuss will help develop these skills. Maybe they will help you answer the age-old parental question, "Why did she (or he) *do* that?" and turn things around. Regardless of whether you have a David, a Barbara, one or several of each, or a child somewhere in between, the family activities that follow can help keep good skills sharp and in use.

How to Help Your Children Look for Signs of Different Feelings

BE A MODEL

When you make a cake, your child can see how it came about. There is a recipe to follow, and he or she observed or helped you in the kitchen. But it's harder for your child to see what your smile means when the cake is finished. How we arrive at our feelings, the events they correspond to, and the labels we apply are things our children must learn. Much of this learning takes place through *modeling*—parents' thinking and feeling aloud so their children can follow what is going on. Following is a conversation between father and son that involves useful modeling.

Sherman: Ben, I've just heard some upsetting news. Your Uncle Charles had a nasty fall in his cellar. He's broken his leg and won't be able to work for a while. Who's going to cover the business? When I hear about things like this, I get hot under the collar. I can picture Charles in the hospital, leg in a cast, uncomfortable. At least Dr. Farrell is looking after him, so I feel he's in good hands.

Ben: Wow! Your face does look red, Dad, and you sure are working up a sweat. You looked that way when I broke your favorite record and when you found out they couldn't fix your bike after you hit that tree.

Besides showing his concern for feelings, how he is feeling, and why, Sherman told Ben about his Feelings Fingerprint. Everyone seems to have one—a characteristic way of showing how one feels when upset or stressed. Sherman got "hot under the collar"—his face gets red and he perspires. Above, we met David, whose Feelings Fingerprint was a certain feeling in his stomach. David's dad's "feeling-print" was the back of his neck. Some people feel it in their shoulders or arms, or get headaches or backaches, tightness in the chest, and so on. All we know is that people seem to be consistent in *where* they feel their stress. By modeling our own Feelings Fingerprint areas and helping our children read and label theirs, we teach them to *look for signs of different feelings*.

ENCOURAGE EXPRESSIONS

When we encourage children to express their feelings, we show them we are sensitive to their signals and that it is all right to share and talk about feelings. Children show their feelings through their Feelings Fingerprint and their words, body posture and gestures. But a more subtle way is through changes in their routine. For example, a sudden stalling or reluctance to go to bed or get ready for school can be a sign of some fear. Changes in eating and sleeping patterns or energy level can also indicate upset or unhappy feelings. You know your children well; when they are "not themselves," it is important at these times to *encourage expression* of feelings. Here are some probes we have found useful:

> "How are you feeling . . . I mean how are you *really* feeling?"
> "You seem (unhappy, upset, and so on)."
> "When I feel sad, I sometimes don't feel like eating either."
> "What seems to be the matter . . . I'd like to know."
> "It seems as if something is bothering you. I'd like to talk with you about it."
> "When I see (describe what the child is doing, such as not getting ready for bed on time, or being irritable), I know something is the matter. When can we talk about it?"

If your child resists, pressing too hard usually doesn't work. Let him or her know you are available and ready to talk, when he or she is. Sometimes, though, words are less effective than a touch or a hug, which says, "I care about you."

ACCEPT AND ACKNOWLEDGE WHAT YOU HEAR

Notice we didn't say "understand" or "agree with" what you hear— sometimes this is impossible. But a feeling is not "right" or "wrong." If we want our children to share their feelings with us, we must be careful not to make them pay for it. Here's what we mean:

Mother: Ronald, what seems to be the matter?

Ronald: Nothing.

Mother: Ronald, I really would like to know. You haven't been eating and that's just not like you.

Ronald: Well, it's Virginia. I don't think she likes me anymore and I'm worried.

Mother: That's the silliest thing I've ever heard. How could you worry about her? Of course she likes you.

Ronald: I'm going inside, Mom.

What if his mother acknowledged Ronald's feelings and praised him for sharing them:

Mother: That certainly seems upsetting. Thanks for telling me . . . I thought you had stopped liking my cooking!

Ronald: (smiling) No, it's not that, Mom.

Mother: What happened between you and Virginia?

Ronald: Oh well, nothing really. (Mother remains silent, looks concerned.) Well, she walked to the bus with Tommy.

Mother: You saw them walk to the bus together. How did you feel then?

Ronald: I was burning mad in my eyes. And you know what else . . .

Later on Ronald's mom might tell him that when he refuses to eat and when he feels "burning in his eyes," these are *signs of upset feelings*. And Ronald will probably *keep* talking to his mom about his feelings, because she accepted them, praised him for sharing them, and asked him questions that showed she was concerned and listened carefully. To help your child learn to *look for signs of different feelings*, we suggest you teach him or her about Feelings Fingerprints and try some of the family activities that follow. Whether you are at home or away, we think your family will have fun and become closer.

Family Activities You Can Do at Home

FEELINGS WORD LIST

How well we recognize feelings depends in part on how many labels we have to stick on them. Gather your family together and try to make a

Feelings Word List. Just try to name as many different feelings as you can. As long as they're not identical, you can include them. We suggest you work on it for fifteen minutes or so and then put your list on the refrigerator. Gradually people can add to it as a new feeling word comes to mind. We've included a list you might find helpful—but try to make yours first! Be sure to keep your list—it will be useful for other activities.

happy	embarrassed	lazy	terrific
angry	disappointed	satisfied	calm
surprised	pleased	ashamed	joyful
bored	mad	important	scared
proud	shocked	curious	worried
sad	loved	excited	frustrated
tense	upset	jealous	serious

USING BOOKS AND STORIES TO LOOK FOR SIGNS OF FEELINGS

A father is reading a book to his daughter before bedtime:

Dad: "And when Geppetto brought in his fishing pole, who was on the end of it but Pinocchio and his conscience, Jiminy Cricket." Before we keep reading, let's look at the pictures. How do you think Geppetto is feeling?

Sarica: Happy.

Dad: What else?

Sarica: Surprised.

Dad: How can you tell?

Sarica: His eyebrows are up and his arms are up, too. He's kind of smiling. Pinocchio looks happy too. Jiminy just looks tired and wet. But I bet he's happy to be out of the water.

Dad: How would you have felt if you were Pinocchio?

Sarica: Smiling and happy inside because I found my daddy.

Even if the book had no pictures, the questions could be exactly the same. Sarica is learning the signs of feelings and also how different events lead to certain feelings. You can use this activity with fiction or nonfiction works (such as biographies, sports stories, and newspaper articles and pictures) and help your children get a human and personal perspective on what they read.

FEELINGS

FLASHBACKS

For this family game, you will need a stack of index cards. On each card write one of the words from your Feelings Word List. One person in the family picks a card and, for the feeling on it, shares a specific time or situation when he or she felt that way. One format is the question, "Tell about a time when you felt _____." Everyone is permitted to ask follow-up questions. Be sure to ask your children occasionally how they knew they felt that way. Feelings Flashbacks can be used with preschoolers, high schoolers, and everyone in between. It builds family sharing. Below is an example of how Joe got his wife, Ellen, and eighteen-year-old daughter, Diana, to give it a try.

Joe: Hey, everybody, I've got a game I'd like to try.

Ellen: Does it involve horses?

Joe: No, just us.

Ellen: No dice?

Joe: No, just us. Diana, come back here, you can make that call later. Okay, now I have some cards here.

Ellen: I knew it!

Joe: Each one has a word from our Feelings List. We'll take turns picking one and then telling about a time we had that feeling. It works well if you pick the card, close your eyes, breathe deeply, try to picture clearly the situation you were in, and *then* tell about it.

Ellen: Are we going to have to chant or anything?

Joe: No, no chanting. Diana, why don't you go first.

Diana: Me? Nah. Why don't you play with my aunt and uncle instead? Oh, all right. Let's see . . . "excited." Hmm. Oh, I can think of a time.

Joe: Picture it as clearly as you can.

Diana: We were at the racetrack and the horse we picked—the long shot with the limp—was in the lead. I was excited then. I remember my heart pounding and I was jumping up and down.

Ellen: I kept saying, "Joey, Joey, Joey," because I was so excited, too. My legs got so weak I could hardly stand up.

Joe: I bet you both can picture it very clearly. Do you remember the horse's name?

Diana: It was Veyzmir, number six, from the last position . . .

With younger children, you may find it helpful to suggest times they have felt a certain way. In any case, try a couple of Feelings Flashbacks when you have some time. It can become habit-forming—so watch out!

FEELINGS DETECTIVE

This is a versatile family game with seemingly endless variations. It is designed to give family members practice at recognizing and labeling feelings. Take out a magazine with pictures in it. Ask each person to write down all the feelings they see in the magazine in an hour (or ten minutes, or in one day). You might want to keep track of the pages, so that everyone's results can be compared. The real fun is in talking about what you find—we think your children will surprise you! Perhaps you might offer a small reward for the person who has the most different kinds of feelings. Variations include cutting out or locating many examples of one feeling, such as happy, sad, or scared, or several feelings on which you might want to concentrate. To help you keep track of your detective work, we've enclosed a chart you can use or adapt to your specific activity.

FEELINGS FOOTLIGHTS

Do you know how many great actresses and actors got their start? They sat down with their families on cold winter nights and played a variation of Feelings Footlights. If your family wants to have fun and learn signs of different feelings, we think Feelings Footlights is for you. There are several variations, but all of them involve showing how feelings are expressed. So get your top hat, put on your makeup, and . . . action!

Warm Up. Ask someone to name a feeling (or use the cards you made for Feelings Flashbacks). Then have that person ask *someone else* to tell everyone how he or she shows that feeling. That person then asks someone else, and so on. Begin again for different feelings.

In the Spotlight. One person decides what feeling he or she would like to show, possibly by picking a feelings card. The rest of the family tries to guess the feeling, but there's one catch—the actor *cannot use any words*. Only gestures, facial expressions, and body postures are allowed! Whoever guesses the feeling can have the next turn in the spotlight.

Quiet on the Set! You may wish to have relatives, friends, and others

TABLE 2
THE FEELINGS DETECTIVE
LOOK FOR SIGNS OF DIFFERENT FEELINGS

This activity is designed to help you identify some common everyday feelings that everyone has. Make believe you are a detective and you have a problem to solve. A good detective has to look for small clues. See if you can find people who show feelings on TV, in the movies, or in real life. First write down where you found the clues. Then write down the clues you found with your eyes (WHAT I SEE) and/or with your ears (WHAT I HEAR).

Feelings	Where	What I See	What I Hear
Example: Happy	Example: newspaper, picture, p. 4	Example: people smiling and waving	
1.	1.	1.	1.
2.	2.	2.	2.
3.	3.	3.	3.
4.	4.	4.	4.
5.	5.	5.	5.
6.	6.	6.	6.
7.	7.	7.	7.
8.	8.	8.	8.
9.	9.	9.	9.
10.	10.	10.	10.

join you for this activity. Divide into teams. One person picks a feelings card and acts it out nonverbally. Whichever team guesses the feeling first gets a point. Play for a set period of time or until you reach a certain number of points, and then let the winning team have a small reward. Maybe they get first crack at the popcorn, or an extra marshmallow in their hot chocolate. If you have teenagers or just wish to play Quiet on the Set! with your friends, you can use movie, book, and song titles and the like with feelings words in them, instead of single words only. Some examples: "Love Is a Many-Splendored Thing," "Happy Together," "Thriller," *The Red Badge of Courage.*

Costumes! Costumes! It can be *very* interesting to give children a feelings word and then ask them to dress up in a way that shows the feeling. Perhaps you can encourage them to develop a little scene or imaginary play around the feeling. You might wish to dress up also!

Run Through the Script. Our final act involves the selection of a passage from a book, comic book, magazine, or other work that expresses some feelings. One person reads and the rest act out silently the feelings they hear, *using only facial expressions.* Children's books are wonderful sources of material. Here is a brief example of the kind of passage that works well (the feelings words are in italics):

Juan and Rosa are in art class, working on a picture together. Rosa is *happy* and *enjoys* herself while she works. Juan is *upset*—he's not sure they're doing a good enough job. Rosa stops and thinks about what to do next. She asks Juan, but he's *annoyed* and answers in an *angry* voice, "I don't care." Rosa looks *surprised.* She didn't realize how *angry* Juan was. She asks him what's wrong. Juan *calms down* a little and says, "I don't feel *proud* of this. I'm *worried* that when we show people, they will *laugh* at us."

As a variation, *body postures* can be used with, instead of, or after facial expressions.

Family Activities You Can Do Away from Home

TEACH YOUR CHILDREN
TO SHAVE

Children anywhere from preschool age through teenage can learn to SHAVE; that is, they can learn to observe in themselves and others:

S   = Shoulders
HA = Hands
V   = Voice
E   = Eyes and face

By observing others' shoulders, hands, eyes, and face, and by listening to the tone and loudness of voice, we learn a great deal about how people are feeling. A quick SHAVE of others can be fun and easy to do, as we will illustrate.

MALL DETECTOR

When you are at a mall, sit on a bench near a busy area, especially near an escalator. Pick a person to observe and then SHAVE him or her: take a quick look at the shoulders, and so on, and evaluate the voice, if you can hear it. Each person should decide what feelings are being observed, and then compare ideas. The first few times you try Mall Detector, begin by reviewing what SHAVE stands for and how it helps us to *look for signs of different feelings.* A wonderful variation of this game is Fast-Food Frenzy, during which you SHAVE fast-food customers. And let's face it—many adults have been SHAVEing others for years in restaurants, bowling alleys, subways, and buses. Why not take advantage of the excellent learning opportunity these places provide to look *(discreetly,* of course!) for signs of different feelings.

SHAVEing IN THE MOVIES

After a movie, ask your children about how characters expressed certain feelings. Use SHAVE as a guideline. You can also model by sharing your observations of how people felt at important points in the movie and see what others observed. Of course, you can SHAVE with your family during and after television and radio programs. But the big screen and loud sound systems of movies often provide the most striking—and lasting—examples of feelings being expressed.

RELATIVE ENTHUSIASM

When families get together for holidays or picnics or birthdays, SHAVEing can liven things up and at the same time teach children something about feelings. Try SHAVEing a cousin or uncle and do some Feelings Footlights activities. These are two exercises that are best saved *only* for family gatherings.

Smiling Faces. Your child's task is to say or do something that will make a relative smile or laugh. You can have your children plan together, work individually, or you can be the team captain. Things like funny faces, compliments, and jokes are all good smile getters. Help your children review what tactics work best with different relatives. You'll also find the good spirit of this activity can be contagious.

Mirror, Mirror. Have your children pair up, perhaps at first with you on some other willing relative. One person is going to be a mirror; the other, a communicator. The mirror can reflect only what it sees. Therefore, the person playing the mirror must watch the communicator carefully and accurately reflect any changes in expression, position, movement, and so on. The communicator can express whatever he or she wishes or can follow some guidelines (that is, go from tired to scared to sad to happy). Roles can be switched, and other relatives can be enlisted as observers to comment on what was mirrored best. If your relatives resist, you may wish to start them on Feelings Flashbacks. Eventually, many will come around and give Mirror, Mirror a try.

FEELINGS ON THE ROAD

When your family is in a car, bus, plane, or train, there is a fun way to approach feelings from a different perspective. Start with a physical characteristic or sensation and link it to a color. For example, "When I say _____ (tall, twisty, hot, cold, wet, dry, and so on), what color do you think of?" After a few of these, move to, "When you see the color _____, what kind of feeling do you have?" It's interesting to find agreements and disagreements with our children. Preschoolers might see blue as cool, red as hot, and yellow as happy. Older children may have more than one color as an answer. You can also reverse the question and start with words from the feelings list:

"When I say _____ (excited, bored, sad), what color do you think of?"
For an added challenge, use something other than colors, such as shapes
(circle, triangle, octagon), types of trees (maple, birch, oak, knotty pine),
muppets (Bert, Animal, Kermit, a Fraggle), sports figures (Babe Ruth, Joe
Namath, Bill Russell), cars (Cadillac, pickup truck, Edsel), or flowers
(daisy, sunflower, tulip). Try selecting categories with which your child is
familiar. There is no shortage of examples to choose from!

Using the First Decision-Making Step to
Handle Everyday Problems

By carrying out the activities in this chapter—Feelings Fingerprints,
Feelings Word List, Feelings Flashbacks, SHAVEing in the mall and movies, and Feelings Footlights—you introduce your child to the first decision-
making step. When your child can *look for signs of different feelings,* he or
she has made a major advance toward becoming successful at making
thoughtful decisions. You guide the process by finding time in your daily
routine for some or all of the family activities we've been presenting.
However, everyday problems which come up provide the most powerful
opportunities to teach the first decision-making step—the feelings step.
Below are examples of how four different families use common situations
to build their awareness of signs of different feelings.

NENA'S HOME FROM SCHOOL . . . AND SHE'S UPSET

Nena lives with her mom, Mary, in a housing project in the city. Nena's
just come home from her eighth grade class. She puts her books down on
the table and doesn't pick them up as they slide down onto the floor. She
stalks into her room and slams the door. When the phone rings, Mary asks
her daughter to answer it. Nena does so, but she speaks very angrily and
ends the conversation with her friend by saying, "Oh, leave me alone . . .
just don't bother me!" See how Mary responds to these signs of upset
feelings:

Mary: Nena, since you came home, your books have ended up on the
floor, I thought the door to your room was going to break off, and

whomever you were talking to heard quite an angry voice. When I notice things like that, I think they are signs of upset feelings.

Nena: Oh, Mom, c'mon.

Mary: Remember when Daddy and I were first divorced? Every time Grandma would call, I'd sound just like you did. I was upset—but not at Grandma.

Nena: Yeah.

Mary: Were you upset at the friend who called you?

Nena: No, she had nothing to do with it.

Mary: Your eyebrows and forehead are all wrinkled up—whatever it is, it must be pretty upsetting.

Nena: Yeah.

Mary: Would you care to talk about it now, or would later be better?

Nena: Later Mom—maybe while we make dinner.

Mary: Fine. Speaking of dinner, I've got to go and get . . .

Mary recognized Nena's signs of different feelings. But rather than interrogate Nena about her feelings, Mary chose to describe what she observed in Nena, using a little bit of humor. Then she combined modeling and a Feelings Flashback to draw a parallel between her feelings and Nena's problem now. Finally she pointed out Nena's signs of angry feelings and then gave Nena the choice of when to talk about her feelings. Note she did *not* ask, "Do you want to talk about it?" It's very easy for young adolescents to say no, out of anger. Sometimes these discussions don't go this smoothly. At other times the child will not even wait until later to start talking. What is most important, though, is that Mary and Nena have a way to handle strong feelings that arise.

THE BEDTIME CHAT . . . WHEN SOMETHING DOESN'T SEEM QUITE RIGHT

Donna knew all day that something was not quite right with her daughter, Jennifer. Jennifer didn't eat much—not even her favorites. She was very quiet and stayed by herself a lot, and this behavior was very unlike her! Robert noticed the same thing. When he got home from work, there was just a quiet "Hi, Dad," instead of an enthusiastic, "Daddy!" When Jennifer was getting ready for bed, Donna sat down next to her.

Donna: Remember some of the games we've been playing the past two weeks, games to help us look for signs of different feelings?

Jennifer: Sure.

Donna: Well, I've seen a lot of signs of feelings from you today, things that you don't usually do. Can you think of what I mean?

Jennifer: Hmm. I didn't eat my dinner or my dessert. And when I spilled the juice by the refrigerator, I didn't wipe it up too well.

Donna: Daddy and I have seen some of these same things, and we think they are signs of upset feelings. What should you try to do when you have upset feelings?

Jennifer: Talk to you or Daddy or someone. But if I have to go to the dentist, it's going to hurt.

Donna: So you've been upset about your teeth *and* about maybe having to go to the dentist. I'm very glad you've told me. Now . . .

Donna found out important information by helping Jennifer use the first decision-making step. Now the family can address the *real* issue. Notice that Donna *didn't* respond, "Why didn't you just tell me?" or "Isn't that silly!" Instead, she tried to help Jennifer see that looking for signs of different feelings is a good and useful activity. Sharing these signs and feelings with other family members can also be helpful. There is a lot of decision making to come, but Donna will probably wait until the morning before she pursues things.

"I DID IT, I DID IT": SIGNS OF PRIDE AND ACCOMPLISHMENT

When Bill came home from the lab, the house was in an uproar. Peter, age five, was running around in circles. Anna, only a year old, was in tears. Inger was just managing to stay a step or two behind Peter and protect Anna from harm. Bill took off his coat, and called Peter. "Hi, Dad!" Peter ran over, jumped up and down, whooped and sang, and ran off, singing, "I did it, I did it." Inger knew that this was how Peter reacted when something especially exciting happened to him. Peter's saying, "I did it," was a further clue that something *really* special had occurred. She saw Bill was looking puzzled and perhaps a bit annoyed. So she began to explain:

Inger: Peter just came back from his soccer practice about ten minutes ago . . . Barbara drove him. He started right in with this and it was all I could do to keep Anna calm.

Bill: Did he finally score a goal in practice? I bet he did!

Inger: That's what I think. I'm going to change Anna. Why don't you bring him closer to earth and see if he can tell us what happened.

Bill: Okay. Peter . . . Pete . . . How can I talk with you if you keep running inside?

Peter: I did it! I did it!

Bill: Hopping, running, jumping, and whooping—when you do these things, that tells me you're feeling, uh, um . . .

Peter: Happy!

Bill: That's just the word I was looking for! You did something that made you happy? What was it?

Peter: At the Pine Grove field, I scored a goal, all by myself! The coach said, "Great, Peter," and then I did it again!

Bill: It sounds like you feel happy and proud of yourself, too. Let's go put that word on our Word List. Mommy and Anna and I would like you to show us how you did it. Before we figure out when, let's Get Calm! for a minute, okay?

Peter: . . . eight, nine, ten.

Bill: Great! When can you show us?

Peter: After we eat.

Bill: Okay, terrific. I'm going to clean up in here before dinner. You can help me, or else maybe you'd like to draw a picture of soccer practice or something . . .

Bill and Inger have a youngster who can't contain himself when he's excited. But sometimes even happy feelings can disrupt a household. Bill helped Peter see the signs of his happy feelings, gave him another label for those feelings (proud), and helped channel Peter's energy into a demonstration and into either cleaning up or continuing to celebrate in a "safer" way. He asked Peter to use Get Calm! (see Chapter 3) so he could talk to him, but certainly Peter's enthusiasm and feelings of pride and accomplishment were not diminished. Over time Peter will be able to tell his parents a little sooner and a little more directly what he is feeling . . . to his and their benefit!

**DO WE HAVE TO GO
TO UNCLE LUIS'S HOUSE AGAIN?**

It's Saturday morning and the Sanchez family (see the chart) is at the breakfast table. They are talking about a trip to the zoo that they've planned for the afternoon. As they are talking, Miriam answers the phone. After a few "buts," Miriam says, "Okay" and hangs up with a pained expression on her face.

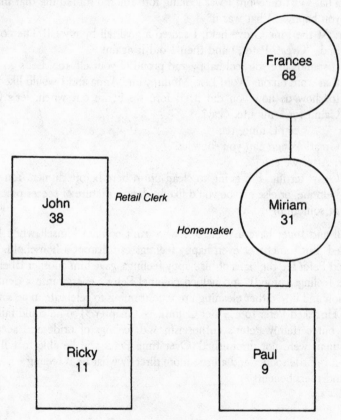

Miriam: I just spoke to Uncle Luis. The party for Tio Edward has been switched from next week to this afternoon.

Ricky: Good. I didn't want to go, anyway. Uncle Luis always tries to teach us to fix things—toasters, radios, shelves. The zoo is much more fun.

Paul: Yeah. Lions and tigers and bears, oh no. Lions and tigers and bears, OH NO. Lions . . .

Miriam: Ricky, Paul, I don't think you understand. We are going to Uncle Luis's this afternoon.

Paul: But you promised!

Ricky: I'm not going!

Miriam: We have to go and that's all there is to it.

Paul: It's not fair. I told my friends we were going to the zoo and I'd show them something I got there.

Ricky: I'm staying home. You said we were going and we're going.

Miriam: Now, I don't want to hear another word from either of you! Get in the living room and quiet down!

Familiar? Kids hate disappointment and parents hate defiance. Fortunately, John has not yet been drawn into this conflict. Once the kids are inside, he approaches Miriam:

John: I haven't seen the kids that upset in a long time. Did you see Ricky's face—how red it got? And Paul made a tight fist.

Miriam: Yes, they were angry. But did you hear what they said?

John: I heard them say they were disappointed.

Miriam: But it's *how* they said it.

John: True. You know, *your* neck was getting kind of strained.

Miriam: Really? Well, I guess so. It just angers me when they talk that way.

John: You know I've been thinking. Maybe if we teach them what their upset feelings mean, they can use different words. Let's call them in and try.

Miriam: Okay. Paul, Ricky—come in please.

John: I was watching you when Mom said we have to go to Uncle Luis's house. Your face got all red and, Paul, you made a really tight fist. Do you know why?

Ricky: We don't want to go to Uncle Luis's house today.

John: You felt that way when you heard the news. I bet you were disappointed and angry.

Ricky: Of course we were. Have you been watching one of your talk shows again, Dad?

John: All right, all right, wise guy. But when you both get upset, you can do something a little more helpful than just getting angry and taking your feelings out on Mom or me or each other. Paul, when Ricky gets mad, how does he look?

Paul: Like a ripe mango.

John: What do you mean?

Paul: His face gets shiny red.

Ricky: It does not!

John: Ricky, how can you tell when *I* am angry?

Ricky: That's easy. You stand up straight and call me like my teacher does, "Rickeee." Or else you use my middle name too, "Rickeee Ernest."

John: And what good things happen after I do that?

Ricky: Nothing.

John: You know, if we all learn to watch for those signs of when we have angry or upset feelings, maybe we can keep ourselves from saying or doing something that will make matters worse.

Paul: Yeah. When we told Mommy that it's not fair and stuff like that, we got her madder and madder.

Miriam: And I don't enjoy getting madder. I'm also disappointed about the zoo. It's my turn to take you both on the skyride!

John: Right! Now, how about finishing breakfast and *then* we'll talk about what to do today.

John has begun to prepare his family to look for signs of different feelings. Over the next week he can start to introduce family activities to sharpen *everyone's* ability to do this. He picked a challenging time to start teaching the first decision-making step. But he waited until he and Miriam were alone and until the situation had calmed down a bit. The Sanchez family can at least get through breakfast before facing the problem again. In the next chapter we discuss how the family uses these skills and others to decide what they should do.

Decision-Making Digest

The first decision-making step—*looking for signs of different feelings*—is the key that opens many doors for our children. Feelings are signs that there are problems to be solved or joys to be shared, concerns to be addressed or challenges to be overcome. As our children look for signs of different feelings in themselves and in others, they can use their thinking skills to help them figure out how to act and how to use the energy of their feelings constructively. Activities such as Feelings Flashbacks, SHAVEing, the Feelings Word List, Feelings Detective, and Feelings Footlights can help all family members become more aware of the signs of different feelings. You can guide your children to pick up on signs of feelings with fewer and fewer hints or prompts. With our feelings in better focus, we can proceed to the next decision-making step.

Before proceeding to the next chapter, take a moment to look at the chart of the main family activities in this chapter. As before, it can serve as a handy reference.

Decision-Making Digest:
Look for Signs of Different Feelings

If you'd like your child to	*Then try these activities:*
1. become sensitive to his or her bodily signs of stress	1. Feelings Fingerprint
2. become aware of a range of feelings one can experience	2. Feelings Word List Feelings on the Road
3. learn different signs that indicate how people are feeling	3. Using Books and Stories to Look for Signs of Different Feelings Feelings Flashbacks Teaching Your Children to SHAVE
4. practice recognizing and labeling feelings	4. Feelings Detective Mall Detector SHAVEing in the Movies

5. learn to express a range of different feelings	5. Feelings Footlights:
	  In the Spotlight;
	  Quiet on the Set;
	  Costumes! Costumes!
	  Run Through the Script
	Relative Enthusiasm:
	  Smiling Faces;
	  Mirror, Mirror

5

*Tell Yourself
What the Problem Is*

"Problem." It's a word we see, hear, and use all the time. If you work in an office, you know that problems are constant: with numbers not adding up, with the typewriter, with the telephone, and with co-workers telling you about *their* problems! When you are a parent, your problems could include dirty diapers, food on the floor, curfew violations, or children sick with the flu. Certainly these kinds of problems are annoyances, interruptions of our routines and activities. Yet there is another quality to the word "problem" that makes it a very special and useful concept.

Problems can be solved! They provide challenges to be met, answers to be found, and circumstances with which one must cope. When we have a problem, and we *know* it is a problem, we can think about ways to solve it. But when something is bothering us and leaving us with vague feelings of uneasiness or discomfort, we're often not quite ready to tackle it. The first decision-making step is to *look for signs of different feelings*. By doing this we prepare ourselves for the next step: *telling ourselves what the problem is*. We do this by *putting the problem into words*—thereby unlocking the door to our decision-making and problem-solving potential.

Researchers and educators like Jean Piaget and John Dewey have spent years watching children solve problems—in the classroom, on the playground, and even at home. They noticed that once children can put a problem into words, take it apart, or look at its specifics, they can begin to *think* about it. This thinking process, however, is rarely taught to children. If they are fortunate, they pick it up through interactions with parents, teachers, other relatives, or friends. But too often children do not learn the value of telling themselves what the problem is. This chapter will teach your children to verbalize what the problem is and will help you understand the importance of teaching your children this second decision-making step.

"Steptalk": Where We've Been and Where We're Going

Learning to *look for signs of different feelings* is like finding yourself in front of an encyclopedia. Information of all kinds is available to you—but you must know what to do with it, and how to make the information accessible and useful to you. The key to putting this information to work is to *tell yourself what the problem is.* "I'm looking at this encyclopedia because I want to know something about the way Alexander Graham Bell invented the telephone." *Now* you have a sense of what to do, where to look, how to solve your problem. Similarly, you can probably recall a time when you had a feeling that was upsetting you, but you couldn't get a handle on what the problem was. Even a mildly distressing problem can illustrate this. Let's say, for instance, that a friend has told you great things about a movie. As you are watching the movie, you feel that you *should* be enjoying it more . . . why aren't you? Then you say to yourself, "I'm feeling this way because Larry said it was so exciting, especially the chase, and I'm not finding it all that special." You've just linked the first two decision-making steps:

1. Look for signs of different feelings.
NEW 2. Tell yourself what the problem is.

Now you can think about what to do next—stop watching, continue watching but with different expectations, have a talk with Larry, and so on.

When we've taught children this second decision-making step, we've asked parents and teachers how it has been most helpful. They tell us that conversations like this happen less often:

Adult: What seems to be the matter?
Child: Nothing.
Adult: What's wrong, I'd like to know.
Child: I don't know.

They are replaced by conversations like this one:

Adult: What seems to be the matter?
Child: Nothing.
Adult: I really would like to know.
Child: I feel terrible . . . Todd didn't invite me to his party.

It is so much more gratifying to have our children share feelings and concerns with us than it is to hear a lot of complaints, "nothings", and "I don't knows". This chapter will help you teach your children to tell themselves what the problem is. Let's see what happens when children do and do not possess this skill.

CASE EXAMPLE: LEONORE TURNS FEELINGS INTO WORDS

"No, no, no. More lift—*more lift!*" Leonore's gymnastics coach had never been easy on her, but this was the roughest day she could remember in her fifteen years. As she kept trying the routine on the uneven bars and as she kept hearing her coach's criticisms, she noticed she was having more and more uncomfortable feelings. "The last time I felt this way was when my friends were sleeping over and Dad blew a make-believe trumpet and said it was time for us to go to sleep—and that was only two weeks ago." Leonore thought this to herself as she put some resin on her hands. She got ready to try again. As she looked at the bars, she imagined herself doing the routine better than ever. She noticed other, good feelings joining the uncomfortable feelings she had before.

When Leonore completed her landing, she knew she had done well. She knew she was feeling proud of what she had done. When her coach said, "Not bad, next time, more fluid, more graceful," she felt a warm feeling that she had come to learn meant "joy." These feelings stayed with her as she changed in the locker room, before she met her friends.

Her friends Raquel and Alicia asked her how her practice went. Their question started Leonore thinking. "It was an amazing day. My coach kept criticizing me and I had all kinds of feelings. I felt *angry* because he kept saying I needed more lift. I felt *disappointed* because I wasn't doing the routine correctly. And I even felt *embarrassed* when I thought about what my father did at my sleep-over party—you remember." "We sure do," they said. "At least he can carry a tune." "Yeah," Leonore agreed. "Well, when I stood at the bar, I told myself why I had all those feelings, and I didn't feel so confused and upset. When I thought about doing the routine well, I felt hopeful. And when I finished and the coach said, 'Not bad,' I felt proud because I knew I had done my best routine today." "What a day!" Alicia said. Raquel added, "It's great to hear. I hope you'll show us the routine . . ."

Leonore enjoyed being with her friends and looked forward to her next practice routine. At age fifteen, Leonore knew she could sort out her feelings, put them into words, and keep things in focus better than a lot of other people her age. As she walked home, there was a bounce in her gait that reflected the smile on her face.

CASE EXAMPLE: NELSON HAS TROUBLE TAKING HIS FEELINGS APART

Nelson liked reading about Indiana Jones, Sherlock Holmes, and other adventurers. They kept cool in the face of danger or mystery. They kept their wits about them; they thought fast and clearly. They could tell what a problem was and ZOOM—they started to deal with it. Sure, Nelson was only sixteen, but it seemed hopeless. Those guys were sports cars; he was a station wagon. They were Lear jets; he was a transport plane. They were filet mignons; he was an undercooked meat loaf. They were . . .

"Hey, Nelson, what are you doing? You look fogged out." "No, Lee, I was just thinking about this book I'm reading." "Are you going to Hollie's picnic next Saturday?" "What picnic?" "Oh, ah, um, I don't know. Listen, I gotta go. See you later!"

Nelson said goodbye and went back to his reading. But he started having trouble—many upset feelings kept him from enjoying Sherlock. When he switched to Indiana Jones, nothing changed. He kept asking himself, "Why do I feel like this??" He became restless and fidgety. Lee came back to see if Nelson was ready to leave. "Hey, Nelson, let's head out, I'm going to the movies tonight." "When I'm good and ready." "What's the matter?" "Just bug off, Lee." "Hey, Nelson, I mean, hey . . . what's going on?" "Hollie's not so nice, either." "Hollie? Nelson, I'm going. You need a good night's sleep—or maybe a shrink." Nelson sat there, his face getting redder and redder, his hands gripping his book so tightly, the pages were getting sweaty and folded.

"CASETALK":
A CLOSER LOOK AT THE TWO CHILDREN

Teenagers like Leonore and Nelson have a lot in common. They are developing a sense of who they are and what they can and cannot do well. They want to be involved with friends, and they are experiencing very strong and sometimes conflicting feelings. Leonore has developed a way to handle these feelings and turn the energy of these feelings into constructive action. Nelson is locked up by his feelings. They are confusing, hard for him to separate, and they cause frustration that spills over onto uninvolved others, like Lee. What does Leonore do differently?

Leonore puts her feelings into words. She tells herself what the problem is that has led to the feelings. She felt angry because the coach kept criticizing. The *criticism* was the problem, *not something about Leonore.* And Leonore learned what we have taught many, many children. What do you do with a problem? *Solve it!* So Leonore took the energy of her feelings, told herself what the problem was, and tried to meet the challenge of solving it. Her feelings of pride came because she improved her performance and because the coach acknowledged it. These positive feelings were not signs of problems—but it was rewarding for Leonore to be able to put these feelings into words and share them with her friends.

Nelson is a sensitive teenager whose upset feelings left him hopeless and frustrated. If he were able to *tell himself what the problem was,* he could perhaps try to solve it. Take a moment and review Nelson's case example. What problems could he have identified? He felt worthless and inadequate *because* he was comparing himself to Indiana and Sherlock. He felt left out and angered *when* Lee asked him to leave, and especially *when* Lee said he might need a shrink. *Nelson's upset feelings needed labels;* then he had to *tell himself what problem his feelings were signs of.* If Nelson could say to himself, "I'm angry because I wasn't invited to Hollie's picnic," he could start to think about the situation and *make a decision* about what to do next. An adolescent like Nelson, unfortunately, is likely to have angry outbursts that friends, parents, other relatives, and teachers do not understand.

It is not unusual for children to have difficulty handling strong feelings. Preschool children and adolescents seem most susceptible. But if these strong feelings often seem to be getting the best—or worst—of a child, and if he or she seems to have difficulty recognizing problems and trying to solve them, then it is entirely possible that they have not been using the second decision-making step—*tell yourself what the problem is.* The general tips and activities that follow are enjoyable ways to strengthen your family and prepare your children for sound decision making and problem solving.

How to Help Your Children Tell
Themselves What the Problem Is

BE A MODEL

Decision making is, essentially, a thinking activity. As such, it is often invisible to our children—they see the *results,* but not the *process* adults go through to reach the result. Unfortunately television often makes matters worse, because problems seem to be solved with little thought, and the methods used on many shows tend to be violent. In the last chapter we talked about the importance of *modeling* as a way to allow your children to learn how to look for signs of different feelings and where you feel stress. The next step is to help your children put the problem they have into words. Let's see how one father did this:

Father: We've been painting for about two hours now. Look at this mess . . . and that hole in the wall. And the paint can—darn!—it's almost empty.

Phil: What do you mean, Dad?

Father: Well, let me see if I can put this into words. I feel a little discouraged when I see the mess we have to clean up. And I feel kind of unsure about how I'm going to fill in that hole before we paint. And I'm feeling annoyed because the paint can is almost empty and I'll have to clean up and drive to the store. So we have a lot of problems to solve.

Phil: Wow! We'd better get started.

As you can see, Phil's father was able to put a number of problems into words. He felt and expressed all of these in his first statement—but not in a way that Phil could understand and learn from. He had to say clearly which situation led to which feeling.

As adults, we have many, many opportunities to model how we tell ourselves what problems we face. Some situations that allow useful modeling include *cooking* ("I'm a little nervous about the vegetable dish because I've got to pour just the right amount in, or the recipe could be ruined"; "My arm is tired because I have to keep beating the eggs until they are very, very stiff."), *car repair* ("I'm annoyed because I have to get past that hot hose"; "I'm confused about how to reattach the fan belt."), and *driving* ("I'm upset because the instructions say to make a left and it's one-way going the other way"; "My head is pounding and I can't concentrate when you're all yelling and screaming in the backseat!").

In each of these instances, we might hesitate or just not think of putting our problems into words. Do the kids really need to hear about these things *all* the time? Certainly not, and certainly not for situations they really cannot understand. But our children *can* benefit from hearing how we use our feelings and tell ourselves what the problems are in common situations such as driving, cooking, and repairing—and they may find themselves doing the same thing more and more often, as they get older.

ENCOURAGE EXPRESSION

With a few well-chosen questions, it is possible to encourage children—even those of kindergarten age—to go beyond upset feelings and put their problems into words. Note that for children up to about age eight, *"put your problem into words"* is probably a more useful activity to encourage, rather than *"tell yourself what the problem is."* The former is a building block for the latter and we recommend its use almost exclusively until age eight or nine, with gradual shifting to "tell yourself . . ." beginning at that time. By about age eleven, children can often "tell themselves what the problem is" in a clear and useful manner.

In the previous chapter we encouraged our children to express their feelings. Now, once we've learned that they are experiencing upset feelings, we want them to get a sense of the situation or problem leading to these feelings. Two ways of encouraging this connection in our children are *asking* and *suggesting*. Let's look first at how a father used "suggesting" with his five-year-old daughter:

Father: Sweetheart, you're stomping your feet—what's the matter?
Daughter: I'm angry.
Father: Your face sure *looks* angry.

Daughter: My silver scissors cut cardboard, not my green ones.

Father: Oh.

Daughter: And my silver ones are gone.

Father: I see. Let me see if I can find the right words to use, okay? Do you feel angry because you can't find your silver scissors?

Daughter: Yeah.

Father: So your problem is that you don't know where the silver scissors are.

Daughter: And I looked in my art box and my desk and everyplace.

Father: Where else besides the art box and desk . . .

Father's suggestion about why his daughter was angry helped her get past her anger and into some problem solving about the scissors. *Suggesting* means *you* try to put your child's problem into words and see if the child agrees with how you've summed it up. If your youngster does *not* agree, then try again.

Chuck: Dad, I'm just not good enough, I just can't cut it.

Dad: Your voice sounds pretty hopeless. Did you start feeling that way when the first band members were announced?

Chuck: No, it was after I finished. I took one look at Mr. Phillips and I knew I had made too many mistakes.

Dad: So you figured it was hopeless because he had a look of . . .

Chuck: Like, "Oh, brother, get this guy off the stage and put his clarinet in the furnace."

Dad: What would you say is the problem now?

Chuck: Huh?

Dad: Well, out of everything that happened, what would you say, is the problem you want to solve? It may help if you start by saying, "The problem is . . ."

Chuck: The problem is . . . that I can't play the clarinet.

Dad: Is that why you went to Mr. Phillips?

Chuck: No—I went to join the band.

Dad: So try again. The problem is . . .

Chuck: The problem is . . . that I'm not in the band.

Dad: What's so special about the band?

Chuck: Well, the guys are in it—and so is Marilyn.

Dad: This is starting to sound like a different problem—and the band is only a part of it.

Chuck: Yeah, well, the problem is that I won't be with the guys or Marilyn two afternoons every week.

Dad: It sounds like you've put the problem into words and you've told yourself what it *really* seems to be.

The father here did not use suggestions as much as he used *asking*. Asking helps a child to generate his or her own ideas, to *think* and build independent problem-solving and decision-making skills. It forces a child's thinking patterns to change and expand. Here the father's questions helped his son move away from his original feelings of hopelessness and the frustrating audition experience. Instead, the problem was defined in terms of spending time with friends—something that is much more solvable.

Here are some "starters" to help you with your *suggesting* and *asking* questions for your children:

Suggesting	*Asking*
1. Do you mean . . .	1. What is the problem?
2. So, is your problem that . . .	2. What would you say is the problem? What *else* could be the problem?
3. Do you feel _____ because . . .	3. How would you put the problem into words?
4. Do you feel _____ when . . .	4. What seems to be troubling you?
5. Would you say that . . .	5. How would you put it into words?

ACCEPT AND ACKNOWLEDGE WHAT YOU HEAR

As discussed in the previous chapter, it is important to be on the lookout for times when your child tries to put a decision-making step into action. Here's another example of how, if we are not careful, we can put out the spark we so much want to nurture:

Father: How was school today?

Mike: Rotten. I don't want to talk about it.

Father: It sure sounds awful. What does the problem seem to be?

Mike: Oh, all right. I feel really low because we were reading "Paradise

Lost" and my essay about the poem only got a B. I don't know how I'm going to get an A in English.

Father: English? Getting a B is good enough. And there are more important things to do than read poetry. You've got to keep those science and math grades up . . .

This father seemed to forget that problems can be *very* subjective—what your child sees as a problem, you might see as trivial or nonsensical. If your children hear that kind of response, it is unlikely that they will go back to you with future problems. Who could blame them? As parents, we want our children to feel as if they can share their problems with us. When children *do* share their problems, our task is to help them *clarify their feelings, put the problem into words,* and *define the problem clearly,* in a way that suggests it might be solvable. We suggest you *praise* your child's *efforts* at sharing problems with you and *ask questions* that will make the situation less confused and cloudy:

Father: English? How are you doing in English so far?
Mike: I was on the border between an A and a B. This essay brings me to a B. I don't know how to get that A.
Father: Well, Mike, you really seem to have told yourself what the problem is. I bet you haven't given up on that A.
Mike: I guess not. You know, I thought of a couple of ideas to try . . .

The following activities, designed for the entire family, will help build your children's second decision-making skill and help *you* practice suggesting, asking, and other ways of encouraging children to think clearly.

Family Activities You Can Do at Home

PROBLEMS IN THE NEWS

If your child is a reader, then he or she is ready to uncover Problems in the News. Read a story together in a newspaper or magazine—let's say it's one about commuter railroad problems. Then use the probes that Don does to help his son define the problem presented in the story.

Don: Okay, what was that story about?
Andy: Trains. Lots of people take trains to get to work.

Don: Yes, they do. What seems to be the problem with the trains?

Andy: They need more money and they need to be safer.

Don: So one problem is that there isn't enough money to run all the trains that everyone needs to get to work. And another problem is that the trains are not as safe as they should be.

Andy: You really picked up on that one! Okay, I think it's time you passed the catsup . . .

Whether it's about trains or electrons or taxes or defense, the news is filled with problems. Each one gives you the chance to sharpen your child's thinking. You might have to question more than Don did and think aloud your ideas at first until your child gets the idea—but it's all part of the learning process. Television or radio news is often not useful because those stories are so brief that they usually define the problem for you. This robs our children (and us!) of a chance to think about and verbalize what the problem is.

HOBBY PROBES

Hobbies provide wonderful teaching opportunities. They involve something we know well and/or something in which we have an interest, something about which we are motivated to learn. A reliable sign that your child is working on a problem of some kind is when he or she is practicing something over and over again—shooting baskets, practicing chess moves, looking through coins or stamps or rocks, or some other activity. Here is a series of comments that will help your child *tell himself or herself what the problem is:*

1. You sure seem to be working hard (a lot, spending a lot of time).
2. What are you working on?
3. What problem are you trying to solve? Anything else?
4. It sounds as if you've told yourself what the problem is . . . let's see if I understand it. (Then summarize what you've heard, using the Suggesting "starters" we've mentioned.)

Watch how Alice first starts to use Hobby Probes with her son, Andy, whose interest in trains extends beyond news stories. Now he's making a model of a train and his face is showing signs of frustration.

Alice: Boy, you sure are working hard! What are you working on now?

Andy: I have to put the locomotive together.

Alice: Oh. It looks hard to do. What problem are you trying to figure out?

Andy: I have to put the wheels on so that they can move back and forth and not fall off.

Alice: Anything else?

Andy: And I have to put the windows in without getting glue on them.

Alice: Any others?

Andy: No, not really.

Alice: It sounds as if you've told yourself what the problems are . . . let's see if I understand them. One problem is to put the wheels on so they stay on, but also move back and forth. The other problem is to put the windows in without getting glue on them. Your face looks calmer now—it's easier to solve problems when you *put them into words* and *tell yourself what the problems are.*

Andy: Yeah, I guess so . . . Mom, can I have the tweezers . . .

PROBLEM FINDING

Problem Finding is a family game you can all play. First you need a list of problem stories, like the one below. You can use a written list with each one numbered, or else put each one on an index card:

1. Someone took Ted's new bicycle for a ride without asking his permission.
2. Someone drew on Martha's new blouse on purpose.
3. Elizabeth has just been chosen for an important part in a class play.
4. Your best friend just told you he or she is going to move far away.
5. Alex and Terry just cheated in a game you were playing.
6. Your poem is going to be put on a special bulletin board.
7. Albert had been doing very well in math, but lately he's found the work to be hard, and his marks have gone down.
8. The teacher just yelled at Leslie for not paying attention.
9. Your friends won't let you play with them at recess.
10. Rico is thinking about having someone do his homework for him.

You can add your own problems to the list. Have someone pick a card or pick a number. Then, have someone read the following Thinking Cards (which can also be put on index cards):

1. How do you think _____ would be feeling if _____ had that happen?
2. What are some *signs* that would tell us how _____ is feeling?
3. If you were _____, you would have a problem. Put the problem into words. Then tell yourself what the problem would be. Okay, what could it be?

Before going on to the next problem story, get everyone's answers to the different Thinking Cards. Praise your children for their thoughtful use of the first two decision-making steps. (You can also do Problem Finding by having family members gather pictures of problems; then start off with a question about what the picture shows.) *Point to the decision-making and problem-solving steps list on your refrigerator (or wherever!) and let the kids know they're in the process of learning them!*

HOMEWORK: PROBLEMS, PROBLEMS, PROBLEMS

There are some households in which the problem of getting homework done with only a minimum of hassles is solved without much effort. But more often homework provides a challenge to parents' problem-solving powers. If we take a closer look at homework, we notice that it is often unappealing to children, especially when compared to being with friends, "hanging out," listening to music, talking on the phone, playing sports, or watching television. The long-term value of "good work habits" or doing assignments to get good grades at the end of a marking period or to get into college is usually less potent than the value of immediate "fun" things. Homework is even less appealing in those subjects in which a child has difficulty (or, at times, excels).

Homework time will lead your child to show signs of different feelings —often, upset feelings. It can be very helpful to have your child put the problem into words and tell himself or herself what the problem is. Once this happens you can negotiate things much more clearly and with fewer emotional outbursts—by you *or* your child! Table 3, the Homework Time chart, can be useful for turning homework conflicts from battles into *problems that can be solved.* It's mostly your child who has the problem—

and you can work toward resolution by handling things similarly to how father Leroy does:

Leroy: Tommie, what did you write on the homework chart?

Tommie: I was working in the dining room and I was feeling angry because I want to watch the after-school program and also because this history stuff takes so long and there's so much.

Leroy: So there are two problems: you'll miss the television program and the homework will take a long time to do.

Tommie: Yeah. Can I watch it?

Leroy: If you show me how you can get all the work done after dinner, you can watch.

Tommie: There's no way.

Leroy: It's unfair of the teacher to give you all that to do in one night.

Tommie: Well, we've had it since Monday.

Leroy: Oh. That was three days ago. So another problem is how you can miss even more things and have to work longer and harder when you leave things for the last day.

Tommie: I guess so.

Leroy: How are you feeling now?

Tommie: Kind of upset at myself. Dad, can we talk later? I have a lot to do . . .

The chart helps focus conversations and reduce tensions and parent blame for homework problems. This activity also forces the child to think about how the situation can be improved, with *telling yourself what the problem is* as an essential step.

Family Activities You Can Do Away from Home

PROBLEMS IN THE CAR

It is rare to take a car ride without something happening that tempts you to say something like, "Look at that jerk. What's his problem?" It is very useful to seek out *answers* to that question. Ideas range considerably, including, "He must be late going someplace"; "He doesn't know how to drive"; and "His mirrors are crooked so he didn't see those cars near him."

Encourage a lot of different problem statements. Also, don't forget to *model* your own problems as you drive. Some examples:

Too Brief:	A Good Problem Statement:
1. "What to do, what to do?"	1. "We need gas but we also need to stop for dinner and I'd like to stop only once. Where should we stop?"
2. "Lousy wipers."	2. "The windshield wipers aren't working well because one of them is loose."

PROBLEMS AT THE DINER

The diner (sometimes called a coffee shop) is a restaurant that has a varied menu, including breakfast, lunch, and dinner meals, plus the chef's own creations. All of these foods are listed in one large menu. The menu contains numerous inserts, and it describes à la carte or a full dinner options. The entire situation can be complicated by the fact that the kitchen might not have all the vegetables listed or the ones you want. Many diners have jukeboxes.

Each visit to a diner challenges us with a complex set of decisions that families cope with in different ways. When it gets out of hand for Al and Shirley, and their children, Lou and Ilene, it can go like this:

Al: I'm in the mood for some breakfast food.

Shirley: I'd like a salad, maybe the cottage cheese plate.

Lou: Dad, can I get the tomato soup?

Al: Sure. Maybe I'll have soup, too.

Ilene: Soup for breakfast? I want this *spanakopita* thing.

Al: What's that? The Greek spinach pie?

Ilene: Yes. It's great!

Lou: They also have a tomato surprise. Maybe I'll have that.

Shirley: Does anyone have some change? I think I'll play some music . . . where's a Frank Sinatra song.

Waitress: Are you ready to order?

Ilene: Sure. Are you ready, Mom?

Shirley: Not yet. I just saw the specials.

TABLE 3

HOMEWORK TIME:
TELL YOURSELF WHAT THE PROBLEM IS

This activity will help you take your feelings and put them into words. Once you can tell yourself what the problem is, you are already on the road to solving it!

Ex. Where were you trying to do homework: in the kitchen.
    How did you feel: angry.
    How could you tell: my fist was tight.
    What is the problem: I felt angry *because* I can't go to the mall
        with everybody else OR I felt angry *when* I was told that the
        TV stays off until homework is done.

1. Where were you: _____
   How did you feel: _____
   How could you tell: _____
   What is the problem: I felt _____
                          (when or because) _____

2. Where were you: _____
   How did you feel: _____
   How could you tell: _____
   What is the problem: I felt _____
                          (when or because) _____

3. Where were you: _____
   How did you feel: _____
   How could you tell: _____
   What is the problem: I felt _____
                          (when or because) _____

4. Where were you: _____
   How did you feel: _____
   How could you tell: _____
   What is the problem: I felt _____
                          (when or because) _____

Al: Maybe I'll have a dinner.
Lou: I'll start with tomato juice.
Waitress: I'll be back later.

But things can be a *bit* different if we apply decision-making steps 1 and 2:

Al: I'm in the mood for some breakfast food and I feel like ordering quickly.
Shirley: It's always a problem deciding what to order here.
Al: Yeah. So let's not make a big deal out of it. How about everyone decide what you feel like eating—then we can decide what music to play.
Ilene: I'm all set with my order.
Lou: So am I. Let's pick three songs to play. How about "Goodie Goodie" by King Sol and the Boys?
Al: Ilene, you and Shirley pick the others. Lou, what did you think of the movie last night?
Lou: It was pretty good.
Al: What problem did you find most interesting?
Lou: Well, there were two . . .

Naturally the waitress didn't come over because she would never suspect any family could decide so quickly. Al modeled out loud his own feelings and the problem of taking so long to order—and Shirley put the problem into words quite clearly. Al also anticipated several other problems (music, specials) and then was able to go on to other things like helping Lou think more carefully about the movie they had seen. This family found creative and useful applications of *telling yourself what the problem is* in diners and similar establishments.

NATURE CHALLENGE . . . WHEN YOU TAKE A WALK

Family walks can be lots of fun. Each season of the year brings new sights to appreciate, new sounds to attend to, and a different feel to the air. The variations nature allows and requires provide opportunities to help your children put problems into words. These problems, however, are better seen as challenges, demands with which people, plants, or animals must cope. Nature Challenge involves having everyone in the family look around during your walk for several minutes while thinking about the following question:

"It's now _____ (name of a season). Let's all try to look around and find _____ (three, four, five, and so on) things that are affected by the change from _____ to _____. Seasons favor some things—plants, animals, even certain people—and lead to problems for others. So our Nature Challenge is to see how many different things have changed that we can see, hear, or feel. Ready? Let's start!"

Here are some Nature Challenge comments we've heard concerning problems that arise in summer:

> Mosquitoes bite people, which can lead to itching or to changing when and where one goes out.
> The sun is out longer, which makes it harder for children to get to bed early.
> Ants come into the basement and then we have to spray.
> Air conditioners use up energy and cost money.
> There's no school and sometimes it's hard to think of things to do.
> If you don't keep covered or use sunscreen, you could get a bad sunburn.
> The weather is so terrific, there are so many things to do and sometimes it's hard to choose.

What is most important is that everyone try to describe clearly and fully the Nature Challenge and how it is a problem of some kind. You might also want to highlight problems that really can't be solved and that we just have to get used to somehow.

EXIT ONLY: LEAVING FROM VISITS WITH FRIENDS OR RELATIVES

"It's time to go now." "I don't want to." "No, it's time." "Please, just ten more minutes." "No, we've been here for hours." "Five minutes?" "Bill and Nancy have to clean up—they have work tomorrow." "Two minutes? Just two? Oh, please, just two? Can I? Please?"

Sound familiar? These encounters often proceed unpleasantly. Many times there is no "happy ending." But there are ways to turn this situation into one that improves thoughtful decision making and at least improves your understanding of what your children have in mind. They might also learn something about you as well. First, let's take the opening dialogue and put it into the language of problem solving and decision making:

"It's time to go now"	=	I'm tired; I don't want to hit traffic; Other people are leaving now; What we came here for is ending.
"I don't want to"	=	It's fun here; I'm tired and I don't want to move myself to get ready to leave; I don't want to go home and have to do homework or get ready for school.
"No, it's time"	=	I'm serious about this . . . but I might negotiate.
"Please, just ten more minutes"	=	I really have a problem with leaving and I want to avoid it if I can.

And so on. Let's listen to Laura using an Exit Only activity with her nine-year-old son, Sam.

Laura: Sam, it's time to go. Finish what you're doing and we'll pack up our stuff. If we stay later, getting home will be a real problem because I'm getting tired and there may be traffic.

Sam: I don't want to go. Can we stay ten more minutes?

Laura: Your voice and face are telling me you don't want to go. What's the problem?

Sam: I just started a game and I want to finish.

Laura: That's a problem, all right. What about my problem of being tired and not wanting to hit traffic?

Sam: Traffic is not much fun. But I just started.

Laura: Let's pack up and think about how you can get some extra game time in the next day or so. What is that game? Maybe you can tell me about it in the car . . .

Some children will be easier than Sam, some will be more ornery. But Exit Only means you *tell how staying would be a problem for you, acknowledge* your child's Feelings Fingerprint, and ask him or her to put the problem into words. Then you make your judgment about how to respond. *Exit Only,* however, means you're definitely on your way out, with mutual understanding and hopefully with many fewer hassles.

Using the Second Decision-Making Step to Handle Everyday Problems

The activities in this chapter have followed a general plan for helping your children *tell themselves what the problem is.* Much of what you do involves putting into words *your own thinking* about problems you encounter. As you do this more and more and encourage your children to do the same, you'll find *they* begin to put *their* own problems into words. As they enter middle (or junior high) school age, they develop the ability to *tell themselves what the problem is.* And that, after all, is your goal: to build your child's *independent* decision-making skills.

There will be times when your child will need to use only the second decision-making step. But often it is important for a child to learn to use the steps in sequence. To help your child build his or her skill in linking the steps together, this chapter (and each one that follows in this part of the book) includes a section on using the decision-making steps to handle everyday problems. Each step is reviewed in order to help make the connections between them. Then two family situations introduced in Chapter 4 are further examined. First, the steps:

1. Look for signs of different feelings.
2. Tell yourself what the problem is.

THE BEDTIME CHAT REVISITED: GOING BEYOND THE FEELINGS

In Chapter 4, Donna and Robert had noticed that Jennifer was not quite herself—she was not following her usual patterns of behaving. Just before bedtime Donna helped Jennifer express her feelings: she was upset about a toothache and the possibility of having to go to the dentist. It's now the next morning, and Donna's going to help Jennifer tell herself what the problem is.

Donna: Ready for breakfast? Good. How are you feeling this morning?
Jennifer: Okay. Can I have hot chocolate instead of cold milk?
Donna: Sure. Your tooth bothers you when you have something cold, doesn't it?
Jennifer: I guess so.

Donna: It seems as if you have a problem.

Jennifer: I don't want to go to the dentist.

Donna: Well, what would *you* say the problem is?

Jennifer: The dentist hurts me.

Donna: That's one problem. But there are others, too.

Jennifer: Yeah, like I can't eat ice cream without it hurting me.

Donna: Anything else?

Jennifer: No.

Donna: Remember what happened to Daddy when his toenail hurt him but he waited and waited before he went to the doctor?

Jennifer: Yeah, he had to have it taken out. Does the dentist take out teeth?

Donna: She does if the tooth is sick and it can't be cured.

Jennifer: I don't want my tooth to come out.

Donna: So there are lots of different problems. Here's your hot chocolate. Which one do you think is the biggest problem—which one do you feel most upset about?

Jennifer: It hurts when I eat ice cream and I don't want to have my tooth pulled out.

Donna: You'd really miss not being able to eat ice cream and it's scary to think about getting a tooth pulled out.

Jennifer: Yeah.

Donna: I also used to get upset when I went to the dentist. But let's try Feelings Flashbacks—remember when you had that cut on your arm and we had to get it fixed? Remember how you felt and what you did?

Jennifer: I was crying so I used Get Calm! and I felt better.

Donna: You *did* feel better—you even stopped crying.

Jennifer: Maybe I can use Get Calm! at the dentist . . .

Donna used good timing and spoke to Jennifer when she was not so tired—and when she was faced with cold milk! Donna helped Jennifer remember her feelings and then think of the different problems she was facing. By putting them into words, Jennifer could think about the problems. When it was time to pick the "biggest" problem, Donna helped Jennifer use her feelings to make that choice. Finally, she used Feelings Flashbacks and *Get Calm!* to help Jennifer feel as if she could cope with her decision to go to the dentist.

Donna isn't always this good at using the decision-making approach.

There are still days when she and Robert are just too tired or upset or overwhelmed to be at their decision-making best. But they've gradually become better at using the ideas in this book by *practicing* a little at a time and by *thinking about how to make the activities work a little better next time.* They've *talked* to each other and to friends and relatives *about what they are doing* and *how else they could try* to teach Jennifer the decision-making steps. Donna and Robert are being problem-solving parents—and the results will often be worth the effort for them!

THE SANCHEZ FAMILY REVISITED: UNCLE LUIS'S HOUSE OR THE ZOO?

Refresh your memory about the Sanchez family by looking at their Parenting Tree in the previous chapter. The family was all set to go to the zoo when Miriam received a call. A party at Uncle Luis and Aunt Maria's house for Tio Edward was switched to that day—a conflict with the zoo trip. Ricky and Paul were very upset, and John helped Miriam get the boys to *look for signs of different feelings.* As we left the Sanchez family, they had all talked about their feelings and were going to finish breakfast before making any decisions. Now Grandma Frances comes into the kitchen.

Frances: What's all the yelling and noise?
Miriam: Mom, the party for Tio Edward was changed. It's this afternoon —but we had been planning a trip to the zoo.
Frances: Well, those animals will be there next week.
Ricky: But we were ready to go today. It's nice out and it may rain next week.
Frances: Is this a way to talk? Do you know how much Tio Edward loves you? And Aunt Maria, she cries when she sees your pictures.

Dad, at this point, has to resist the temptation to roll his eyes in dismay. How can he move in before the situation deteriorates? How would *you* get everyone back to thinking about the problem at hand? Let's see how John does it.

John: Well, everybody, I think there are a few problems we have to deal with. Let's everyone tell ourselves what the problem is and then put the problem into words.

Paul: Like we've been doing in the car and on our walks?

Miriam: That's right!

Frances: These boys don't know how to behave and listen.

Miriam: Oh, Mom! The problem is that we're all set to go to the zoo and now we can't.

Paul: The problem is there's nothing fun to do at Uncle Luis's house.

Ricky: The problem is you broke your promise.

John: Well, there seem to be lots of problems. I'm upset because the party time was changed. But Tio Edward would have a problem if we didn't come.

Paul: I bet he'd be sad.

John: What do you think, Ricky?

Ricky: I guess he'd be disappointed.

John: What will this feel like for him?

Ricky: Like we feel about the zoo.

John: Which problem seems to be the biggest one?

Paul: How do we know?

John: Which one do you think is most upsetting? I think it's Tio Edward's problem.

Ricky: I guess so, too.

Paul: Me, too. Can we stop on the way and get some zoo books so we'll be ready for the zoo next week?

Miriam: Sounds like a good idea to me . . .

The Sanchez family used the first two decision-making steps to keep the problem in focus and provide a way for them all to express their views in a constructive way. The problem looks like it may be on the pathway toward a solution. But the most important point to note is how John kept Frances and the boys from getting into an emotional quarrel. He moved in and used modeling and suggested everyone get involved in the task of defining the problem. Perhaps you thought of other ways you might have stepped in at that moment. Certainly there are a number of ways to do this. One final note: we find the first two decision-making steps to be especially useful if other relatives or friends are involved. The steps can help maintain a problem-solving atmosphere and work toward making an actual decision. It won't always go smoothly—but you can add some stability, sharing, and fun to your family routines!

Decision-Making Digest

The second decision-making step, *tell yourself what the problem is* (or, "put the problem into words," for younger children), is like a compass or gyroscope. It helps make your child's mind work in a more focused way. It points attention to the problem so that we can go about solving it. If our feelings are too vague or overwhelming, we can't always figure out what the problem is. But as our children learn to put feelings and problems into words, they can begin to steer through tricky currents and rocky waters— on their way to a sound and reasoned decision about how to take care of their difficulties.

For parents, the family activities provide a way of building these essential skills. To help you decide which activities you might choose for particular purposes, review the following chart. You'll be ready to read on and see how to teach children to take problem statements and transform them into blueprints for action.

Decision-Making Digest:
Tell Yourself What the Problem Is

If you'd like your child to	*Then try these activities:*
1. learn how to clearly define a problem	1. Problems in the News Problems in the Car
2. put his or her problems into words instead of acting out in frustration, disappointment, and the like	2. Hobby Probes Homework Time Problems at the Diner Exit Only: Leaving from Visits with Friends and Relatives
3. realize that upset feelings are signs of problems	3. Problem Finding
4. learn that problems and changes are a normal part of everyday life	4. Nature Challenge

6

Decide on Your Goal

"If you don't know where you're going, you'll never get there."
—Almost everybody's parent, at one time or another
"If you don't know what you want, you'll never get it."
—Everyone else's parent, at one time or another

Perhaps these ideas are a bit overstated. But society is getting more and more complicated. The amount of information and technological change with which we must contend grows constantly. Our children will be adults in a world vastly different from the one we now live in. To prepare children to manage as adults, it is important to build their ability to *decide on their goals*. Children need the opportunity to lead and not be led. They need to know they can decide and not simply follow; that they think and create, and not passively accept and consume. To accomplish this requires their ability to select a goal—the third decision-making step.

Our use of the word "goal" is very broad. As an example, think about your usual mail, either at home or at the office. Most of it is "junk mail." But what *is* junk mail? Usually it is requests from people and organizations whose goal is for you to send them money. What are your feelings as you sort through the junk pile? Anger? Amusement? Boredom? Uncertainty about which cause or group is worth supporting? In addition to the daily mail, the mass media contains constant barrages of goal-directed messages: watch this, go here, buy that. How do we, as adults, sort all this out? Certainly, it is a struggle. Imagine, though, how our children will cope when an older child comes up—as is almost inevitable—and offers them cigarettes or alcohol or drugs, or pressures them to join a delinquent group. What decision will they make? Will they recognize the goals of the peers pressuring them and check their own goals to see if they differ?

In our research, work with schools, and clinical practice with troubled families, we have been consistently struck by the frustrations and turmoil caused when youngsters act prematurely or impulsively, or fail to act—all because they did not have their goal clearly in mind. The skill of *deciding on your goal* is perhaps the greatest gift parents can bestow on a child. It is *our* goal in this chapter to share with you many of the ideas and activities we have found valuable for helping children learn our third decision-making step. First, we review the path we've taken to get to *goals*.

"Steptalk": Where We've Been and Where We're Going

Up to this point we have been preparing our children for action. *Readiness* activities focus their attention, memory, and concentration and help them accept praise and assistance. *Looking for signs of different feelings* provides children with critical information about themselves and those around them. It is like an "early warning system." The information is then put into words as our children *tell themselves what the problem is*. When children *decide on their goal*—the third decision-making step—they are taking the problem and turning it into an action statement, a statement about *where or how they would like things to end up*. Once the goal is selected, decision making moves into high gear—how to make that goal happen.

When decision making is working well, children move from feelings to problem to goal almost instantly. We also observe when decision making is *not* working well. We can illustrate this by noting how three children present the same problem to a parent. In each case the child bursts into the house, visibly upset. The parent asks, "What happened?"

> *Solution Jumping:* Mitch was teasing me and I'm upset. I'm going to tell his mother. He should be grounded for life.
>
> *Goal Paralysis:* Mitch was teasing me and I'm upset. He's my friend and he shouldn't. I don't like him any-more. I'm staying in the house. But my stuff is outside. I don't know . . .
>
> *Decision Making:* Mitch was teasing me and I'm upset. I don't want to get upset by Mitch anymore.

Solution jumpers go right from the problem to suggestions for action. They are the people you know who often wind up saying, "I didn't really mean to do that. You know how it is, things got out of hand." It's also easy to spot people who are paralyzed because they do not know which goal to choose. Their thoughts are racing, but their ideas are not *anchored* by having a goal in mind. So they end up taking no action, or else following others' urgings. The decision maker takes the problem and turns it into a goal statement: *What do I want to see happen?* The child in the example just given also could have chosen a goal of having Mitch not tease anymore—after all, in many situations there can be more than one goal. Regardless, having a goal in mind readies a person to take initiative for constructive action.

The next two children we will describe are struggling with the question of goals. Perhaps these children will remind you of someone you know. First, here is a quick review of the decision-making steps thus far:

1. Look for signs of different feelings.
2. Tell yourself what the problem is.
NEW   3. Decide on your goal.

In the following examples, try to notice the number of different goals there could be for different people at various points in time.

CASE EXAMPLE: JACQUELINE'S GOT HER GOALS IN FOCUS

Jacqueline is one of several children at East Gate middle school who has very poor eyesight. Although she is not blind, she must sit in the front of her classes and sometimes she has trouble getting around the school without bumping into people or objects. Jackie takes the bus to school and sits in the front, next to the driver, so she doesn't have to walk so much in the narrow aisles. The bus ride is a time when some of her schoolmates tease her. They say things like, "Hey, four-eyes!" "Watch out you don't trip on your feet"; and "Look out for that thing on the floor. Watch out!"

These comments lead Jacqueline to have some upset feelings. Some of the most uncomfortable feelings emerge on the bus ride home, during which she hears everyone talk about what he or she is going to do that day. Bicycling, shopping, walking around in the mall, playing ball—these are all activities that are very hard for Jackie to do. Jackie feels left out.

But Jackie does well in school. She spends a lot of time reading and studying, and she learns things quickly. Jackie can also sing exceptionally well. Her teachers and parents praise her often, and she has learned to accept that praise and enjoy it.

It's Thursday and Jackie has just come home from school. She looks particularly upset, and her mother decides to talk to her about it.

Mother: Jackie, it looks like the bus ride was pretty rough.

Jackie: No, not much worse than usual. Cathy and Teri were calling me names like "teacher's pet" and "brainy"; even Maryanne called me something. But I'm not too upset at that.

Mother: Well, your voice is shaking a little—something must be bothering you.

Jackie: I want to go to my room and think, Mom. I don't want to talk now.

In her room Jackie starts to think. She tries to use her decision-making steps to help her understand why she was so upset. Nothing different happened on the bus. She felt upset when she was teased, but she feels wonderful about her schoolwork and her singing projects. "What's the problem?" she asks herself. She even uses Get Calm! to help keep her from getting upset because she can't think of the problem. And then she put it into words in a way that felt right. "I'm upset because I'm alone so much. No kids hear my singing. No one even asks for my help with homework. My problem is that I'm lonely!" Then a smile appears on her face as she walks out the door. "My goal is that I make some friends who will share things I like to do."

Her mother took one look at Jacqueline and realized that the tension and stress she brought into the house had almost vanished. "Jackie, you seem so much more relaxed." "Yeah, I guess so." "Where are you going?" "I'm checking my assignments for the week to see when I can invite some friends over after school."

Jacqueline knew she had a strategy she could use when she was upset. She had learned that once she put her problem into words and decided on a goal, she felt relief. She could then take whatever action might be necessary.

CASE EXAMPLE:
MARYANNE DOESN'T KNOW WHAT HER GOALS ARE

Those bus rides to and from middle school were awful, thought Maryanne. People throwing things out the window, taking each other's books and hats, calling people names—Maryanne wished she could just be invisible and sit in her seat without being noticed. Most of the time she could get away with it. Every so often, though, Cathy would get her involved in something terrible.

"Hey, Maryanne. What do you think of four-eyes?" "What?" Maryanne feels her heart pounding. "Everybody in this row has to say two things to four-eyes or else their books are going out the window," says Cathy. "And it's your turn!" Maryanne's heart keeps pounding. Her throat is dry. Teri keeps saying, "C'mon, Maryanne. It's your turn. It's your turn." "Open the window," says Cathy. It had never been this bad before, thought Maryanne. "Where'd you get those ugly glasses?" screams Maryanne to Jacqueline. "They make your eyes look like peas," she adds. Everyone laughed and laughed. She was congratulated so much, she found herself smiling!

At home Maryanne starts to feel uneasy. She can't quite figure out why. "It's wrong to call her names. But how could I let them throw my books out? Jackie's nice, though. She once helped me with a math problem. And I made fun of her glasses! But Cathy and Teri sure were proud of me. They'll probably let me eat lunch with them. Maybe they'll leave me alone on the bus. But what if they bother me more? Jackie did look surprised when I yelled at her. What if Mrs. Morgan finds out—she thinks I'm nice, and pretty smart!"

Maryanne's heart again begins to pound and her mouth is dry. She gets a soda from the refrigerator and puts on her favorite radio station, loud. Pretty soon, she is repeating some lyrics and isn't noticing her heart, mouth, or her problem anymore.

"CASETALK": A CLOSER LOOK AT THE TWO CHILDREN

Both Maryanne and Jacqueline experienced stress. And a frequent cause of stress is *goal confusion*. Goal confusion occurs when we have too many conflicting goals, or our goals are too vague to give us a clear direction. Goal confusion can also occur when we do not have goals, such as in persons who seem to just "go with the flow" and do not follow a consistent direction that is *theirs*. Before we take a closer look at our two young ladies, take a moment to write down the different goals you observed for the different people in our two case examples.

Let's concentrate on Jackie first. Jackie had several major choices: (1) get people to not tease her, (2) be like "everyone else," (3) not get upset by teasing, and (4) develop positive, sharing friendships. Jackie kept thinking about her different feelings and possible ways to put her problem into words until she found one that seemed right to her. *Her goal was a reversal of her problem, a positive statement of how she wanted things to be.* Problem: I have no friends; Goal: that I get friends. She left her room ready for action!

Maryanne had a clear case of goal confusion. Did she want Cathy and Teri to like her? To keep her books on the bus? To "do unto others"? To make sure her teacher thinks well of her? To be nice to Jackie? To be left alone? Maryanne really didn't know *and Maryanne did not have a way of finding out*—she had no decision-making strategy to turn to. So she did what many sufferers of goal confusion do—avoid the stress by drowning it out—with music in this case, but in more severe cases, with alcohol, delinquent acts, or drugs. Maryanne would feel less stressed if she could *decide on a goal*, especially a goal that would move her closer to people whose approval and friendship would be good for her.

For parents it can be a new experience to hear about children's goals. And sometimes their goals will not agree with parents' goals for them—an issue we will discuss shortly. But it is important that children learn how to *decide on their goals* and *develop confidence in their ability to decide on goals*. The rest of this chapter contains general guidelines and specific activities to teach your child the third decision-making step. As you put these into practice, you will introduce your child to a method that can allow him or her to handle stress constructively and prepare for positive action!

How to Help Your Child Decide on a Goal

BE A MODEL

Much of what we do has a goal, and often more than one goal. However, the goals of adults are often invisible or confusing to children. Here's a taste of what we mean.

Father: Eat your vegetables, will you please?
Son: I hate lima beans. They taste awful.
Father: Then have some artichoke.
Son: Artichoke? Don't they eat that in Beverly Hills?
Father: They're good for you.
Son: But they taste lousy, I don't like them. I'll gag and be sick.
Father: Eat it anyway.

How about this exchange?

Mother: We're going out now. We'll be back about 10 P.M.
Daughter: It's Sunday night. Where are you going?
Father: It was a busy weekend and we have a busy week ahead, lots of
    work. So we're going out, probably to the diner.
Daughter: Boy, was it ever busy. I'll get my coat and be right with you.
Father: Hold on! You've got studying to do for next week and you can do
    it starting now.
Daughter: You're getting ready by going out—why can't I?
Mother: I've heard enough. We're leaving. You're staying.

The parents wind up with stress, the kids see things as unfair or, at least, unreasonable, and goals were never mentioned. If we add some *modeling, some thinking out loud about goals*, the situations change:

Father: Eat your vegetables, will you please?
Son: I hate limas. They're awful.
Father: Well, I'd like to see you be healthy and vegetables have vitamins
    that will help you grow up healthy. My goal is for you to be healthy,
    not to eat horrible food.
Son: They're really bad, though.
Father: Well, I think they'll help you grow.
Son: Maybe a couple, just this once . . .

Several things happen when goals are modeled. First, the situation is *clearer*. The *goal becomes the issue*, not the personality of the people involved. Your child is respected, in that you imply that he or she will have the good sense to accept and follow your intention. Finally *thinking will occur*—is this a decent goal? Let's replay our Sunday night outing:

Mother: We're going out now. We'll be back around 10 P.M.

Daughter: It's Sunday night. Where are you going?

Mother: It's been a busy week and your father and I would like to have some time alone, out of the house, before we start the new week.

Daughter: Can't I come?

Mother: Tonight we'd really like to go out alone. Next time it can be a family outing.

Daughter: Okay.

You will note that the side issue about studying was never even mentioned. One goal emerged: the parents want to be alone. Certainly parents' goals aren't always as readily accepted as in our replay example. But *modeling of goals leads to clarity, reduces misunderstandings,* and *starts children thinking about goals.*

Perhaps the best time to model goals is when you are having a problem with an involved, sequential task like cooking, fixing something, sports, or preparing to leave the house to get someplace on time. Here are some samples:

After you say your problem:	*Say your goal:*
1. The last egg we need for this recipe is no good.	1. I need another egg.
2. This screw doesn't fit in the hole.	2. I need a screw that fits that hole.
3. My serve is all off.	3. I need to get my serve working right.
4. We're late, but it's dangerous to rush.	4. We'll get there safely and as soon as we can.

We didn't say that modeling had to be complicated! What does have to happen is that *you remember to say your goal out loud.* As you can see from even these few examples, *when you decide on a goal,* you are already *providing a blueprint for action.* This is a valuable addition to what your child learns from the second decision-making step: *"problems can be solved, and here is what I want to have happen!"*

ENCOURAGE
EXPRESSION

Because our children rarely think about their goals, encouraging them to express their goals can have an interesting effect. Here is an example with one of *our* children, at dinnertime. Sara is now almost five and a half years old. She will, at times, begin to tap different objects with her fork to the beat of the music we usually listen to while we eat. Her tapping usually begins with the table, and then rapidly moves to her glass, the catsup bottle, a parent's glass, her sister's limbs—and anything else within reach. After the second tap, we begin a chorus of, "Sara, would you please not do that—it's annoying." This request continues, with increasing intensity for six or seven taps. By this time indigestion begins to set in. Within the past month we have tried several probes that have had a dramatic effect on Sara. Simply put, we've *asked* her to tell us her goal. *Some probes to help your child think about goals are:*

"What are you trying to do?"
"What do you want to have happen?"
"How do you want this to end up?"

The first time we asked Sara, "How do you want this to end up?" she stopped tapping and looked extremely puzzled. It seemed to us that we had introduced a totally new thought. She was not really able to respond to an *ask* probe, so we did some *suggesting:*

"*Are you trying* to get Mommy and Daddy upset?"
"*Do you want to* be so noisy, we can't hear the radio?"
"*Is that your way* of breaking glasses and plates?"

Sara's answer: "No." "Well, then what are you trying to do?" "I don't know." "Why don't you think about what you want to do, instead of tapping?" The fork went down. We have *asked* and *suggested* that children from preschool through high school age think about their goals, and we find that this helps children be more aware of the fact that their actions have goals.

Another time to encourage expression of goals is during *sibling conflicts.* There are two rules parents can follow that will help children become more aware that *others have goals and these may differ from theirs.*

1. A person in a particular situation may have *more than one goal.*
2. *Different people* often have *different goals.*

This mother brings out both of these points after her sons, Rudy and Seth, ages six and nine, start arguing and pushing each other. It seems as if Rudy was using Seth's school pen without asking, and Seth had taken Rudy's book without asking.

Mom: All right, all right, stop this pushing now. Seth, what happened?

Seth: He took my pen without asking.

Mom: What were you trying to do by shoving him?

Seth: Get my pen back.

Mom: What else?

Seth: Er, um, blurble.

Mom: I can't hear you.

Seth: Get him back.

Mom: Rudy, what were you trying to do?

Rudy: He's trying to break my book.

Mom: He is? *How do you know?*

Rudy: He took my book and put it under his homework papers.

Mom: What else could Seth be doing with your book?

Rudy: Huh?

Seth: She asked what else I could do with the book—like I told you, I needed something to lean on and your book was out. I don't care if you take it back—I'll get another book to lean on.

Mom: Rudy, what were you doing with Seth's pen?

Rudy: When you asked me to write down "meat" so you'd remember to take it out of the freezer, his pen was out and I used it. Then I went to do my puzzle book, I took it, and I just forgot.

Mom: We'll talk about this more later. But I hope you both realize that your brother may not have the goal you think he does—he may have a different reason for doing something than you think. And next time, before you start pushing, first think about what you want to have happen and how pushing will help you get there.

Encourage your children to express their goals. As you do, you will provide them with the awareness they need to be able to *decide on their goals*—a skill you will especially want them to have as they become older and more independent.

ACCEPT AND ACKNOWLEDGE
WHAT YOU HEAR

One of the most powerful ways to build a new skill in children, such as deciding on a goal, is to acknowledge their attempts to use the skill. Acknowledging often means pointing out that the glass is half-full, rather than half-empty. Let's look at the difference:

Mom: Ben, what on earth are you doing?

Ben: I was really bored. I was going to watch TV, but I figured I'd fix the chair. You said it was a pain, so I took the scissors and cut a hole and put in some padding I cut off the rug pad—no one will see it. Now I'm taping it up and coloring it with magic marker so it will be the same color as the chair.

(Half-empty) Mom: How could you do such a thing? Weren't you thinking? That chair is ruined. What's wrong with you?

(Half-full) Mom: So all this work is because you were bored and you decided that instead of watching TV, you wanted the chair to be less of a pain for me? I hardly know what to say.

Ben: What do you think, Mom?

Mom: (trying to keep from fainting) You know, I'm afraid I can't try it because the marker isn't dry on the tape, see? I'm glad you were trying to make me more comfortable. Let's talk about how else you can try to do it next time.

Ben's mom, when seeing the glass as half-full, understood the kindness Ben showed in passing up television to do something for her. Although his method wasn't the best (see next chapter), Mom let Ben know that his decision about a goal was fine, especially when the goal is to help someone else. Ben will feel good about what he tried to do: *put his problem* (being bored) *into two goals* (pass the time or be busy doing something constructive), *decide on one goal* (be constructive), and *then try to do it.* The half-empty approach will produce shame, anger, and an "I'll show her" point of view partly because it focuses on the unfortunate choice of *what* to do, rather *than how to do it.*

It's a challenge for parents to be able to keep a sense of humor and look at both the shredded furniture and rug pad and also a *set of decision-making skills* the child is showing that should be nurtured. You will have to find your own balance between the present and future. However, we have found that family activities that encourage children to become aware of goals and decide on goals have value for the future *and* for the present.

Family Activities You Can Do at Home

GOAL ANALOGIES

Sometimes it can be easier to learn a new idea—like *goal*—by showing how it is similar to something already familiar. Goal Analogies is an activity that helps do just that. The next time your family is watching a sports event, ask, *"What are the players trying to do in this game? What's their goal?"* There are generally two goals—an overall goal that they *win* and a short-term goal that they *score* (or stop the other players from scoring). Other things that can be mentioned—pass the ball, make a good play, block a shot—will probably be actions toward the goal. It's worth an extra moment or two to help your children be clear about the difference between *goals* and actions *toward* goals.

As you watch, it can also be interesting to ask, *"What was he or she trying to do?"* There are lots of examples of situations where a player cannot *decide on a goal,* with unfortunate results. Turnovers in basketball, quarterback sacks in football, steals in soccer and hockey, and other points of hesitation usually signal goal confusion or goal paralysis. It can be useful for children to see what happens when goals are unclear. You can, of course, use something other than sports for Goal Analogies—musical performances and parades, for instance.

It can also be fun for your family to keep a list of as many *goal* words as you can think of to help you see how the goals fit into so many aspects of our everyday routine. Some examples we've heard include:

target	computer output
destination	deadline
last stop	ideal
end point	final product

Adolescents find it useful to have alternative ways to think about goals. You'll find one or two terms that seem to catch on well—"target" is a particular favorite—and you might use those instead of "goal."

GOAL X RAY

Research sometimes confirms what many of us believe from our experience. One example is that a sense of humor seems to contribute to positive, healthy relationships within a family. So in the spirit of humor, we introduce Goal X Ray. Goal X Ray involves stopping the action—whether it's in the kitchen, the yard, the hallway, or anywhere—and asking aloud, *"Goal X Ray: What am I trying to do?"* It's especially useful when you're feeling hassled and trying to do several things at once—eat dinner, read the mail, feed the kids, and answer the phone. Once you've modeled the Goal X Ray, you can then ask other family members, "Goal X Ray: What are *you* trying to do?" It's best if you begin Goal X Ray with some kind of "zzzip" or "zzzap" sound. This kind of goal clarification can help your family to relieve hassles and stress. Here's a brief example:

Tim: I did not!
Tom: You did to!
Tim: Did not!
Tom: Did to!
Dad: Zzzap, Tom: What are you trying to do?
Tom: Tim broke it and keeps saying he didn't.
Dad: You've been zzzapped, Tom: What are you trying to do?
Tom: I, uh, um, I don't know.
Tim: Zzzip, Dad: What are you trying to do?
Dad: I'm trying to help you stop your argument and get on to something more useful.
Tom: Gee, it's great having a dad who's a zzzapper!
Dad: Okay, okay. I need some help in the garage. Let's see if you . . .

Once everyone gets the idea, you'll only need to "zzzap" people to get them to stop and think and *decide on their goal.*

AD ATTACK

Television and magazines assault us with their cleverly constructed attempts to influence our actions. Children are especially defenseless against this assault, particularly between the ages of about four and nine. Ad Attack is a simple activity that can help break the spell a bit. When a commercial comes on television, say, "The people who make this commercial want us to do something, like buy something or go someplace. What do they want us to do now?" After a while, you'll only have to ask, "What are they trying to get us to do?" Commercials become less real, less magical if we "unmask" them. You can follow up, as your children get older, with questions like, "How do they make _____ look so good?" "What makes _____ something you'd want to buy?" Then explain how a commercial is a little show, and help your children begin to recognize that ads have goals and we don't have to accept them. Of course, radio, magazine, newspaper, and other ads can be subjected to Ad Attack.

GOAL DRILL

In the previous chapter you prepared some cards or pictures with brief problems on them. Well, dust them off! Gather the family around for Goal Drill. The rules are simple. First, shuffle the cards. Then, ask someone to pick one and read it aloud. Everyone has to try to *tell what the problem is* and then *decide on a goal*. Each person should have a *different goal*, although the problem can be the same. For example:

"Peter saw Michael taking something out of Peter's desk."

Problem: Peter's desk is wide open and things can get stolen.
Goal: That nothing gets stolen.
Problem: Michael's a crook.
Goal: That Michael doesn't steal anymore.
Problem: Michael took something from Peter.
Goal: That Peter get it back.
Problem: Michael took something from Peter.
Goal: That Michael learn his lesson.

It's often more fun if you have a family goal, like "after we all do two cards (or pictures) with different goals, we'll go have dessert."

JIGSAW PUZZLES

For children from preschool through high school age, especially those needing to build up their readiness skills, jigsaw puzzles provide countless examples of chances to ask, "What's my goal?" Of course, the overall goal is to complete the puzzle. But at many points along the way, smaller goals are set, such as: do all the edge pieces, find all the blue pieces, do the upper left section. *Modeling* your own strategies out loud using *suggesting* and *asking* during puzzle time can help your children practice setting and meeting goals.

SELECTING A PRESENT, PREPARING FOR A TRIP: LIST THE GOALS

Tasks that require careful decisions—like selecting a present for someone and preparing for a trip—can sometimes get out of hand if we lose track of our goal. We've probably found ourselves, at one time or another, packing four outfits for an overnight trip, or walking in and out of stores, wondering why we went in to begin with. When these kinds of tasks face your family, it's time to List the Goals. On a piece of paper write the *problem:*

1. We've got to pack for our trip.

1. We've got to buy a present for Aunt Julia.

Then your *goal:*

2. That we pack enough but not too much.

2. That we get her something for her new house.

Then *some facts* related to each goal:

3. We'll be away four days and three nights.

3. It's got a big living room window and a screened-in porch.

4. It's warm all the time.

4. She likes to sit out at night and talk.

5. We'll go out dressed up once.

5. She's keeping all her old stuff.

6. We'll probably go swimming.

6. We'll go there next week.

Now you can proceed with a bit more focus! List the Goals can be done separately by each family member, by pairs, or by everyone together. After some modeling and practice, your child may be ready to List the Goals to help bring the right materials to school, to a friend overnight, or to a family gathering. In time you may notice your child thinking in a more focused way, without lists or other prompts.

Family Activities You Can Do Away from Home

SUPERMARKET SCRIBE

How do you do your shopping? One weekly trip? A major monthly trip? Lots of little stops during the week? And how does your family decide what to buy? Is one person largely responsible? Does everyone have input? Do you use a list, or rely on your memory and what you see on the shelves? For many families we work with, shopping is either a burden, an incidental task, or an annoyance. Particularly when there is one parent at home, or two working parents, shopping can be difficult. Supermarket Scribe is an activity to help clarify and balance family goals concerning shopping. The next couple of times you go shopping, ask family members to *keep track of the problems* shopping presents, such as the time it takes, the need to cut down on junk food, the need to figure out what junk food to buy, the expense, or whatever is a problem in your family. Then have everyone help *decide which is the biggest problem*, then the next biggest, and so on. Finally, *write down a goal for each problem*. This list of goals, plus your list of which problems are biggest, should serve as an anchor for your shopping trips. But perhaps most important, Supermarket Scribe helps your family see that shopping is a cooperative activity, one that should reflect and meet family goals.

BACK AT THE DINER

Because we have worked with families who have had some dining-out disasters, we use the diner as an "ultimate test" of the usefulness of a decision-making step. After feelings have been examined and problems put into words, you may still be deciding what to order or which records to play. Here are some probes we've found useful to bring *goals* into the family picture:

"*What kind* of food do you most feel like having this time?"
"*What kind* of music do you most want to hear this time?"
"*Do you feel like* having a big meal, small meal, or middle-sized meal? A breakfast, lunch, or dinner meal?"

"*Do you feel like* listening to fast or slow music? One person or a group? Loud or soft?"

(only kiddingly!) "How about if we never eat out again?"

If you review our previous diner examples, you'll remember that Lou's goal was clear: he wanted something with tomato. Of course, there are still many tomato alternatives—but our next two chapters cover the topic of examining a variety of different ways to meet your goals and coming to a final decision. Overall, we do find that once goals are set, diners become reasonable places for a nice family meal.

AT THE BARBERSHOP: THE GOALS OF NEW EXPERIENCES

Our children face many new situations, such as the first day of school, the second day of school, the first time meeting a new sibling, the first time sleeping overnight at a friend's, the first stay at a hospital, the first bicycle ride without training wheels, and so on. Each one of these situations may lead a child to have uncertain or uneasy feelings, and naturally so. Helping children to *talk about their feelings, say what the problem is,* and *decide on a goal* allows them to enter the new situation with a little less uncertainty and a little stronger sense that they will be able to get through it.

Let's look in on Gene, a five year old getting his first haircut by a regular barber, before his first day of kindergarten:

Mom: Gene, do you know where we're going this morning?

Gene: Yes—to the barbershop.

Mom: We visited there last week and watched the barbers giving haircuts, remember?

Gene: Yes.

Mom: You're going to sit in the barber's chair, he'll put a smock on you— like your painting smock—and he'll cut your hair.

Gene: It won't hurt, will it?

Mom: I know it can seem a little scary—but do you think it hurt the people we saw getting haircuts last week?

Gene: I guess not.

Mom: Anything else you want to say about it?

Gene: Do I have to go?

Mom: Well, our problem is that your hair is long and we'd like it to look nice and neat for school.

Gene: I guess so.

Mom: So, when you're finished, you should look very handsome for school . . . and that's what we want, right?

Gene: Uh-huh. Are we going soon . . .

Mom reviewed what would happen and what the goal was twice more, in the car and in the barbershop. She also had to ask Gene to Get Calm! before he actually sat in the chair and *say the goal out loud and then to himself several times.* Gene felt less anxious because he had his goal in mind and kept himself calm—and all went well.

In new situations having a goal in mind gives a child something to think about, instead of just concentrating on uneasy feelings. A goal can build confidence as well. With older children you may want to ask them to *picture their goal* and *keep the picture in mind.* *Your* goal is that your child enter new situations without being overwhelmed by his or her feelings— the first three decision-making steps can certainly help.

TEAM GOALS: USING GOAL X RAYS OUT OF THE HOUSE

In sports, coaches have a "game plan"; in music, conductors have a "score." Game plans and scores reflect *group goals.* When everyone on the team carries out his or her part, then the goal is met. Certainly families work this way as well. But sometimes these goals are hard to see. For example, sometimes conductors don't read a score in a performance. They've memorized it, and our children may not realize that. To make goals more visible, we recommend a sophisticated piece of apparatus: the Goal X Ray.

Before X-raying, it's useful to talk to your child about the coach, manager, conductor, and so on. Who is this person? What does he or she do? What is his or her overall job? What does it mean to work as a team? Once you get these ideas across, you can begin X-raying the game or performance.

"*What is he trying to do* by taking that pitcher out of the game?"

"*What is she trying to do* by calling a time-out?"

"*What is he trying to do* by pointing to the trumpet players?"

"*What is he trying to do* by asking everyone to stand up at the end?"

In contrast to what we see as a large emphasis on *individual* excellence in our society, Team Goals emphasizes how *each of us relies on others* to accomplish important tasks. Once you've practiced the Team Goals X Ray on sports, music, and other team activities, you can begin to apply it to how your family works as a team.

Using the Third Decision-Making Step to Handle Everyday Problems: Choosing Goals for Your Child's Academic Performance

You may already see the benefit of just trying out one or two of the family activities in this chapter. These activities bring *goals* into the family spotlight. Usually a goal is found only in the mind and heart of an individual. But in your family, goals can now be shared, talked about, and better understood. The stress of goal confusion or goal paralysis can perhaps be prevented, or at least reduced.

In the previous chapter we gave an example of how telling yourself what the problem is could help make homework time less troublesome. In a growing number of families, however, problems around homework create lasting tensions that harm the relationships among all family members. As technology advances, automation increases, and competition for colleges and jobs becomes more intense, homework and related problems will loom larger and larger. We've worked with many families who are encountering difficulties with some aspect of school. What we have found is that families benefit from having their goals about education X-rayed and brought out into the open. The first three decision-making steps have been our tool for teaching families how to *put the homework problem into words* and *decide on family goals*. Having come this far in teaching your children decision making, you are probably ready to see how the Johnson family uses the steps. As you read our example, think of *your* family; think about which of the issues raised affect you or your children, and how you will handle it.

THE JOHNSON FAMILY: WHERE DOES EDUCATION FIT?

Frank and Shirley Johnson live upstairs in a two-family house. Frank works for the city, in the transportation department. Now thirty-nine years old, he's been the assistant operations planner for the past four years. Shirley works part-time as a hospital technician. She spends much of her time working with schools—on parent committees and boards and volunteering as a class aide. Shirley also visits her downstairs neighbors a lot— Rosemary and Ronald Riggs, her parents. Ronald is a gentle, thoughtful man who works in the post office. His wife is a bundle of energy—cooking, shopping, sewing, never seeming to stop. She enjoys all of her grandchildren: Vanessa, age nine, in second grade; Frank Jr., age eleven, in fourth grade; and William, age fourteen, just beginning high school. Vanessa loves school and is well above average in her test scores. Frank Jr. (Frankie) works right at grade level. William is finding high school to be a bit more than he bargained for. He had always been a B+ student—until now. We look in on the Johnson household on the evening after three of William's teachers delivered very negative progress reports. First, take a look at their Parenting Family Tree.

Shirley: I don't understand it. William may fail three courses this marking
    period! I . . . I . . . I just don't know what to say.
Frank: Have you forgotten what it was like when you started high school?
Rosemary: Well, I know what to say. That boy is heading for big trouble.
    He's not the boy he used to be. We're going to lose him for sure if we
    don't get him back into this house nights and . . .
Ronald: Hold on now, Rose. You're going to pop your cork. You chain that
    boy to a desk and he'll be out so fast, your toast won't even be warm.
Shirley: Dad, you just don't realize what it takes to be successful now.
    It's . . .
Rosemary: It takes backbone. And that boy needs calcium—and fast.

These family members really differ in their reactions to William's progress reports. Shirley and Rosemary show signs of upset feelings. To Shirley the problem is that William is going to be a failure in life. Rosemary would agree but sees the problem as a lack of good character. Frank isn't alarmed. To him the problem is temporary: starting high school. Ronald does not seem to see a problem at all. If William were to enter the room, the result would be chaos. Let's see what could happen if Frank were to be the decision-making parent, with the goal of helping William clarify *his* goals.

Frank: All right, we're upset about this report. What do we want for
    William?

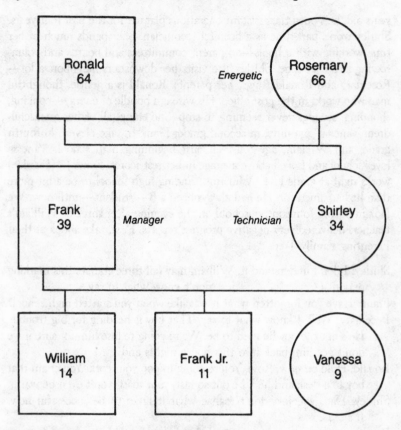

Rosemary: Frank, have you been taking those vitamins again?

Frank: No, Rose. I mean that William is in high school now and he's responsible for what he does.

Shirley: All well and good, but we can't let him ruin his entire future. We can't watch him fail!

Frank: Do you think William wants to ruin his future?

Shirley: Of course not, but . . .

Ronald: The boy has a mind of his own. Let's just try to find out what's in it.

Rosemary: I tell you he's going to follow the crowd . . .

Frank: Well, our first step, I think, is to find out what William is trying to do in school, to see what *he* wants to have happen.

Frank has tried to find a common goal that will allow the family to keep a problem-solving outlook. He's asked people about their goals and brought issues to the surface in a way that is not destructive—and we have seen too many families become unintentionally destructive when trying to cope with a child's educational problems. Frank's next task is to talk with William. Notice how he uses modeling, suggesting, asking, and the Goal X Ray to help William *decide on a goal.*

Frank: William, I've just read your progress reports. I'm not pleased. How are *you* feeling about it?

William: I guess I knew they were coming.

Frank: Well, they're here. Are you feeling proud or upset or nervous or what?

William: I'm upset and nervous.

Frank: Okay, let's use our decision-making steps, okay? What problem are you nervous about?

William: I'm nervous because you and Mom and Grandma Rose and Grandpa Ron have been talking about this and I don't know what's going to happen to me.

Frank: And what are you upset about?

William: I'm upset because my grades are going down.

Frank: You put that into words pretty clearly. All right, I'd like to zzap those problems—remember?

William: Oh, yeah, yeah. My goals, right?

Frank: Right.

William: I don't want everyone mad and disappointed at me. But if I'm going to be successful, I've got to do more than get good grades. I've got to join a club or a team. And the guys, you know, they like to fool around sometimes, so I join them. If I don't, they throw my books around the bus and stuff. So I have so much to do and then I fall behind but if I go up to teachers after class the guys get on me and . . .

Frank: Hold on, hold on. I think I heard about four goals, but maybe I lost count. Willy, you're gonna be like someone whose left leg wanted to go one way and his right leg wanted to go the other—dead stuck in your tracks.

William: Every time I try to think about it, I get a headache.

Frank: Well, this is complicated stuff. When I have times like this, I try to write down my goals on a piece of paper. What do you say?

William: Hey, Dad, it's worth a shot.

Frank: Okay. Then we'll look at them, figure out which are most important, and you can decide on one or two goals to go after . . . unless
you can figure out a way to do everything at once.

William: I don't think so, I'm not another Grandma Rose . . .

How things proceed from here depend on the values of a family. But
the energy of William and his family's *feelings of concern* were channeled
into *telling what the problem was.* Then a Goal X Ray found goal confusion—so many conflicting goals that William wasn't really meeting *any* of
them. *He was ready to have his stressful feelings relieved.* And this is the
case with so many children who experience school-related problems. Next,
William is going to look at his goals on paper and *decide what he wants to
have happen*—and perhaps admit that he must *choose his goals.* To try to
meet them all, at once, may well be beyond his capability right now.

If you've brought your children along to this point—decision-making
step 3—you now have begun to give your child the tools needed to get
"unstuck" when faced with problems and upset, stressful feelings. At first
your modeling and suggesting and use of family activities to get across the
basic readiness ideas and steps will be necessary. But shortly your children
will acquire the signs and vocabulary of decision making, much as William
has done. Get Calm!, Feelings Flashbacks, Feelings Fingerprints, Problem
Finding, Goal X Ray, and other terms will become signals, and eventually
your children will *ask themselves* questions that get them to use the decision-making steps. For William that would be *most* helpful. Then he can
prevent problems from building up during the whole school day—he can
sort out his goals even before he gets home.

Decision-Making Digest

The ability to *decide on the goal* allows your children to focus their
energy instead of spreading it out and spending a lot of time bothered by
vague, upset feelings. With a goal in mind, your children are now ready to
blast off into the exciting world of generating alternatives—finding ways
to meet goals that have been decided on. You have already, in a subtle

way, begun encouraging your children to think flexibly and creatively. Now they can use this creativity to solve problems and make decisions. The chart at the end of the chapter highlights the main activities you will probably use most often.

Decision-Making Digest:
Decide on Your Goal

If you'd like your child to	*Then try these activities:*
1. learn what a "goal" is and how common it is for people to work toward goals	1. Goal Analogies Goal Drill Jigsaw Puzzles Team Goals
2. think about his or her goals and put them into words	2. Goal X Ray Back at the Diner
3. recognize when others are trying to get him or her to follow their goals	3. Ad Attack
4. decide which activity he or she wishes to complete, and focus on it	4. List the Goals Supermarket Scribe
5. decide on goals as a way of making new experiences more manageable	5. At the Barbershop: Goals of New Experiences

7

Think of As Many Solutions
and Consequences
As You Can

Believe it. If you've helped your children identify their *feelings*, *problems*, *and goals*, you've done a lot of problem solving. You've taken them from having mixed up, confused feelings to being focused and objective. They can better state what they feel and what they want in a commonsense way. They're more organized. Now it's time to expand their thinking in a directed way. How? By encouraging them to think of as many possible solutions and consequences as they can.

Imagine that you've been cleaning up at home and also trying to keep your restless child busy. The phone rings and the voice of a man asks you to donate money to a charitable cause. Your child is growing cranky, you want to get back to your work, and you've already donated money to another charity. The voice on the phone is happily insistent. You're feeling frustrated at not being able to help your child and a bit guilty about the request of the phone caller. You're probably tempted to act impulsively: donate some money to the man's cause or yell at him.

Acting in an impulsive way often means acting on feelings alone. We know that feelings are important because they help get us interested in problem solving. But—acting on feelings alone can create problems. Thought needs to be added. In an important way, stopping to think of alternative solutions adds the *thought* dimension. This creative thinking process is what we call *generating alternative solutions*.

Generating alternative solutions reduces the likelihood of impulsive behavior. We all know that some social problems emerge because people "did not think before they acted." That is impulsive behavior. If your children (as we all do at times) tend to act impulsively more often than you would like, teaching them to generate solutions can be of great help. Why? The mere act of children generating solutions buys time. They won't try out the first solution that quickly comes to mind if they are spending time thinking of other ideas. In fact, research tells us that the quality of the solution that youngsters ultimately select improves as the youngsters generate more than one idea.

Considering consequences is where your child can practice "predictive" thinking. It is a critical decision-making step. Why? First, because it involves the idea of "fairness." Your child will be best served if he or she can select a solution that solves difficulties with the least chance of hurting himself, herself, or others. Considering the consequences is a step that develops what we call social awareness: thinking of the other person. By considering consequences, we also have a check on whether the action being thought of will help reach the *goal* that was set. In that way we keep our decision making focused and on target.

"Steptalk": Where We've Been and Where We're Going:

Let's review where we've been and take a look at the two new decision-making steps covered in this chapter:

1. Look for signs of different *feelings.*
2. Tell yourself what the *problem* is.
3. Decide on your *goal.*

NEW 4. Stop and think of as many solutions to the problem as you can.

NEW 5. For each solution, think of all the things that might happen next.

It would be natural to wonder why steps 4 and 5 are so important. When we are adults, things seem clearer, and more self-evident than they do for developing children. If any of us can recall our adolescence, we would most likely find ourselves experiencing a great deal of emotional upheaval, constantly involved in decision making about what to say, what to wear, what to do now, and what to do next.

It would also be natural to think that children just "grow out" of this way of feeling and thinking into a more mature, adult pattern. But our clinical work with families and the years we have spent consulting in the schools have shown that many children do not grow up to think clearly. There are so many stresses in life, and so many pressures to learn new things, that many children become "stuck," or hesitant about what to do next, and this pattern can persist into adulthood.

From ancient times educators have emphasized the ability to think flexibly and creatively, to consider many possibilities and their consequences. Socrates was perhaps the first to teach flexible thinking by asking his students mind-expanding questions. Many of his students went on to contribute to major advances in philosophy, science, and human relationships.

In our century John Dewey was a champion of the need to teach children *how*, not *what*, to think. He found that children who had a habit of thinking of alternatives and consequences did well academically and interpersonally. We have adapted many of his ideas about how to teach children to think into the activities presented here. Recently, there is even more reason for parents to be concerned about how their children will learn these life-enhancing skills. In our public schools children often do not learn how to problem solve and make decisions. There is a larger concern with covering the basics and learning facts that may come up on standardized tests. But we know that many of today's facts will be tomorrow's relics—how much time did we spend learning geography only to have the map change more often than a chameleon in a paint store! Someone must ensure that children learn to think—and until the schools can do this more systematically, it is up to parents to see that their children are not left "stuck."

Stop and Think of As Many Solutions to the Problem As You Can

CASE EXAMPLE: STEVE THINKS OF MORE THAN ONE SOLUTION

Consider Steve, age nine. Steve is a likable youngster in Mrs. Hartwick's fourth grade class. He moved into Cedar Grove when his father was transferred. Steve misses his old friends and is planning on making some new ones (goal). It was Wednesday and recess time at school. Steve asked Bob if he could join him and his friends playing kickball. Bob said, "No, we have enough players." Steve moved in along-side them, anyway. He began to chime in with his comments. Occasion-ally Steve's observations were well received, but he never really felt part of the conversation. Steve then saw Mike walking out of the school building. He recognized Mike as someone in his class who was also on his school bus. Steve approached Mike and asked, "Hey, Mike, does Mrs. Hartwick give hard tests?" "Yeah, she sure does," answered Mike. The two began to talk about their class and school. They even made plans to sit together on the bus ride home.

In the span of a twenty-minute recess period, Steve exemplified a major decision-making skill. He was able to generate a number of solutions to-ward his goal of wanting friends.

CASE EXAMPLE: MARCIA'S STUCK AND COULD USE SOME ALTERNATIVE SOLUTIONS

Now think about Marcia. She is also nine and in Steve and Mike's class. Marcia has attended Cedar Grove Elementary School since kindergarten. She would like to play a position other than right field during her regular recess kickball game. There she seldom gets a chance to touch the ball because it rarely ever gets out of the infield. It's usually handled by Fran who also seems to be the one who decides who should play what position. The routine is that after lunch, the girls will gather by the fence and decide on what position they will play. Marcia will usually hurry through lunch to be one of the first at the fence, hoping that she'll be picked to play first or third base. Typically, positions are decided with Marcia just waiting . . . patiently hoping that her promptness will propel her into a good position. Inevitably, Marcia is almost always stuck playing right field. To the outside observer she appears cooperative and content. Inside, how-ever, she is often a frustrated and disappointed little girl.

"CASETALK": A CLOSER LOOK AT THE TWO CHILDREN

Steve and Marcia are miles apart in their ability to generate alternative solutions to a problem. They do about equally well academically. Both will certainly have a number of nice friends over the years. Yet Steve will continue to be a happier person than Marcia, because he has watched his parents and learned from them that there is always more than one possible solution to a problem. Marcia single-mindedly and repeatedly tries her same solution of arriving early each recess time. She does not choose to expand her thinking to generate other ideas about how to get to play the infield. The result? A youngster whose life will be more limited than it has to be.

Steve does not get overly discouraged at not reaching his goal after he's tried his first idea. He can consciously think of a series of other possible solutions. He channels his disappointment into an energy that works for him.

Like Marcia, Steve is persistent. But he's persistent in brainstorming alternative solutions. In many ways you, as parents, can help your children learn that they have the ability to think of a variety of solutions to a problem. In our teaching of decision making to children in schools, we have consistently been impressed with the number of solutions that children can come up with. We might challenge them to come up with three solutions . . . then extend those to six solutions . . . then to ten—they always seem able to use their creativity and surprise us with interesting new solutions.

How to Teach Your Children to Stop and Think of Many Different Solutions and Their Consequences

As you read this section, we encourage you to practice this important step yourselves. Think of alternative ways that you can teach this step!

If you were our friend Marcia's parent, there are a number of ways that you could help to loosen up Marcia's single-minded approach. First, however, your home is probably as busy as most. Consequently you need some techniques that do not require a good deal of time. Also, Marcia may not be particularly eager to tell you about her kickball problem. She may be sensitive about discussing it with you. Marcia may even think that she would be burdening you with her problem. That's okay and not an inappropriate way for a nine year old to feel. Even if she were willing to talk to you, you may not always have the time for a detailed dialogue. Therefore, try generating alternatives with situations that are somewhat removed from real-life encounters. Often, it's safer to start there and it's fun.

There are a few general tips for encouraging children to generate alter-

natives and consequences. Below are some practical ideas for parents to
try.

BE A MODEL

In Chapter 1, we talked about how most of us learned to be parents: by
watching our own parents. It's a deceptively simple idea, but a powerful
one. All of us, and children especially, can learn new behavior *by observing
and listening to someone else.* This principle is not just someone's good
idea; it has been confirmed in scientific tests. We encourage you to take
advantage of this powerful learning principle to teach your youngster to
practice generating alternatives and considering consequences.

With this in mind, if your child gets stuck in generating alternatives,
get the ball rolling yourself. Offer your own alternative ideas. Even when
you are not directly getting your child to practice himself or herself, you
can model "out loud" your own decision making. For example, imagine
that you are trying to figure out what the family could have for dinner.
You could say out loud, "Let's see, I suppose we could have hamburgers or
spaghetti or maybe chicken." Even that little contribution will have its
impact. Your child listening to you will understand that adults use alternative thinking all the time. Another example: "Hmm . . . how should I
spend my time this afternoon? I could cash a check at the bank, pick up
some food at the supermarket, or stay home and do some work around
here."

The power of modeling is not only confined to what parents do; after
all, there are the other important influences on a child, such as characters
from television and books. One parent reported a wonderful example of
how his daughter was helped to generate alternatives by reading *The
Three Little Pigs.* In the version of the story they read, the two pigs who
built their houses of straw and wood preceded their decision by saying,
"Ho." But the third pig preceded his decision by saying, "Hmm." As we
all know, future events clearly favored the "hmm" pig over his "ho"
friends—something the daughter could easily notice. Now when decisions
are about to be made, the entire family says, "Hmm," as a cue to stop and
think of different ways to handle the situation. As the child grew older,
the parents have explained that "hmm" means "Stop and think before
you answer." Most important is that we should think creatively about
finding models of alternative thinking, and of considering consequences,

for our children. Look for expressions such as "hmm" that your family could use as reminders to pause and think of alternatives.

ENCOURAGE EXPRESSION AND ACCEPT WHAT YOU HEAR

Remember: we are teaching children *a way* to think, not *what* to think. So we want to increase the likelihood that they will say their ideas out loud and not fear criticism of those ideas. Thus when they do come up with ideas, even if the ideas are not right on target, let the children see that you are pleased they made an *effort* to generate ideas. In generating alternatives, we are most prone to be critical when our child has offered an idea that is very similar to one already mentioned. ("Aren't you listening? I just said that!") Instead, you can be a powerful influence in encouraging creative thinking: "That's one idea . . . what else can we think of?"

For example, imagine that you are outdoors with your child. You decide that this is a good time to teach the use of alternatives. You look up at the cloudy sky and have this dialogue with your son:

Mother: David, those clouds look almost like pictures. *What kinds of things* do those cloud shapes remind you of?

David: I don't know.

Mother: Well, let's see. That one straight up looks like it could be a snowman. *What do you think?*

David: Yeah . . . it looks like it could be a snowwoman too!

Mother: (smiling) That's a great idea, David! *What about that one* over there?

David: Wow! That looks like a horse—or maybe a racing car!

Mother: I never thought of that! *I wonder what else* is up there today . . .

David's mother is subtly encouraging him to come up with new ideas. She is actually using *modeling* ("I wonder . . ."), *suggesting* ("That one looks like a snowman. What do you think?"), and *asking* ("What kinds of things . . ."). If David gets enough experience in having his mother encourage alternative thinking, he'll be better able to think creatively when he might really need it, in some kind of difficult situation when his mother is not around. In a similar way we can encourage thinking about consequences by asking:

"What if . . ."

"How will that get you to your goal?"

"Are you saying that _____ might happen if you do that? What else could happen?"

By using *modeling* and by *encouraging* children to think of a variety of alternatives and consequences, parents can bring out the creative thinking potential they have. Below are specific activities that we have used with children and have found helpful and fun in teaching these skills.

Family Activities You Can Do at Home

USING PICTURES TO TEACH ALTERNATIVES

One easy way of generating alternative ideas is in reacting to pictures. Draw some pictures like these and have your child generate ideas with you. We have used this exercise with all ages of children and adults. Note the different ways you can ask your child to share his or her ideas with you —keep experimenting until you find the ones he or she responds to best.

Parent: "What could this be?"

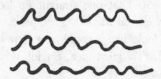

Possible alternatives: waves, snakes, eyebrows, TV test pattern.

Parent: "What does this look like to you?"

| |

Possible alternatives: a street, a worm crawling up the sidewalk, a tree trunk, a navel.

Parent: "What are all the different things this might be?"

Possible alternatives: four bald men, hills, bows, buttons on a clarinet.

Parent: "I wonder what this is . . . what do you think?"

Possible alternatives: a hot dog, a pool of water seen from an airplane, a potato, a surfboard, an open mouth, a face without features.

Parent: "How many different things do you think this might be a picture of . . . shall we write them down?"

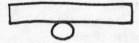

Possible alternatives: a man wearing a hat, a wagon, a seesaw.

Parent: "I bet I can think of three things this could be . . . how many can you think of?"

Possible alternatives: a smile, whiskers, a parade, grass, dominoes in a row, pretzels.

Parent: "Gee whiz, I just can't figure out what this might be . . . what are your ideas?"

Possible alternatives: a Ping-Pong table, an upside down *t,* a racquetball court, a plant growing, a thin man standing sideways, a worm coming out to see the sun.

Parent: "Hmm. This looks like a lot of different things to me. Over here it looks like a key hole. What do you see over there?"

Possible alternatives: a raft on a lake, a doughnut with a square hole, a steering wheel, an eskimo's hood, an opening to a cave.

Another way to use these picture activities is to ask your child to draw a design or pattern. Then both of you can practice imagining what images you see. As your child draws a variety of designs, that, in itself, is generating alternatives! As in our example of looking at clouds and guessing their images, the environment can offer many opportunities to practice generating alternative ideas. In our families we've been known to guess what new object a cookie resembles as we take succeeding bites.

Encouraging your child to generate alternatives will greatly boost his or her confidence. If you practice this approach often enough yourself, generating alternatives will become a natural part of how you converse with your child. It's often easier, when practicing this skill, to start with activities that don't involve people. Thinking up different uses for a shoe box or what a drawn shape could be is easier than thinking up a variety of ways to handle being teased. As you grow comfortable in engaging your child in our alternatives exercises, you'll want to graduate to situations that are more realistic.

Television and movies provide a fine opportunity to begin practicing generating alternatives to interpersonal situations. You are doing a number of beneficial things for your youngster when you start practicing alternative thinking to these two media. At the very least, by watching a program or movie with your youngster, you're showing him or her how important he or she is to you. You do not have to create a situation that you hope will interest your child. Consider a popular movie, *The Wizard of Oz.* Your youngster is probably already greatly interested in Dorothy or the Wizard, or some other favorite television and movie characters. Your job is to take this interest and expand upon it, in this case by encouraging alternative thinking.

To make television and movie viewing an active rather than passive activity, you can ask questions like, "What are some other ways Dorothy could handle the Wizard?" or "How else could the Lion, Tin Man, and Scarecrow save Dorothy?" Some people see no harm in asking while the relevant action is still going on. The action is fresh in mind, and it conveys to the child that TV or movies are not "sacred," but something to think about carefully. In other families such questions are held off until commercials or the end of a show. Each child responds differently, and we find it best to be flexible.

Family Activities You Can Do Away from Home

STORY STEMS: I KNOW SOMEONE WHO . . .

We have made extensive use of hypothetical stories and story stems in our classroom work. You can, too. A story stem is best described as part of a story. It is often easier at first for children to react to brief hypothetical situations that they are not involved in. They can answer "as if" they were one of the people in the story. Next, they can gradually tell what they might do in the hypothetical situation, and eventually respond to these questions: "Has anything like this ever happened to you? How did you handle it . . . what else might you have tried . . . what would you try if it happened again?"

Story stems such as the ones we will describe can be used with your children to practice generating alternative solutions. Introducing a story stem in a natural way makes it more likely that your child will become engaged in conversation about it. From our experiences we have found several types of lead-ins to be useful.

The Rumor: *"I heard that* a girl in the middle school was being bothered by other kids on the school bus, and it was really upsetting."

The News: *"In the paper,* there was a story about how hard it is for some children to do well in sports—they try to catch and hit, but they can't, and they feel badly."

The Out-loud Muse: *"I was just thinking* about how important it can be to be in a band. *I wonder* . . . if a child wanted to get into the band, how could he or she do it? . . . What if he or she didn't get accepted?"

As before, you will find other ideas for lead-ins that occur to you, and you will find your child responding to one format or another. When you do a story stem, your child may give what you consider to be an undesirable solution; if so, encourage his or her willingness to be creative, but have your child examine the possible consequences. We describe how to do this in the second half of this chapter. On the next pages however, you will find some specific story stems of commonly occurring situations for children.

Story Stem: Breaking in the Line.
"Another child pushes to be in front of you in line at school."
Goal: Not to be taken advantage of.
Alternative Solutions: (1) tell your teacher, (2) push back (examine the consequences), or (3) talk to that child directly.

We have found, surprisingly, that being at a certain position in line is very important for our younger elementary school children. Some of the situations that we will begin to describe may be a real problem for *your* child. At some point, out of worrying about your child's hurt, or your wish to help, you might be tempted to solve your child's problem for him or her. Try to avoid that when you can. Remember, he or she may not come up with the solutions which you might have thought of. But if your child has generated a few of his or her own ideas, he or she is succeeding in building this important decision-making skill. The point is *how* your child thinks, as much as *what* he or she thinks.

Story Stem: Classmate Spreading Lies.
"You think Jennifer, a girl in your class, has been saying untrue things about you."
Goal: To find out if this is really going on.
Alternative Solutions: (1) don't say anything, just be on the alert, (2) ask your best friend, Mary Anne, if it's true, (3) ask your teacher, or (4) ask Jennifer directly.

That kind of situation is one we have found to be of particular concern for children as they near the fifth grade. It's a difficulty that can linger in one way or another, as children may become distrustful of others or doubt their feelings about themselves. You can help solve the problem merely by talking about it. For those children who silently suffer with problems like this, hearing their mother or father bring up the topic suggests that "I'm not the only one who has felt this way." This is the value of the story stem activity. Your child, especially as he or she nears the teenage years, will have a way to help share situations with his or her *parents*, as well as being able to confide in friends. Story stems can allow you to practice problem solving and decision making around a neutral, "hypothetical" situation, without your child feeling that he or she has to always reveal "personal" information to you.

Story Stem: New Child in the Neighborhood.
"A new boy just moved into your neighborhood."
Goal: You would like to be his friend.
Alternative Solutions: (1) go over to his house and wait for him to come out, (2) knock on his door and introduce yourself, (3) find out his phone number and call him up, (4) ask your mother to take you over, or (5) wait for him to introduce himself to you.

Making new friends. This is a challenge that has confronted us all from early childhood on. And we know that it is often not the easiest social situation to handle. Some of us grow shy, some of us wait for the prospective friend to make the first move, and so on. Because it is a situation that children always find themselves in, the need to "make new friends" can become a cue to click into thoughtful decision making. Again, if your children can consciously draw upon such decision-making steps as thinking of a variety of solutions, they're less likely to be passive and helpless. They'll be more confident, in control, and less likely to let opportunities slip by.

ALTERNATIVE ALTERNATIVES

You might try this game with your children the next time you go for a ride or walk.

How many kinds of soda can you think of?
(1) orange (2) grape (3) ginger ale (4) cream (5) cherry (6) cola

Let's think of all the games you can play with a ball:
(1) football (2) soccer (3) pinball (4) baseball (5) polo

How many ways can you think of to prepare eggs?
(1) poach (2) scramble (3) fry (4) as an omelette (5) as eggnog

Think of all the different uses you could have for an old tire:
(1) a backyard swing (2) a giant doughnut (3) a steering wheel

Name some different ways that you could use a shoe box:
(1) as a house for a turtle (2) as snowshoes (3) as a hat

What could an empty ice-cream cone be used for?
(1) a microphone (2) a telescope (3) a baseball bat for a tiny person (4) a scoop (5) a horn

Think about how you could use the inside roll from a package of paper towels:
(1) as a telescope (2) as a microphone (3) as a telephone

When you try activities like Alternative Alternatives, be patient. Your youngster will certainly enjoy some of the items more than others. Keep in mind that the games should be fun and should not be forced. Your children may be able to come up with only one alternative or two. That's fine. Consider new ways of stimulating their thinking. Remember, encouraging their effort is your goal.

If we can help our children realize that they are able to think of more than one solution, this alone will be of great help to them. But it is only another part of the picture. Youngsters also need to learn the importance of trying to consider the consequences of their ideas.

For Each Solution, Think of All
the Things That Might Happen Next

It's important now to review what has been presented so far. Your children are beginning to see the value of knowing their own and others' feelings. We know that feelings serve several purposes. Expressing feelings is a way to reduce tension. More than that, recognizing our own and others' feelings can be very motivating. If a fourth grader did not feel happy when he or she got an excellent grade in language arts, then he or she might not be motivated to try hard to capture that feeling again.

With your help the children are also beginning to practice putting their difficulties into concrete words. This skill alone helps reduce sad and unhappy feelings because it makes the "problem" look solvable.

Deciding on a goal organizes us even further. It asks the children to think about what they want, thus reducing the likelihood that they'd become scattered and frantic in their thinking and activities.

Thinking up as many solutions as you can is a tremendously powerful step to remember. If your children remember that step and use it, they will begin to see themselves as problem solvers. But as you know, generating multiple solutions will go only so far. Youngsters need to learn the importance of *considering consequences.*

We like to think of this skill as a way to forecast what might happen. It is one of the most abstract ideas to teach and you may need to practice this step frequently with the children.

Because it is so empowering to generate solutions, your youngster might be tempted to rush in and select a solution without carefully examining it. This is a time for you to help them slow things down.

Case Example: Steve Can Consider Consequences, Too

Imagine that it had gotten to be midafternoon. Our friend, Steve, was now sitting on the bus with Mike. Steve felt pleased inside. He was beginning to make a friend in his new school. Steve still had this goal in mind when their conversation turned to bikes. Mike was excitedly telling Steve all about the new one that he had just gotten for his birthday. As Mike's stop neared, he turned to Steve and said, "Why don't you come to my house now? I'll show you my bike and you can ride it. We can practice some tricks with it." Steve hesitated. He recalled promising his mother that he would come home right from school. Steve quickly ran through some alternative solutions:

1. If he decided to go to Mike's right now, they might become even better friends, but his mother may be very angry.
2. He could tell Mike the truth, that he couldn't come that day.

Mike might get upset and might not be as willing to extend such an invitation the next time.
3. He could tell Mike that he had to go home first and ask his mother. If she okayed it, he would come over then.
4. He could tell Mike that his mother wanted him home but maybe he could go to Mike's house now and call home from there. It was hard for Steve to figure out how his mother would react to *this* idea.

Steve saw that many of his choices were risky. He decided to tell Mike that he had to go home first and then ask his mother. As it turned out in this case, Mike expressed his disappointment but said he would wait for Steve's call.

In this situation Steve was demonstrating the decision-making skill of being able to *consider the consequences*. It is important to note that our minds work rather quickly—the reasoning that Steve did took about a second or two. That is the time frame that is most often available to us when we have to deal with daily problems. Our sense is, however, that Steve was able to handle this situation in a quick, confident, and fair way because his parents had encouraged this decision-making skill. They did this for him over the years by modeling their own decision making and by playing decision-making games with Steve like the ones we have been describing. At this point generating alternatives and consequences was becoming a rather natural strategy for Steve.

CASE EXAMPLE: MARCIA HAS TO THINK ABOUT CONSEQUENCES MORE CAREFULLY

Remember Marcia? She has been sitting several seats behind Mike and Steve on the bus. Marcia was still feeling frustrated about being stuck in right field again. She still wanted a chance to touch the ball more. Fran was sitting directly across the aisle from her. Too many times had passed with Marcia unsuccessfully trying that same old solution of waiting patiently by the fence. That solution was just not working. Because Fran was one of the leaders, Marcia began to generate some alternative solutions. She could

1. make a demand to Fran that she be allowed to pitch the next time.

2. flatter Fran and then hope that Fran would like her and get her a better position.
3. tell Fran that she would do her math homework for her if she could play third base tomorrow.

Marcia was clearly making progress in her decision-making skills. She was not "stuck." Marcia was being creative and generating multiple ideas. In the long run this change would clearly work to her advantage. Continuing to do that kind of alternatives generating will boost up her confidence. But, unlike Steve, she was not good at considering the consequences of her proposed solutions. For example, Marcia decided to offer to do Fran's math homework for her. Marcia was actually a conscientious little girl. She did not foresee the guilt that she would be feeling as a result of that decision. Nor did she anticipate the fact that Fran would be expecting her to do her language arts homework as well from now on. That is indeed what did happen, thus creating a *new* problem.

Family Activities You Can Do at Home

WEATHERPERSON

Here's a simple way you can help your child anticipate consequences. Talk to your youngster about forecasting the next day's weather. For example, imagine that it is late afternoon. You and your child are inside. Look out the window together and using the clues, try to predict the weather.

Father: Lynn, what do you think it's going to be like tomorrow?
Lynn: I don't know.
Father: Let's look out the window and check it out.
Lynn: It's cloudy out.
Father: What might that mean?
Lynn: Maybe it will be cloudy tomorrow too, or even rain.
Father: Yes, maybe you're right.

This particular game might be set up nicely by watching some of the television weather forecasts with your youngster. It's our feeling that it's difficult for many adults, and certainly children, to understand how the

TV weatherperson uses natural signs and so on to make forecasts. You might simplify the process for your child by offering some comments during or after the show. For example, "It looks like strong winds will blow away the rain clouds, so we'll have sunny weather tomorrow." After some brief discussions like this, you might go into the routine of playing weatherperson. Often it's a helpful game to play right before your child goes to bed, when he or she is involved in deciding what kind of clothes to wear the next day. You might be the person forecasting the weather for a while, modeling how to do it. Then give your youngster an opportunity to be the weatherperson. When your child wakens in the morning, and the weather is indeed as he or she predicted, you have a great opportunity to compliment the child's capacity to anticipate and think ahead.

TV AND MOVIE CONSEQUENCES

Besides television or movie plots providing an opportunity for decision-making practice, as we have mentioned, stories offer a good vehicle for practicing a variety of decision-making steps. Ask your child, "What do you think will happen next?" and then entertain all of the ideas. You might be more specific with questions like, "If Dorothy (in *The Wizard of Oz)* clicked her heels together now, how might the story be different?" Here is where you can take advantage of the suspenseful moments when it's unclear about the fate of the heroine. Again, you don't want to interrupt unduly the children's concentration on the story. When this is a concern, state out loud, "I wonder what's going to happen next?" The children don't have to say anything. Just raising the question will stimulate their thinking about consequences.

Family Activities You Can Do Away from Home

THE "WHAT IF" GAME

One of the best ways we have found to help your child anticipate consequences is to play a game like What If. This is a good activity to use when you are in the car, or are waiting for dinner in a restaurant, or are elsewhere waiting for some activity to begin. The idea is to first have fun and second to practice considering consequences. With this game and with other such exercises, you can begin to see how several decision-making rules can be taught at once. For example, when you play a game like What If you can encourage alternative thinking *and* the consideration of consequences. Here are some What If questions and some answers we've heard at different times:

What if . . .

What if you could read minds?

1. I'd be surprised at what people think.
2. I could rule the world.
3. I'd be really smart.
4. I'd have too much on my mind.

What if you found a thousand dollars?

1. I'd play video games all day.
2. I'd put it in the bank.
3. I'd find out whose it was.
4. I'd buy presents for all my friends.

What if you could breathe underwater?

1. I'd see all the fish.
2. I'd live down there.
3. I'd swim to Europe.
4. I'd help the whales.

What if you could jump as high as a house?

1. I'd go on television.
2. I'd have a lot of fun.
3. I'd play professional basketball.
4. I'd always be outside.

What if you had your own horse?

1. I'd take care of him.
2. I'd race him.
3. I'd give my parents a ride.
4. I'd find a barn for him.

What if you had a car?

1. I'd need a license.
2. I'd visit my grandparents.
3. I'd give it to my father.
4. I'd drive myself to school.

What if you could run as fast as a deer?

1. I'd enter the Olympics.

2. I'd never just walk again.
3. I'd get tired.
4. Some people might be jealous of me.

What if birds could talk to us?
1. They could tell us what they see.
2. I'd ask them about all the places they've visited.
3. They could tell us what the weather would be.
4. It would be noisy.

What if it snowed every day all year?
1. I could build the world's largest snowman.
2. I'd get tired of not having a summer.
3. We might not have to go to school all the time.
4. My back would hurt from shoveling.

What if babies could read?
1. They'd know a lot.
2. They couldn't tell us much because they don't talk.
3. Someone would still have to hold the book up for them.
4. They'd be reading strange things.

What if fish could walk?
1. The streets would be crowded.
2. They'd be able to jump out of fishermen's boats.
3. They would have fins and legs then.
4. They would be able to run too.

What if you met someone from outer space?
1. I'd try to talk to her.
2. I'd run away.
3. I'd see if she were lost.
4. I'd be frightened of her.

What if you had your own television show?
1. I'd be famous.
2. I'd have my friends on as guests.
3. I'd have all my favorite singers and actors on.
4. I'd watch myself.

What if you were the President?
1. I'd stop making nuclear weapons.
2. I'd live in Washington, D.C.
3. I'd be very busy.
4. I'd need a lot of help.

What if the New York Yankees wanted you to play for them?

1. I might play in the World Series.
2. I'd leave school.
3. I'd be excited.
4. I'd have my own baseball card.

What if it rained roses?

1. The sky would be beautiful.
2. It would feel nice.
3. The streets would be a mess.
4. The air would smell sweet.

Your child may "miss" some of what you might think would be obvious consequences. Use your judgment about how to best handle this. Keep in mind that one goal of the What If game is to keep the children interested in doing that kind of forecasting. If you can offer that "obvious" consequence in an encouraging way, by all means do so. But if you think your child will see you as critical, consider holding your comment back. You want your child to feel successful in these activities. In the game we've offered you four responses that we've heard. It's fine if your child volunteers "just" two or as many as ten. It is also likely that many youngsters will not be thinking of the same consequences that we did. That's fine, too. You can also encourage your youngsters to practice "alternatives and consequences" by making up their own What If questions and offering their own forecasts.

We've done a lot of work with exercises and games that stimulate generating alternatives and consequences. Let's take a look at how a mother can teach these skills in a real-life situation.

Using the Fourth and Fifth Decision-Making Steps to Handle Everyday Problems: When Siblings Battle

Marlene is a thirty-five-year-old divorced mother of two boys. Danny is her eight-year-old third grader and Jason is four. Danny, as is the case with many eight year olds, is very possessive about his things. Marlene is a teacher. Lately she has been arriving home at 4 P.M. to find Danny and Jason intensely fighting with each other. A four year old contesting with an eight year old can be a very difficult situation to encounter. Developmentally a four year old can get overexcited, excessively active, and can easily be perceived as a nuisance to an older brother or sister. It's Tuesday afternoon and school is over. Marlene is picking up the boys at her mother's. She is greeted at the door by her mother, Joan, who is looking quite frazzled.

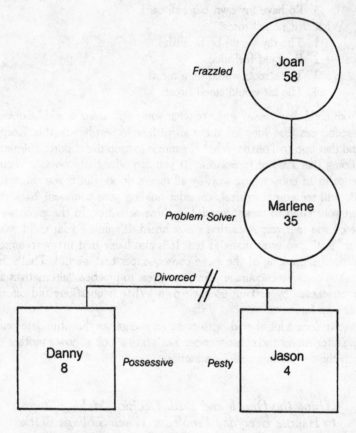

Joan: Marlene, I just don't know what to do. Danny never lets Jason play with him . . . Jason starts to scream . . . then I get upset . . . It's a real problem.

Marlene often has been letting her boys settle these disputes themselves. She realizes that she will not be stopping this kind of fighting behavior completely, especially at their ages. However, Marlene decides to take this opportunity to help Danny, her eight year old, sense some decision-making opportunities.

Marlene: Danny, what happened?

Danny: (angry) Jason's always bugging me, Mom. He's a pest. He's always fooling around with my stuff.

Marlene: Looks like you're pretty angry at your brother.

Danny: You bet.

Marlene: Well, what do you want to have happen?

Danny: I want you to punish him.

Marlene: No, I mean if you weren't fighting with him, what would you really like to be doing?

Danny: I wanted to play in peace with some of the stickers and cards I've been collecting.

Marlene: Well, tell me what the problem is.

Danny: I hate it when he butts in and tries to grab my cards and stuff.

Marlene: I wonder what you could do to be able to play in peace.

Danny: I don't know.

Marlene: Well think about it a little.

Danny: I guess . . . I guess I could take my collection into the bedroom and play there.

Marlene: That's a good idea. Tell me more.

Danny: What do you mean?

Marlene: I mean, what else could you do?

Danny: Oh . . . I guess I could try to get him to play with some of *his* things.

Marlene: That's great. You've thought of two ideas. Anything else?

Danny: Well, maybe I should give him a couple of my old cards . . . the beat-up ones.

Marlene: Yes, that's another idea. Well, what do you think would happen if you tried out your ideas?

Danny: If I went to the bedroom, he'd just follow me there and keep on being a pain.

Marlene: What about your other ideas?

Danny: He'd never listen to me if I tried to get him to play with his things.

Marlene: Uh . . . huh.

Danny: I guess I'll just have to let him play with a couple of my old cards that I don't need.

Marlene: Would that be your best idea?

Danny: Yeah, I guess so.

Marlene: (gives him a hug) Danny . . . terrific job on thinking this
through.

In this exchange, note that Danny did not offer his mother perfect
solutions. At several points he did not understand what his mother was
asking him to do. For example, when Marlene asked him to offer more
alternatives by saying, "Tell me more," Danny responded, "What do you
mean?" Marlene did not let that throw her and rephrased her question,
that is, "I mean, what else could you do?" Marlene also did something else
that was useful. She carved out a chunk of this episode and dealt with one
piece of it at a time, helping Danny practice problem solving. For the
moment, at least, she did not choose to calm her mother down or discuss
the matter with Jason. It would have been a too scattered or too shallow
approach. Rather, she chose to let her mother stay frazzled for a bit while
she spoke to Danny. Finally, although she was confronted by this minica-
tastrophe about her children misbehaving, she was able to refrain from
rushing in and solving the problem for them. She could have, at the
outset, suggested that Danny give Jason some of the old, beat-up cards.
The immediate problem would have been solved but she would not have
given Danny practice in operating independently. Because she is also
working outside of her home, Danny needs to be able to act independently. By solving Danny's problem for him, she would have missed a
chance to equip him with decision-making skills. Fortunately Marlene
made the time to have this kind of a conversation with Danny. We
painted this scene to give you a sense of what an extended problem-solving
conversation can look like. There will be many more times that Marlene
will have only a moment or two to spend on decision making with Danny.
In that case we'll offer you a shortened version:

Marlene: Danny, what happened?

Danny: Jason keeps bugging me, Mom. He's a pest. He's always wanting
to play with my stuff.

Marlene: Well, what are some things that you could do that could help it
work out?

Danny: I don't know.

Marlene: Think about it.

Danny: I could leave the room.

Marlene: Yes.

Danny: I could let him play with some of my older cards.

Marlene: What would happen if you tried these ideas?

Danny: He'd just follow me to our room anyway. I guess I could give him some of the old cards. But, Mom, he's still a pest.

Marlene: I know he can be pesty . . . but you've done a good job thinking this through. I'm proud of you. I'll talk to your brother later.

Note that Marlene concentrated on Alternatives and Consequences. Depending on what she felt was important at the time, she could have elicited other decision-making steps. For example, if she felt that Danny was unclear about what he wanted, she might have concentrated on Feelings and Goals, another appropriate approach to this situation.

Marlene could also have used problem-solving skills with her mother, who may have been stuck about what to do.

Marlene: Mom, what happened?

Joan: Jason and Danny are always fighting.

Marlene: What did you do?

Joan: I yelled at both of them.

Marlene: Did it work?

Joan: No.

Marlene: Mom, this is a tough situation. This goes on here a whole lot. Do you have any other ideas?

Joan: It's hard to handle them when you're not here. Maybe I'll just put them in separate rooms for a while or not give them their snack if they fight.

Marlene: Well, what would work out the best do you think?

Joan: Don't give them their snacks. They're too big for me to separate them.

As we imagine Marlene and her mother having this dialogue and trying to be helpful to one another, we again think about how important generating alternatives and considering consequences are in the decision-making process. We also realize that considering consequences brings us closer to the next step in our decision-making strategy: choosing your best solution, which is discussed in the next chapter.

Decision-Making Digest

We can do much to prepare our children for an uncertain future by teaching them to think in a flexible and creative manner. Perhaps there is no more important set of skills than the ability to have many ideas to choose from and to know how to evaluate the consequences of each one. We have shared some parent-child conversations and some family activities that can become a part of your everyday routine. The major ones are summarized on the chart at the end of this chapter. We hope you'll find the time to use at least some of them regularly. In the following chapter, you will see how to help your children choose from among the many alternatives and consequences they will think of.

Decision-Making Digest:
Think of As Many Solutions
and Consequences As You Can

If you'd like your child to	*Then try these activities:*
1. practice thinking in a creative, flexible, mind-expanding way	1. Using Pictures to Teach Alternatives Alternative Alternatives
2. learn to generate alternative solutions in conflict situations involving other persons	2. Story Stems
3. anticipate future happenings	3. Weatherperson
4. learn that there can be more than one consequence to a particular solution	4. What If

8

Choose Your Best Solution

When you start teaching alternatives and consequences, your children are at the heart of decision making. There are many enjoyable ways to teach these skills. It is at this point that we can finally feel like we are making some headway. And we are. But, this decision-making process can be deceptive. Why? You have already carefully gone through identifying feelings, problems, and how to select a goal. You have also taken a close look at alternatives and consequences. At first glance, it seems we've learned about anticipating all the possible outcomes to your several solutions. Isn't that enough? In many cases, when we do have to move quickly, that may be enough. But it has been our experience that there are other steps that need to be taught to children in order to better prepare them for the job of implementing and acting on their good ideas. This and the next chapters will help move us from *ideas to action*. Developing these skills can be smoother with some parental assistance.

"Steptalk": Where We've Been and Where We're Going

Many of us—including our children—may have a tremendous knack for generating solutions and consequences. If we are given the time and the encouragement, we could really go on for a long while generating solutions and their accompanying consequences. But the next challenge for us and our children is to know when to stop. At some point we will want to put to practical use some of the good ideas that we have generated. Of course, there are even alternative expressions to describe this step of *choosing a best solution!* First, let's review our decision-making steps.

CASE EXAMPLE: ANDREA THINKS ABOUT OPTIONS AND CHOOSES WISELY

Think about Andrea Meyers. She is an eleven year old who is now in the sixth grade. Andrea and her good friend, Michelle, who is also eleven years old, are still adjusting to a school year with many big changes. They are getting used to their middle school, which is a much larger building than their elementary school building. Many of their classmates are new to them, having come from other elementary schools. These two girls have always been good students. The biggest challenge this year has been to try to deal with eight different teachers for their eight different subjects. It has not been easy.

It is now eighth period and that means language arts with Mrs. Vance in Room 202. "Class," says Mrs. Vance, "one of the words that we have been studying is procrastination. For homework, due on Monday, I would like you to write a five-hundred-word essay on 'What procrastination means to me.' Okay? All right then, you can go back to your homerooms when the bell rings. Have a nice weekend." Waiting for the change of class bell, Andrea and Michelle eyeball each other with quiet displeasure at the sound of this weekend assignment.

Because they have different homerooms, the girls part company. Andrea is feeling somewhat anxious. "When am I going to get the time to do that essay?" she thinks to herself, as she packs her books from her locker. "I'm supposed to go shopping tonight," she thinks, "and I think that Mom and everyone else have some kind of family outing planned for this weekend. Sometimes it's easier to have homework due the next day . . . then you don't have to make these kinds of choices. Why does Mrs. Vance give us weekend homework anyway? What a pain!"

Once home, Andrea learns that her family evidently does have plans this weekend. They are going to visit Andrea's grandmother all day on Sunday. "Let's see," Andrea thinks to herself, "that leaves this afternoon, tomorrow, or Sunday night to write the essay. Well, none of those times are great but maybe I'll start it right now. Mom is home and she looks like she's in a pretty good mood today. Maybe I can convince her to give me a few good ideas, too."

As you might expect a scenario like this to unfold, Andrea was able to get herself a snack at the kitchen table and, with some encouragement from her mother, was able to finish the essay by dinnertime. Her anxiety lessened and she was able to enjoy the rest of her weekend. Incidentally, Andrea's mother did let her know how happy she was that Andrea had done the assignment early. Although we are not able to get inside Andrea's mind to explore her thinking more, we'd make a good guess that there was a lot of decision making going on. She was in touch with her *feelings* about the assignment, knew her *problem* and goal of trying to get it done over a busy weekend, and *generated solutions*. In fact, she introduced a topic we will talk about later: *the solution review*. That is, she was able to call to mind all of her solutions before choosing. And then she was able to *choose* her best solution. Any one of her proposed homework slots may have worked out well. But she didn't procrastinate on the procrastination assignment. The result? She was a much more relaxed eleven year old when she comfortably chatted on the telephone with Michelle later that evening.

CASE EXAMPLE: MICHELLE PUTS OFF MAKING CHOICES

When Michelle heard from Andrea that evening that her assignment was done, she was genuinely surprised. "I can't believe you've already done it!" she said. "Maybe it won't take that much time after all," she thought to herself. The girls talked for about forty minutes, until they were asked by their parents to get off the phone. "I'll talk to you tomorrow, Andrea," parted Michelle. It was now about 9 P.M. "I'm tired of school stuff," Michelle thought, "but I guess I have to figure out when I am going to do that essay. Really, maybe it won't take that long to do, if Andrea got it done so quickly. I could do it tomorrow when I come home from shopping *or* there's always Sunday night." At this point Michelle yawned and thought, "Hey, that's not so bad. I've got three times at least that I can do it this weekend." She yawned again and said to herself, "Tomorrow morning, when I'm not so beat, I'll decide about when I am going to do it."

Tune in Sunday night for the finish of the story! In this case we see an irritable sixth grader unhappily remembering that she put off doing the procrastination assignment. She gets it done, but at some cost to herself, her parents, and her family.

Like Andrea, Michelle had done some good problem solving, up to a point. She felt purposeful, powerful, and organized after generating some good alternative solutions. But these feelings were deceptive, *because she never chose.* We can speculate why. We all know people who have a difficult time bringing things to closure and how needlessly unhappy they become at those times. We can help our children avoid that problem by working with them to have confidence in their capacity to *choose a best solution.*

"CASETALK": A CLOSER LOOK AT THE TWO CHILDREN

The Monday morning finish to our story is that both Andrea and Michelle handed in good essays and they both got good grades. What was probably less obvious to others, though, was the fact that Michelle was somewhat sleepy and grumpy for having stayed up late the night before. Also the quality of their weekends was much different because Andrea's willingness to *make a choice* freed her from feeling anxious and guilty. The "choice" that Michelle made, we suppose, was to put off making a choice until she was stuck with Sunday night!

The focus of this chapter is to teach our children to choose their best solutions and try them. One of the best ways to start is to begin raising your child's awareness that he or she has actually been making a number of decisions during the course of the day, and that those decisions have generally been good ones. What we would like is for our youngsters to begin to regard themselves as "decision makers," individuals who are confident because they have already been making decisions. Here are some tips about building your child's ability to make choices. Then we'll describe some examples of activities your family can *choose* to try.

How to Teach Your Child to Choose the Best Solution

BE A MODEL

Think of all the choices and selections that you make during the course of your busy day. Consider letting some of your silent choices gain a voice as you *decide out loud* for your child's benefit. Here are some examples:

I like both colors but I think I'll pick the blue because it goes with my dress better.

It's between watching the news and the end of the football game; I think I'll watch the news so I can watch the President's news conference.

Even though I'd love to go shopping, I've decided to stay home for a while and clean up before our guests arrive.

There're so many people I'd like to invite, I think I'll ask Irene and Patrick to come over for cards because I haven't seen them in months.

ENCOURAGE EXPRESSION

When we think that our children need to make a decision, we can move them along by encouraging them to express their choices. One way to do this is to ask questions. For example:

Do you think you might choose _____?
    Tommy, to stay outside, the book about stars, Channel 2, to get ready, and so on.
Which idea will you choose?
What do you think you'll do?
Which one best reaches your goal?

There is another approach that appears to help a number of children make progress in choosing a best solution. It's called the Solution Review.

Solution Review. In order to make a good choice, we need to keep in mind alternative solutions that we generated. Sometimes in the excitement and enthusiasm of getting unstuck in a problem, our child can momentarily forget what his or her good ideas were. At this point you can help out, by prompting a *Solution Review*, encouraging your child to call to mind his solutions. For example, a parent might use such prompts as:

Could you tell me the solutions you thought of?
What were those ideas again?
I forgot some of your solutions. Could you go over them again?

Sometimes youngsters might generate a number of solutions. In their excitement at doing so well, they might select the last one they thought of. That may not be the best solution. A Solution Review can be done efficiently and in a way that is thought-provoking. Think of the Solution Review as a way for your children to get their thoughts in order. Here is an example:

Susan: (sad) I promised Diane that I'd come over today but I don't feel like it anymore.

Mom: Well, what are some solutions that you have?

Susan: Well, I could go to her house and tell her, or I could call her up, or maybe I'll just not show up . . . yeah, that's what I'll do, just not show up.

Mom: Susan, slow down a little, think, and say them again.

Susan: I could go to her house.

Mom: Okay.

Susan: I could call her up.

Mom: All right.

Susan: Or I could just not show up.

Mom: Well, which of these will lead to what you would like to see happen?

Susan: What do *you* think?

Mom: It's not for me to say. You have to choose what's best for you.

Susan: Hmm . . .

ACCEPT AND ACKNOWLEDGE WHAT YOU HEAR

A good way to do this is to compliment your child's efforts at choosing. Remember, the key here is to not make these kinds of remarks constantly. If you do, your child can *choose* to ignore you. Your good intentions will become frustrated. Rather, from time to time tell your child you are pleased that he or she has made a decision. Here are some examples of what we mean:

> "I like the pants that you *selected* today."
> "Looks like you have *decided* that the cornflakes taste better than the other kind."
> "Oh, you *prefer* jelly, just like Dad does."
> "You know, you really *chose* a good friend in Robert."

"I am really glad that you've *decided* to clean up after your snack."
"Mom and I are so pleased that you've *decided* to stay out of trouble at school."
"When you *chose* to ignore your sister's teasing, she seemed to stop doing it."
"Even though Tommy didn't stay to help clean up, I'm glad that you *decided* to stay and help out."

In each case the comment follows a *choice* by a child. This clearly respects and supports a child's feeling good about making decisions.

Family Activities You Can Do at Home

THE CHILDREN'S CHOICES CHART OR THE TYPICAL DAY IN THE LIFE OF A DECISION MAKER

Many choices that we have listed are those that children do silently and quickly. Our contribution as parents is to make our children aware that they have made good choices. We've used a Children's Choices Chart to remind ourselves from time to time of those occasions when even our very young children have successfully made decisions.

Getting Up:

Should I get up now	or	stay in bed?
I wonder if I should go to the bathroom first	or	take off my pajamas?
Should I brush my teeth	or	wait for Mom to remind me?
What should I wear today?		
Should I wear my		
blue jeans	or	green pants?
sneakers	or	shoes?
checked	or	plain shirt?
Should I wake up Mommy first	or	Dad?

Breakfast Time:

Let's see, should I watch TV	or	should I eat breakfast?
What should I eat—		
toast with butter	or	toast with jelly?

cornflakes	or	wheat flakes?
Should I drink milk	or	orange juice?
Shall I clean up my breakfast	or	watch television?

Schooltime:

Many decisions occur here, but we have listed some of the ones that occur when you are able to be with your child and compliment the choices that your child makes. Certainly you can compliment your child after the fact about school decisions if you know about them.

After Schooltime:

I wonder if I should say, "What's to eat?" first	or	talk about all the homework that I have?
I have to decide about whether I should do my homework first	or	go outside.
If I go outside, should I call for my friend	or	should I wait until he calls for me?
I wonder whether I should		
play hide and seek	or	play house?
ride my bike	or	play with my trucks?
play kickball	or	play soccer?

Dinnertime:

Should I go in the first time that Mom calls me	or	the third time that Mom calls me?
I wonder if I should wash my hands	or	skip it?
What should I eat first—		
potatoes	or	meat?
Should I leave when I am done eating	or	should I stay until everyone is finished?

After Dinnertime:

Should I help clean up	or	should I just go?
Should I watch television	or	should I do my homework?
I have to decide whether to do my math first	or	my social studies.

After Dinnertime:

I wonder if I should take a break from my homework now	or	wait until I finish it all?
What television program should I watch—		
the movie	or	the half-hour comedy show?

Bedtime:

Should I try to get Mom to let me stay up	or	is it better to just keep quiet?
What is the best way to get Mom to let me stay up?		
Offer to let her teach me decision making	or	tell her I would like to talk about the news?
Should I go to bed the first time I am called	or	the seventh time I am told?
I wonder if I should put my pajamas on first	or	should I brush my teeth first?

The important point here is to raise our awareness of how many times during the course of the day our children are actually making decisions and, for the most part, making good ones. Again, our job is to let our children know how helpful it is that they have been making decisions. From time to time you can let your youngster know that you feel positively about his or her decision making. You are calling attention to a growing capacity to *decide*.

VISUALIZING YOUR GOAL

Another activity that has helped children *practice how* to learn to choose the best solution is to visualize the goal. This skill is an effort to get your youngster to go back and think again about what it was that he or she wanted to have happen in the first place. Sometimes in the swiftly moving world of decision making we can forget what we were shooting for in the first place.

Visualizing our goal refers to (1) pausing for a moment, (2) closing our eyes, and (3) "seeing" as vividly as possible what achieving our goal would look like. This activity seems to restore clarity and direction to our thinking and make us more confident about making our choice.

For example, a boy whose goal is to get his homework done by the end of the day could take a moment to imagine what he'd be doing with his free time *when that work was completed.* He might, for instance, visualize playing soccer outside with a friend. With that kind of a goal vividly recalled, he may be better motivated and prepared to select a solution that would get him there.

There are also several ways that you may be able to use the media at home, to teach your child about the importance of making choices.

MEDIA CHARACTERS MAKE CHOICES TOO

While watching television with a child, we have found it helpful to point out from time to time how these television characters are actually making a number of decisions. For example, for younger children a puppet character might *decide* to sing a song for the audience or dance for its public. Now this may not look so visible because typically (and perhaps unfortunately?) you don't hear a frog or a mouse puppet talk out loud and say, "I think I will go over there and put on a funny hat." And yet, actions like this do occur and, since our children see them, you should consider making a comment about them. "Oh, it looks like he's *decided* to tell his friend after all. That looks like a good decision to me, too." Again we're not suggesting that you pepper your child's television viewing time with too many interruptions. Yet we feel that from time to time you can "think out loud" for the television character that is making the decisions. According to the ages of your child, you might be doing this with cartoon characters, puppets, super heroes, situation comedy persons, soap opera characters, movie actors, or sports figures. The point is that there is a good deal of "silent" decision making going on that could be highlighted to reinforce the idea that it is good to put well-thought-out ideas into action.

DIFFERENT PEOPLE MAKE DIFFERENT DECISIONS

The next step in using media as an example of decision making is to point out that in the same story, activity, or plot that *another character* could have made a different choice. For example, imagine that you are watching a situation comedy with your child:

Mom: It looks like Bart has *decided* to apologize to Lisa.
Anne: Yeah.
Mom: If it were Tom that had to make that *decision*, do you think that he would apologize to Lisa?
Anne: No way. Tom would never do that, especially because she's the one who is wrong.

Or, *your children themselves* may have *their own* ideas about what would be a good decision. Imagine this discussion going on during a televised basketball game:

Dad: It looks like the coach has *decided* to call a time out. What would you do if you were he?
Ben: I don't know.
Dad: Do you think you would decide to substitute a new player?
Ben: No, I would keep everybody in.
Dad: It looks like a tough decision.
Ben: Yeah.

We are proposing some home situations involving real-life people where you could encourage decision making or choice making. The situations here are examples of discussions that you might have with your child over meals, getting ready to go somewhere, or doing some work at home.

INVITING FRIENDS OVER

Here the parent is focusing on reinforcing her child's good work in generating solutions, asking her to review the solutions, and supporting her for being able to make a choice. Notice that this mother may have had her own preferences about which friend should be coming over. She is careful, however, with her own parental goal of reinforcing that a *choice* has been made, not to make an issue about which friend was selected.

Mother: Kathy, have you decided who it is that you'd like to have sleep over for your birthday?
Kathy: Not quite.
Mother: Well, what do you think?

Kathy: Well, it's down to Mary Jane, Susan, or Karen—I just don't know.

Mother: Well . . . it's nice that you've thought of several possibilities.

Kathy: Yeah, I guess so.

Mother: Well, you know that anyone of them is really okay with me.

Kathy: Okay. You know, I think I'd like to invite Mary Jane over. I think I'd have the most fun with her.

Mother: Well, it's great that you've made that decision. Maybe we can talk about what we can have for dinner if Mary Jane can come over.

RECREATION WITH THE FAMILY

For young children there are many opportunities to *choose a solution,* such as deciding where they want to sit at a family outing. Choices like this often involve some sibling tensions. But notice how, in this kind of situation, a minor quarrel that could emerge about who sits where (or who gets dessert first, or who gets the rest of the ice cream) can turn into a quick practice situation for choosing a solution. Consider how this father uses a solution review, and also notice how he has chosen to emphasize selecting a solution as opposed to consequences.

Mark (age five): Dad, I want to sit on the aisle when we get to the movies.

Steve (age seven): Oh, you always get to sit on the aisle.

Dad: Listen, guys, what are some solutions to this situation?

Mark: I could sit on the aisle just like I said I wanted to.

Steve: That's not fair. What about me?

Dad: Well, are there any more ideas? You guys have been getting pretty good lately at coming up with a list of ideas.

Steve: Well, what if I could sit next to the aisle for the first half of the movie and then Mark could have it for the second half. We could change.

Dad: Other ideas?

Mark: I could sit in the aisle this time and then Steve could the next time we go to the movies.

Dad: Both seem to be good ideas. But I am forgetting them. What are they again?

Mark: Come on, Dad, don't drag this out.

Dad: Okay. One idea is that Mark can sit in the aisle. Another idea is that you can change seats halfway through the movie. And the other idea is that one of you can take the aisle for the whole time this movie and the next time the other person can take the aisle seat. You guys *decide.*

Steve: Mark can take the aisle the first half of the movie and then I'll take it the second half. Okay, Mark?

Mark: Okay.

Dad: Good job. You boys really made a decision. Let's get ready to go.

It is time now to think about some conversations and some activities that you can have with your youngster when you happen to be away from home.

Family Activities You Can Do Away from Home

Decision making does not have to become overcomplicated. When you engage in these decision-making conversations and activities, keep one goal in mind yourself. For example, we are talking about ways to teach your child the importance of *making a reasonable choice.* So one simple goal might be to let your child know that he or she does make a lot of decisions and usually does it well. A parent who gives a youngster that message is developing the child's sense of self-confidence. A child who begins to see himself or herself as a decision maker gains confidence and is more resistant to negative peer pressures when that becomes an issue. With that goal in mind, let's discuss opportunities that you could have to practice encouraging choice-making behavior with your child.

DRIVING IN THE CAR

When you're driving, there are many decisions that need to be made. These include choices about what direction to take or even what kind of music to listen to. Notice how subtly and quickly these parents, while driving, let their children know how pleased they were that a choice had been made.

Dad: What do you think? Should we take the main road or the back way?

Ginny: How about the back way?

Dad: Sounds like a good *choice* to me.

or

Mom: Should we put the radio on or not?
Pat: Let's put it on.
Mom: Fine. What station? Why don't you *decide* what station.
Pat: Okay, how about that rock station that I like?
Mom: Fine, just keep it down low.

SHOPPING

Mom: Well, have you *decided?* Do you want the blue one or the red one?
Peg: I like the blue one, Mom, it matches the rest of my outfit.
Mom: That sounds like a good *decision* to me too.

or

Dad: Should we pick up some doughnuts here or should we go to that
    bakery we went to the last time?
Mikie: Let's get them here, Dad, I like their jelly doughnuts the best.
Dad: Good idea.

Again, we see here a low-cost but high-yield example of how parents can
comfortably compliment their child for making a choice. Also consider
how highly regarded these children might feel being allowed to be decision makers with their parents.

GOING TO A RESTAURANT

Mom: (before starting the car) Well, what do you think, should we go out
    for a hamburger or a pizza?
Donna: I'm in the mood for a hamburger.
Jason: I want pizza.
Mom: Well, we have to come to some kind of a *decision.*
Jason: Well, we got hamburgers last time, remember? How about some
    pizza?
Donna: Oh, okay, but next time, let's get hamburgers.
Mom: I'm glad you've been able to decide. Let's go.

We're not suggesting you allow your child to take charge of all family decision making! If you feel that your own idea about what route to take, music to listen to, or restaurant to go to should be selected, it's best to wait for another opportunity to invite your child's participation. But we *are* suggesting that when you have the time to engage in the kinds of discussions just presented, and honestly feel either way about the choices that are available, you might let the children practice making choices for the family.

DECISIONS DECISIONS

Here is a game that can be played in the car, while you are taking a walk, or on a trip somewhere.

In Decisions Decisions, one person is the "Problem Giver" and another person is the "Decision Maker." The Problem Giver thinks of a situation that requires a decision. The Decision Maker must give a response. This exercise is designed primarily to give a lot of practice in making choices. To help you get started, we have listed some examples we've heard, according to the developmental age of the youngsters:

Preschool Youngsters:
    What's your favorite color?
    What's your favorite TV show?
    Who do you like to play with the best?
    Tell me what your favorite food is.
    Where do you like to visit the best?

Middle-Elementary-Aged Youngsters:
    Who do you like to talk with on the phone the most?
    Name your two best friends.
    What teacher do you like the most?
    Tell me your favorite singer.
    Tell me your favorite musical group.
    What person would you like to be more friendly with than you are now?
    What's your favorite thing?
    What do you like to do the most with your sister?

Upper-Elementary/Junior High/Middle School-Aged Youngsters:

For children this age, include more complex, people-oriented problems suitable to their age. You could allow some more time for responses to these and related choice-making opportunities.

It's two o'clock in the afternoon and you are at school and you have just ripped your pants. What can you do?

It's the first week of school. Your books are in your locker and you have forgotten the combination. How do you handle this?

Your best friend wants to see one movie and you want to see another. What do you do?

It is ten o'clock at night. You've just remembered that tomorrow is your mother's birthday and you've forgotten to get her a gift. What do you do?

Your teacher has just given you detention for talking in class. You feel that you are innocent and that it is unfair. What do you do?

Decisions Decisions is the kind of activity that can be flexibly used. You may just do one or two items, you can do it with humor, or you can have your youngster volunteer his own dilemmas or even propose some for you!

PREDICTING PEER PROBLEMS

As parents, we often know, before our children do, what pressures await them at different ages. We also know that clear-headed thinking is sometimes at risk when our child is in the stimulating and exciting company of his or her friends. It is sometimes helpful to anticipate some of these situations for our children. Engaging in brief, anticipatory problem-solving discussions with our children will start preparing them to make those choices.

Predicting Peer Problems is an activity that often works well on walks or when the family is driving in the car, although it can certainly be used whenever you think it is appropriate. We emphasize the Solution Review here, where we ask our child to quickly tick off the ideas he or she has generated.

Early Elementary Exercise: You can start this exercise something like this. Imagine that you are driving with your five or six year old to the supermarket. You know that teasing is a phenomenon that begins early on in a child's life and stays around for many years. At times our children witness teasing, tease others, or are teased themselves. Problem-solving discussions with a focus on choice making can help out in this common childhood problem situation. The following is an example of a parent-child dialogue accenting decision making.

Mother: Do any of your friends ever get teased at school?
Ray: What do you mean?
Mother: Well, like some kids making fun of other kids.
Ray: Yes, sometimes the kids make fun of Steve.
Mother: How does that make you feel?
Ray: I don't know.
Mother: Bad for Steve?
Ray: Yeah.
Mother: What would you like to have happen?
Ray: That they don't tease Steve.
Mother: I wonder what ideas you have that could help him out?
Ray: I could yell at them.
Mother: Uh-huh, what else?
Ray: Tell the teacher.
Mother: That's another idea. Anything else?
Ray: I could tell Steve to yell back at them.
Mother: Wow, you can think of a lot of ideas. Could you say them all again?
Ray: Yeah . . . I could yell . . . tell the teacher . . . and I forgot the other one.
Mother: Tell Steve . . .
Ray: Oh yeah, tell Steve to yell.
Mother: Well, time for a choice. Which one sounds the best to you?
Ray: Tell Steve to yell back?
Mother: You've really thought that through, that's terrific.
Ray: Thanks. Oh, here we are at the store.
Mother: Great. Listen, Ray, if you ever want to talk about teasing . . . just let me know.
Ray: Okay.

LATER ELEMENTARY YEARS: CIGARETTE SMOKING

One of the inevitable trials our children have to experience is the pressure they get from peers to become involved in cigarette smoking and alcohol and drug abuse. As is true with teasing at an earlier age, it is a healthy thing for parents to engage in some preparatory decision making with their children. The idea here, of course, is to help get them started in organizing their thinking about how to handle these pressures when they present themselves. Here we will discuss cigarette smoking, although talking to your child about alcohol and drugs could be added or even substituted in this particular kind of exercise.

There are so many situations that we as parents can use to kick off a discussion about cigarette smoking. These situations or environmental prompts could include passing a billboard advertising cigarettes or just witnessing someone else smoking. For example, imagine that you are in a fast-food hamburger restaurant with your eleven-year-old, sixth-grade son. There are some folks who are smoking cigarettes in one section of the restaurant. As you sit down to eat, you have this dialogue:

Dad: Do a lot of the kids at school smoke, Matthew?
Matthew: What do you mean?
Dad: Cigarettes.
Matthew: . . . yeah some do.
Dad: Any of your friends?
Matthew: Not really.
Dad: What have you decided to do?
Matthew: What do you mean?
Dad: I mean if someone offers you a cigarette.
Matthew: What difference does it make, you and Mom wouldn't let me even if I wanted to.
Dad: Well, yes . . . but we really don't know a lot about what you think about it. We were wondering how you'd respond if there were any pressure at school to smoke.
Matthew: You sure you want to talk about this?
Dad: Yes.
Matthew: Well, I would probably say no.
Dad: Uh . . . anything else?
Matthew: I could say I don't want to get into trouble.
Dad: What if it's your best friend?
Matthew: Well, I could just say it's bad for you and walk away.
Dad: Well, they all sound like good ideas. Could we go over them again?
Matthew: Say no . . . say I don't want to get into trouble . . . say it's bad for your health and just walk away.
Dad: Well, what is the best choice?

Matthew: A little of each. I'd say no, that it was bad for your health, and then I'd leave.

Dad: All good ideas . . . I'm glad that we talked.

Matthew: (smiling) Well, Dad, I'm glad you feel better. Now can we eat finally?

How the Sixth Decision-Making Step Can Help You Handle Everyday Problems: Choosing Which Friends to Play With

Here is how one parent emphasized *choose your best solution* in a discussion he had with his eight-year-old daughter. Mike is forty years old and works as a sales representative. He has been divorced for three years now. His ex-wife, Joan, (age thirty-eight) is a teacher. She has custody of their eight-year-old daughter, Samantha. Mike tries to work it out so that Samantha can stay at his apartment every other weekend. He also tries to call her at least two times a week.

Mike and Joan have been getting along fairly well. They have some occasional arguments when Mike asks to take Samantha more frequently. They also argue about some of the child-support payments, which at times arrive late from Mike. All in all, however, they seem to be reasonably amicable (see their Parenting Family Tree).

It is 6 P.M. on a Friday in July. Mike has just pulled onto the street where Samantha and her mother live. He notices that several groups of children are playing. Mike walks up to the door and greets Joan. Samantha says goodbye to her mother and now father and daughter are in the car and off. It's about a fifteen-minute drive to Mike's apartment. On the way to the apartment Mike starts a conversation with Samantha.

Dad: It looks as if there were about three different things going on at the same time outside tonight.

Samantha: There were. There's a lot happening these days and I don't know what to do.

Dad: I don't understand, Samantha. Sounds like there's a problem.

Samantha: There is. Michelle and her friends want to play house all the time. Jeff wants to play kickball. And the other kids, especially Rachel, just want to hang around and talk about the boys.

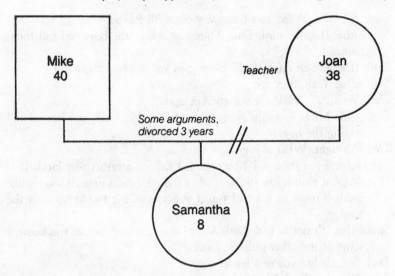

Dad: How do you feel about all of this?

Samantha: Mixed up because I don't know who to play with sometimes.

Dad: Well, what would you like to have happen?

Samantha: For everybody to all play together.

Dad: That might be tough.

Samantha: I know.

Dad: Well, what would be something else that you would want?

Samantha: Just to play with somebody and have a good time.

Dad: Well, you've always been a pretty good decision maker, Samantha. Maybe I could help you be better able to pick your best solution. Okay?

Samantha: Okay.

Dad: First though, I have to stop for some milk, eggs, and bread.

Dad: (settling back into the car with Samantha, placing the groceries on the floor of the car) Okay, now where were we? Well, what if you played house with Michelle and the other girls?

Samantha: It's fun for a while but it gets boring, Dad. I don't know why but she always wants to get me to do things her way.

Dad: Well, what would it be like to play kickball with Jeff?

Samantha: It's really the most fun. Sometimes though the other girls tease me for playing with the boys.

Dad: All right. What about hanging out with Rachel?

Samantha: It gets weird, Dad. They just yell at the boys and call them names.

Dad: It looks like some of the older girls are involved there too.

Samantha: Yeah, they are.

Dad: Well . . . what are our choices again?

Samantha: Michelle and playing house, Jeff and kickball, and Rachel and teasing the boys.

Dad: All right. What is it going to be?

Samantha: Even though I'll be teased, I think I'd rather play kickball.

Dad: Well, it sounds like you've made a thoughtful decision. It sounds like kickball must be a lot of fun if you are willing to put up with the teasing.

Samantha: It's not so bad, Dad. After I start doing it, before you know it some of the other girls are joining.

Dad: Sounds like you're a leader too.

Samantha: (smiling) Oh, Dad.

There are a few things in particular that are worth noting in Mike's effort at encouraging Samantha's problem-solving skills. First, as the parent who does not see her everyday or know in great detail the ins and outs of the neighborhood cliques, Mike used a lot of sense in acting as a *guide* through the forest of concerns that Samantha had. He recognized that Samantha herself was the expert on how she was feeling and on the activities of her friends. His respectful attitude allowed Samantha to open the door for him and encourage a discussion. He was the expert on teaching problem solving. His role in helping her clarify her own concerns helped her to make a choice. These are the kinds of respectful decision-making encounters that go into a quality parent-child relationship. It is likely that Samantha will feel comfortable in the future in approaching her Dad about school, career decisions, geographic moves, and whatever other problems come up. A second point is that there was a natural interruption to their conversation when Mike had to stop at the store for groceries. This situation was treated as a natural pause in the decision-making dialogue. Mike got right back on the track when he returned to the car to say, "Okay, now where were we?"

Let's imagine that Mike has a *much more shortened interaction* with Samantha. It is a Tuesday afternoon. Mike calls Samantha at home from his office to say hello. The phone rings.

Samantha: Hello.

Dad: Hi, Samantha, it's Dad. I had a few moments, so I thought I'd call to say hello. How are you?

Samantha: Oh hi, Dad. Fine, I guess.

Dad: What's the matter? Your voice sounds a little shaky.

Samantha: Everybody has been playing different things outside and I don't know who to play with.

Dad: I only have a few moments, Sam, but maybe I could help by asking you a few questions.

Samantha: Okay.

Dad: What are your choices?

Samantha: Kickball with the boys, I can be with some of the other girls who are calling out to the boys, or I can play house with Michelle.

Dad: Samantha, will you hold on for a moment? Someone is asking me a question here.

Samantha: Okay, Dad.

Dad: All right, I'm back now. Are you still there?

Samantha: Yes, Dad.

Dad: Well, you did a good job of coming up with three choices. No one answer is perfect, but which one looks like it would be the most fun for you?

Samantha: I think playing kickball would be the best.

Dad: Well, it sounds like you think that would be the best idea. Maybe when we have some more time, we can talk about it longer or you could speak to your mom about it.

Samantha: Okay, Dad.

Dad: Samantha, I have to go. I'll call you later when I have more time. Take it easy, now.

Samantha: Bye, Dad.

Mike's conversation with his daughter was best described as "decision making on the run." Nevertheless it *was* a decision-making conversation. Sometimes we have to work quickly in a situation. For many of us parents who are quite busy with our work at home and away from home, we can make fine use of our brief contacts with our children.

Decision-Making Digest

Teaching your child to "choose your best solution" is one step that we feel can particularly lead to self-confidence. A major teaching strategy we feel is to let words like *choose, decide,* and *select* crop up more and more in our everyday conversation. As you reflect back to your child and your observations that he or she has made a choice, the subtle message gets across that your youngster is achieving mastery of an important skill. As your child grows in confidence that he or she is a decision maker, then your child will be more and more likely to fulfill that role and act accordingly. As before, we have included a summary chart for your reference.

Decision-Making Digest:
Choose Your Best Solution

If you'd like your child to	*Then try these activities:*
1. remember the solutions that were just generated	1. Solution Review
2. identify himself or herself as a decision maker	2. Children's Choices Chart
3. keep goal-focused	3. Visualizing Your Goal
4. see that individuals familiar to him or her make decisions too	4. Media Characters Make Choices Too
5. learn there often is not a "right" or "wrong" decision	5. Different People Make Different Decisions
6. see how choosing a solution is helpful in everyday situations	6. Inviting Friends Over Recreation With The Family Driving in the Car Going to a Restaurant Predicting Peer Problems Cigarette Smoking
7. get practice in making a number of decisions	7. Decision Decisions

9

Plan It and Make a Final Check

In previous chapters you learned about, and have started to use, six of the eight decision-making steps. That's a real accomplishment for you and your children. You've spent a lot of time understanding how important it is for them to choose one solution from among many. They are much less likely now to be confused when a variety of good solutions emerges. Your children have been getting the feeling from you that they are decisive. From your out-loud observations, the children are noticing that they are *always* making choices, and most of them are good ones, thereby boosting their senses of self-worth. There are two more steps in the entire decision-making approach. These next two chapters advance your children to a more important and more sophisticated level.

"Steptalk": Where We've Been and Where We're Going

Right now we need to focus on "what to do" with that good idea that your youngster has selected. Children benefit from practice in carefully and sensitively *planning out how to put their good solution into practice.* When our children are able to solve their problems, it is not only because they have thought of a clear and logical answer. When a child's good solution has "worked," it is because the feelings and perspectives of others were considered. Too often (and we have learned this the hard way) children can encounter difficulty because they have acted on a good idea, but in an impulsive way. Our fast paced, computerized, televised society encourages quick action. We've found that, for too many youngsters, quick action even on a carefully selected idea leads to trouble, such as angry friends and teachers. But more of these troubles can be avoided with some hard work in teaching our youngsters *planning and checking*—our seventh decision-making step:

1. Look for signs of different feelings.
2. Tell yourself what the problem is.
3. Decide on your goal.
4. Stop and think of as many solutions to the problem as you can.
5. For each solution, think of all the things that might happen next.
6. Choose your best solution.

NEW   7. Plan it and make a final check.

Here is an example of how step 7 fits into the decision-making process. Three fifth graders (ten year olds) were feeling unhappy because they were doing poorly in a special math class. This trio painstakingly went through all the decision-making steps, ultimately selecting what they thought was their best solution, which was to have a direct talk with their teacher and ask her to slow down the pace a bit. They felt good about this idea, and the three of them strided into the teachers' lounge to express themselves to their teacher. Unfortunately their math teacher was taking her first break, a ten-minute lunch break, in a rather hectic day. In addition, she was finally getting a chance to chat with several of her colleagues. Before even two words got out of these well-intended students, they were firmly asked to leave the teachers' lounge by all of the teachers. These children felt discouraged and confused. The children became so wrapped up in their excellent decision making that they did not consider the feelings of their teacher by their interruption of her break. The step of *plan it and make a final check* refers to the politics and diplomacy of decision making. After youngsters select a good idea, they need to plan how they will carry it out. *Planning* is related to another important skill: anticipating obstacles that might get in the way of carrying out good solutions. Tony's situation provides a closer look at how attending to the *planning and checking* step can help.

CASE EXAMPLE: TONY PLANS HOW
AND WHEN TO ASK FOR SOMETHING

It is a Tuesday in early November. The air is cooler now. After school many of the children are playing out of doors. There is a lot of running, jumping, and kicking footballs and soccer balls going on. It is a wonderful time of the day for most youngsters.

Lunchtime recess at Swampnut Elementary School is, unfortunately, not that much fun for ten-year-old Tony. He's in Mrs. Pittman's fourth grade classroom. Today he is wandering about during recess time with no lively activity appealing to him. Occasionally he enjoys the talking that he does with his classmates and from time to time he starts running around. But today he's just not feeling like it. Tony's mother, Pam, has been learning a lot about decision making. Pam has been doing a good deal more of her own decision making in an out-loud fashion over the year. Trips to the store are her favorite time to practice decision-making skills with Tony. Two years ago Tony would have felt quite stuck in knowing what to do about what he currently describes as "boring" recess time. Now, however, as he walks around during recess he begins to act on his problem. He thinks to himself:

1. I *feel* bored during recess. I wish it were more fun.
2. I *feel* bored during recess *because* there is just running around and talking and not a lot of fun things going on.
3. I want to have more fun in recess!
4. A. I could talk to some of the guys about what to do.
   B. I could just not let it get to me. What's the big deal about recess anyway?
   C. Maybe I'll talk to Mrs. Pittman about bringing in my soccer ball tomorrow.
5. A. If I talk to the guys . . . they'll just keep on complaining. That's how they are.
   B. It would be really hard to just "ignore" the bored feeling that I have.
   C. If we could play soccer, we'd have a great time.
6. I think bringing in a soccer ball is the best idea yet.

NEW STEP:
PLAN IT AND MAKE A FINAL CHECK

7. *Planning it:* I'd better talk to Mrs. Pittman first. And I'd better wait until school is over before I talk to her. She's too busy during regular schooltime. If I were she, I'd get mad if I was interrupted by one of my students during academic time. Besides, Mrs. Pittman seems to be in a better mood when school is over.

Making a Final Check: Sometimes she leaves for home right away. If she does that, I'll try to catch her when she first lets us go for lunch. She usually sticks around to talk to some people for a little while.

What a difference it can make to go that extra step! With his mother's encouragement, Tony has practiced "putting himself in someone else's shoes." He recognizes the importance of careful planning and anticipating the obstacles that may get in the way of his good ideas. Tony is a likable boy with a lot of playmates. He continues to develop his self-confidence and his capacity to care for others with his mother's help. His good ideas often work out well because he has taken the time to *plan.*

As it turned out in Tony's situation, Mrs. Pittman was unavailable after school. As planned, however, Tony did speak with her the following day when she was dismissing the class to lunch. She approved his idea of bringing his soccer ball on Thursday. As a result of his plan, Tony found recess time at Swampnut School much improved starting on Thursday.

The next youngster we will meet has also become a good decision maker. This boy, however, gets confused and upset from time to time because his well-chosen solutions have backfired on him when he implements them. Unfortunately he gets so excited that he puts his good ideas into practice too quickly.

CASE EXAMPLE: MARK NEEDS TO PLAN A BIT MORE

One of Tony's classmates, who was particularly enjoying the soccer games at recess, is Mark Jackson. Mark is evidently one of the smartest students in Mrs. Pittman's class. In fact, he is in the "gifted and talented program" and consistently gets top grades. One of the reasons that Mark is sought out as a friend is because he has a fine capacity to churn out a lot of ideas. His parents are that way too. Mark's dad, in fact, uses a form of decision making quite regularly when he is stuck in his work as a mechanical engineer. Even at an early age, Mark heard questions such as, "What's your goal?" and "How many good ideas can you think of?"

As the boys and girls were playing soccer on the Swampnut Elementary School field, they were having a terrific time. A goal was scored if it went between two small stones that the children had placed on the ground at either end of their "field." Mark, however, was getting frustrated. Members of his team, he felt, had kicked at least two goals that they weren't given credit for and it was causing some tension. Mark and his teammates unsuccessfully argued their point and recess time was over. Feeling upset, Mark began to think about what could be done to improve the situation. Here's what Mark's reasoning looked like as he trudged toward the school building for the afternoon session.

1. Everyone *feels* bad.
2. . . . *because* those two goals that we kicked were never counted.
3. We need a better way to decide if a goal was made or not.
4. A. The captains of the team should decide.
   B. When it's a close call, we could decide by chance somehow. We could do "heads or tails" with a coin or something like that.
   C. (As Mark walks into the building, he sees two large empty cardboard boxes by the school custodian's room.) Or, maybe, we can use those boxes to serve as the goals.
5. A. It would be better than what is happening now *but* who's to say the captains might not just keep on fighting.
   B. It's boring to stop the game to flip a coin. Besides, what if no one has a coin. There should be a better way than that. In fact, it still doesn't seem fair. Also some kids will want to flip a coin at every close call.
   C. If we could use those two big boxes, that would be great. No one could ever argue whether a ball went in or not. If it's in the box . . . it's a goal. Simple as that.
6. Let's use the boxes.

As the children settle down into their seats, Mark manages to tell Ruth, one of his teammates, about his idea. They're excited about the possibility.

The following day most of the students have heard of the idea and like it. As recess begins, Mark and Ruth each take a box out to the field. Play begins and everyone is having a great time. Out of the corner of his eye, Mark sees Mr. Bregan, the school custodian, walking toward the game. Mr. Bregan looks irritated—his face is all wrinkled and his shoulders are hunched up—and indeed he is irritated. "What are you kids doing with these boxes? They're supposed to be used for scenery for the school play. Who's idea was this anyway?" Mark unhappily steps forward. "Next time, *ask* young man! Now give me a hand bringing these boxes back. Thank goodness they're not ruined."

"CASETALK": A CLOSER LOOK AT THESE TWO CHILDREN

Mark is feeling somewhat embarrassed. He is not devastated certainly. But it's unfortunate that this had to happen to a youngster who is such a thoughtful decision maker. Mark was just not coached in the importance of *carefully planning out a good idea* or *anticipating obstacles.* If he had questioned Mr. Bregan about the boxes, he might have saved himself from embarrassment. Perhaps Mr. Bregan could have generated another idea that could have helped, that is, to use another box. Mark is a resilient boy and he bounces back well from such setbacks. He is a good candidate for learning about the politics of decision making: planning and checking the "good" solution. With some practice of this step, he will be fine.

What we are discussing now are the subtleties in decision making. Mark, in fact, being the good decision maker that he is, is probably trying to generate solutions to his latest problem: getting embarrassed at recess time. With a number of setbacks like the soccer situation, he'll probably figure out on his own that there is "another step" that he should attend to. Our guess is that, in part, what happened to Mark was that he received a lot of encouragement in the kind of decision making that does not involve other people. For example, his dad uses some decision making in his engineering work, as we have mentioned. Mark has seen how his dad selects from among a group of ideas and tries it out right away on blue-prints or on a drafting board. In decision making where people are imme-diately and directly affected, however, Mark needs to learn to consider taking things a step further. Other people's needs and feelings should be considered. A sense of timing is also important.

Tony, in our first case, exemplified a youngster who can take other people's feelings into consideration. He was able to "step out" of his own immediate concerns and see the situation unfold. It is almost as if Tony were able to look at himself in a movie, as he watched *when* and *where* and *how* he might approach Mrs. Pittman to see if he could bring in his soccer ball. Moreover, he went a little bit further by thinking on his feet: what if she wasn't available after school? He developed a contingency plan for an obstacle that he had anticipated: seeing her before recess on the following day. As it turned out, the obstacle he foresaw did emerge and Tony was prepared.

How to Teach Your Child to Plan It and Make a Final Check

BE A MODEL

Again, planning and making a final check are activities that many adults do "in their head." In that sense we have to figure out ways of making the invisible visible. Consider some ways to show children how we plan and check. Think about times that you can think aloud so your children can see the "inside story." Here are some suggestions.

Shopping lists:

I don't have much time to spend in the store. I'll go tomorrow and if I plan ahead of time what I need, I'll be able to do it quickly. I'll make a list now.

Preparing breakfast for the family:

Okay. I'll put the coffee cake and juice out now. That way Mary can have something to start on while Jim's still in the shower. I'll put the eggs on last so they don't get cold.

Anticipating an interview:

I'll get my clothes out tonight so I won't have to rush around tomorrow morning. Maybe the blue suit and black shoes would be best. I think I'll just relax then and maybe try to get to bed early.

The first day of school:

Mom: (talking from the kitchen) Patrick, what time are the freshmen supposed to be there for orientation?

Patrick: (calling from his bedroom) Eight-thirty, Mom, in the gym.

Mom: Do you have everything you need?

Patrick: I'm doing okay. I have my new sneakers, the money for my football jersey, notebooks, and pens. I'm set.

Mom: Great. Good *planning*.

Patrick: (emerging from his bedroom) Oh, Mom, I just remembered.

Mom: What, Pat?

Patrick: I need to bring in a lock for my locker. Do we have one? What about that one that Jack used?

Mom: Good idea. It's where your father keeps the tools. Take that one.

Patrick: Okay. Thanks, Mom.

ENCOURAGE EXPRESSION, ACKNOWLEDGE, AND ACCEPT WHAT YOU HEAR

Let's review for a moment exactly what goes into a plan . . . the parts that we want our children to consider. For each part there are questions you can ask to encourage your child to become a better planner. Here are some examples.

Plans	Questions and Prompts a Parent Can Use
1. When?	When would be a good time to try that? Will you be doing that today or tomorrow? I wonder if it would be good to do that before or after dinner.
2. Where?	Where do you think you could do that best? Should that be done inside or outside? Will you try that at Julia's house or home?
3. How?	What materials are important to have? Do you have everything that you need? Is this the kind of thing that needs practice?
4. With whom?	I was wondering if you were planning on doing that alone or with Matthew? Will you need to do it with anyone? Betsy, Joey, and Melissa are outside, are they part of the plan?

Remember to use gentle questioning and praise when your child embarks on some planning of his idea. Recall, from our dialogue, Patrick's mother making comments such as, "great" and "good planning!" Plan as they might, things always don't go so smoothly. But there are ways to help your child *make a final check* of his or her plans. One of the best occasions to do this might be when your child is trying to do something particularly important. It may be his or her first effort in a new area like going out on a first date, trying out for a play, or getting ready to have a difficult talk with a teacher. We encourage you to ask a few What If questions to help your child anticipate that things might not go so smoothly. Gently suggesting that it's normal to encounter obstacles is an important contribution you can make. Here are two brief examples. Notice the subtle questioning and the praise used by the parents as they help their child *make a final check.*

TRYING OUT FOR THE SCHOOL PLAY

Julia: Mom, tomorrow's the day that I'm trying out for the school play. It's going to be after school so could you pick me up at four?

Mom: Fine. Sounds like tomorrow's going to be an exciting day. Did you get a chance to prepare?

Julia: Absolutely. In case Miss White asks us to sing a song, I've got one all set and I even wrote the words down in case I forget them.

Mom: Good planning!

Julia: I convinced Jennifer to try out too. I think I'll be less nervous that way too.

Mom: Didn't Jennifer try out last year?

Julia: Well, she was going to. But at the last minute she got too scared.

Mom: Could that happen again?

Julia: I guess so. But if it does I'm just going to take a deep breath and do it on my own.

Mom: That's great, Julie. Looks like you've really prepared. You'll be fine.

GOING OUT ON A FIRST DATE

Dad: What will you and Ginny be doing?

Jack: We're going to the school play. Ginny's sister Julia's in it.

Dad: Sounds like fun. How will you get there?

Jack: I'm going to ride my bike and meet Ginny at the door. Her parents are supposed to drop her off at two.

Dad: Good planning. Are you set for money?

Jack: Well, I'm pretty set. I already bought the tickets. They're in my wallet.

Dad: What if you want to buy something to eat or drink at intermission?

Jack: I've used up all my money on the tickets, Dad. Could you lend me some?

Dad: I'll tell you what. Empty the wastebaskets and give your room a good cleaning, then I'll give you some. It's always good to have some extra money in case something unexpected comes up.

Jack: It's a deal, Dad.

Look at some ideas that you might use to encourage your children's planning out their solutions and anticipating obstacles.

Family Activities You Can Do at Home

GAMES THAT REQUIRE PLANNING

Board games and table games can be very valuable tools to help teach planning and dealing with obstacles.

Checkers: Children who play checkers learn how to plan their moves and look out for obstacles. For example, "If I move my piece to this square on the right, she can jump me. I better move to the left." Along the same line, chess can also be used in this regard.

Tic-Tac-Toe: Similarly, planning and dealing with obstacles comes up all the time in this ageless game. In some way we have all thought something like this at some time or another. "Uh, oh . . . she put her X in the space that I wanted to go in . . . maybe I should put my O in the other space."

Dot-to-Dot: The game Dot-to-Dot is a paper and pencil activity. A series of numbered dots are scattered on a page. The job is to use a pencil to connect the dots in their correct order. The result is a picture. You can buy Dot-to-Dot books where coloring books are sold. It's a terrific activity to assist younger children in planning and anticipating their next move. For example, "Let's see . . . I connected dot 19 to dot 20, now I can't just move my pencil anywhere, I have to find dot 21 and go there."

Your contribution as a teacher of decision making in these table games is to comment out loud about your own and your child's moves in a timely way. Simply state something like, "Oh, I've really got an obstacle now that you've put your piece here." Basically what you'd be doing is labeling for your child in decision-making terms what he or she is doing. That's sometimes very helpful, because it's basic training for the world of people. At certain points a parent can remind a child of that child's capacity to plan and deal with obstacles in a table game. A parent could encourage the use of that same skill in a real-life situation. Following is a look at planning skills and anticipating obstacles in more complicated situations.

PLAN AND PLAY

Here is an activity that a number of parents have used with their elementary school age children at mealtime. It's known by various names. Because we emphasize planning out ideas, we call it Plan and Play.

In this game someone (probably you) starts off by stating where he or she would like to go for a trip or vacation. The rest of the group then begins, one at a time, naming what they think would be important to bring along in order to have a successful experience. Here's an example of one way that you might introduce an idea that encourages planning. By the way, you can make up an exotic activity or vacation for this game. The main point, of course, is the planning activity.

Mom: I've decided to go to Hawaii for a vacation. I know I have to plan before I play. What do you think I should bring with me and how should I best prepare?

Family responses: Get luggage, swimming suit, beach hat, sandals, beach umbrella, suntan lotion, beach towel, sunglasses, contact a travel agent, select an airline, and leave word with relatives and friends regarding where you are staying. (At various points here, Mom and/or Dad can compliment the children for their good ideas.)

Here's another situation.

Dad: I've decided to play some tennis. I know I have to plan before I play. How should I prepare?

Family responses: Make sure you have a partner, put gas in the car, make sure that there is an open court, get your sneakers, find your racket, and tell others how long you'll be away.

At some point, when you think that your child is ready, you may want her or him to generate the play activity. For example:

Janet (age seven): I've decided that I'd like to go on a rocket ship to a planet far away. I know I have to plan before I play. How should I prepare?

Family responses: Get a space helmet, learn how to pilot a rocket ship, bring some food, let your teacher know what you will be doing, make sure you have air to breathe, and get permission from your parents to go.

ROADBLOCK

Ever drive somewhere only to find that the road you usually take is closed? Well, in decision-making terms you've met an obstacle—a "roadblock." This analogy is wonderful for teaching children to anticipate that something may occur to get in the way of even the most well-thought-out solutions. In our clinical and research experience, we have found that this is a significant decision-making skill. If children can be prepared by their parents to *expect the unexpected,* then they are miles ahead in their decision making. The more practice the children get in anticipating and learning how to think on their feet, the more chances they have of getting things to work out in real life. Anticipating and dealing with obstacles is a skill that we cannot over emphasize. As a family teaching activity, Roadblock means that after someone has a solution and a plan, you offer an Obstacle to think about. Usually a Roadblock is a "What if it doesn't . . ." kind of question. We will give an example of how this skill is practiced in a family.

You can use Roadblock in activities such as Plan and Play. It's as much a teaching style as an activity in itself. For example, as a follow up to the family's planning Mom's Hawaiian vacation, Mom can say, "Let's make believe. I'll come up with some problems with my plans, and then you see if you can help me out."

Family's planning ideas:
1. Pack your swimsuit.
2. Contact a travel agent.
3. Get three suitcases.

Roadblock generated by Mom:
1. What if it doesn't fit?
2. I don't know of any travel agent I can trust.
3. But I only have one suitcase.

Family responses:
1. Lose weight, Mom; buy a new one; don't swim. (Mom and Dad can compliment these ideas).
2. Look in the yellow pages; ask Grandma; take a chance.
3. Take fewer things, Mom; use some shopping bags; borrow a bag from Aunt Susan.

Whenever your children have chosen an action and are planning something, especially something important, give them a Roadblock to think about. Knowing they can overcome obstacles will give them a lot of confidence and pride. We now move to some practice situations that involve other members of your household.

PARTY PLANNING

At various age levels an activity such as Party Planning can take a conversational form. It can allow parents to encourage planning and dealing with obstacles. Here's how younger, elementary-age children and preschoolers can practice the skills.

Planning a Parent Party:

In this situation a father encourages his six-year-old, kindergarten-age son, Danny, in planning a January birthday party for his mother. Dad generates a few roadblocks that allow Danny to think on his feet. Incidentally, Danny's four-year-old sister, Jeannie, is also involved.

Dad:
Tomorrow's Mom's birthday. Let's plan a nice surprise for her. What are your ideas?

Danny's solutions:
I think the best idea is to surprise her and give Mom breakfast in bed. If that isn't good I guess we could clean the house up or take her out to eat.

Dad's Roadblock:
Well, let's say we use your favorite

Danny's responses:
I know! Maybe I could talk to her

idea. Giving Mom breakfast in bed. What if she wakes up and comes into the kitchen? and keep her busy if she wakes up. Meanwhile you and Jeannie can get breakfast ready. (Dad can compliment Danny here).

Older children, as they move into more adultlike social activities such as, having a friend sleep over, sleeping over at a friend's house, learning how to baby-sit, figuring out clique situations in junior high or middle school, trying to decide who to invite over for a party, and so on, can all practice overcoming obstacles and developing a plan.

Also it can be helpful for the children in the fourth and higher grades to begin practicing "anticipating obstacles" *themselves*. Here is a family activity dialogue called Double Check that illustrates a mother using some probes to help her daughter anticipate on *her own* some possible obstacles to her well-planned solution.

DOUBLE CHECK

Mom: Kristen, you had a lot of good ideas about what to do for your science project. Have you decided on a topic?

Kristen: (nodding her head) Yes. I'm going to do "How Crystals Grow." I've got some instructions on how I can grow some crystals with just sugar and water. Also I have my poster all designed.

Mom: Terrific.

Kristen: Oh, and the book about crystals I have says that there's a kind of candy called rock candy that is made of crystals. I saw pictures and it looks beautiful. I thought I'd buy some and include that in my display.

Mom: It all sounds really well-planned. I'm really proud of you. Maybe you can *double-check* your plans just to make certain.

Kristen: Well, I could have some trouble finding rock candy. I've never seen it.

Mom: What then?

Kristen: Maybe I could just make more crystals myself or show pictures of the rock candy from my book.

Mom: Kristen, you really *double-checked* everything very well. That's good thinking.

Your children have seen and heard how you have gently generated obstacles and they can begin to do it too in some of these family activities. In real-people situations these kinds of family activity dialogues work well, when the content of the discussion relates to an activity that really interests your child. Specifically, your child's interests in dialoguing with you will wax and wane depending upon whether you're discussing how to negotiate his or her getting a ride home from an after-school function or how he or she gets homework done on time.

We can move to some activities for building your child's skills in developing plans and dealing with obstacles that can be used when you are away from home.

Family Activities You Can Do Away from Home

Once again, think of yourself in the car, bus, or train with your child. Imagine that you are heading for or returning from the store or a relative's or friend's house. As we've indicated, busy parents can make use of limited intervals of time. You can actually prompt decision making in even the few moments that you do have. Here are some of our favorite examples.

ROUTE PLANNING

This activity is an elaboration on activities that we presented earlier. In the previous chapter we had our children select the best of two routes to take on a trip. For example, we would have them choose between taking a highway or taking the back way. If *planning* a solution is your major objective, you can ask your child to generate ideas about how to arrive at a destination. He can pick out the roads himself without hearing from you the multiple choice situation.

Here's a brief "in the car" example that a mother had with her six year old.

Mom: Let's see, the construction that they're doing on the highway has really added to the traffic problems. I wonder if there's another way to go.

Sam: You could go the Tillett Road way, Mom.

Mom: Tell me what you mean.

Sam: It's the way I get to Bruce's house. Take Tillett all the way to Livingston Avenue. Make a right on Livingston and take that to North Washington. Bruce's house is right on the corner and the store's very close.

Mom: Thanks, Sam. Let's try it.

ASPIRING ARCHITECT

When your youngster is away from the house—at the park or near the water—he or she might construct bridges, roadways, buildings, castles, or something equally creative. In observing your youngster's play, you can reinforce planfulness with such observations as:

Mom: I wonder what you'll need in order to be able to build a tunnel.
Sandy: Oh, I'll need some more dirt (sand), my big pail, and my shovel.

or

Dad: If I wanted to get from the house that you just built, back to the water, how would I get there?
Barry: (demonstrating with his toy car as he talks) Take this road right here, Dad, away from all the creatures.

MAPMAKING AND PATH PLANNING

Once children have been in school for a few years, they often have learned something about maps. Maps used on trips away from home provide excellent opportunities to practice planning. You might want to consider bringing a map with you in the car, train, or bus. Bring it out at an appropriate moment and point out with your child your intended route. Imagine for example, that you're on the train with your child and the train has stopped for a moment.

Dad: (bringing out his map) Jimmy, here's where we are and there's where we want to go. What are some of the ways we could get there?
Jimmy: (pointing to a particular route) How about this way?
Dad: Well, that's certainly one we could consider. Any others?
Jimmy: Others? Oh yeah—how about on the green road?
Dad: Hmm . . . I didn't notice that one! Let's take a closer look . . .

Some elementary school children enjoy the activity of making their own neighborhood map. They can then proudly bring it along with them for trips to school, the library, or to a friend's house. This is an example of a child's map.

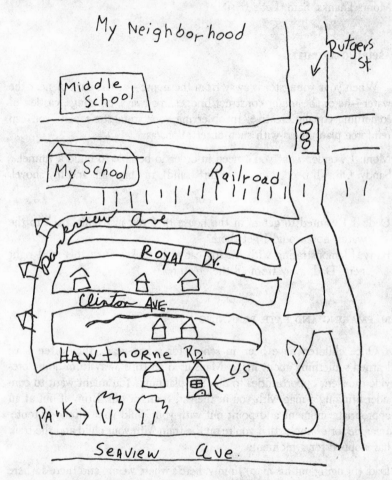

Your middle school/junior high youngster can take on a more sophisticated planning role when you are on a family outing. Imagine that you are at a new shopping center, new department store or, in this example, at a zoo.

Dad: Okay, Tommy, you're in charge. How do we get to the section that has the reptiles?

Tommy: I know! First we go to the lion's cage, then we go on that big sidewalk where they sell all the hot dogs and stuff. It's right behind there.

Dad: We'll follow you, then.

Tommy: Okay, let's go.

Incidentally, in many of these "route" and "map" activities, where your children are gaining confidence in planning, you can also help them practice overcoming unexpected obstacles. For example:

Tommy: (unhappily) Uh . . . oh . . . I thought that it was behind the big sidewalk where we bought those hot dogs. I forgot.

Dad: Take your time, maybe you'll figure it out.

Tommy: Okay, let's see. The only other big sidewalk is the one by the band shell. Let's go over there.

Dad: Good figuring! Let's try again!

One of the best ways that we have found to reinforce the "planning" solutions step is to train our children in home safety.

Raising happy and competent children does involve preparing them to act appropriately in potentially dangerous situations when they are away from home. We have found that giving our children safety skills also provides us with a good opportunity to teach them *planning* skills. Here are some activities that we have used with preschoolers and elementary children.

PLANNING HOW TO DEAL WITH STRANGERS

Parents have always been concerned about their young children potentially being victimized or abducted by strangers. It's surprising, though, how little time we spend with our children, developing with them a plan to help them avoid such difficulties. Here is a father talking with his seven year old, emphasizing the development of a *plan*. Notice how he asks for a *final check* of the plan.

Gina: Dad, some of the kids at school were talking about strangers and they said they were scared of them.

Dad: Are you a little confused about it?

Gina: Yeah.

Dad: Well, a stranger is a person you don't know. *Some* strangers are mean to children. Some try to take children away from their families.

Gina: (silent)

Dad: Your face looks kind of scared.

Gina: Yeah.

Dad: Maybe we can think about what you could do if a stranger comes up to you. We could work on a plan.

Gina: Okay.

Dad: The first part of the plan should be that you don't talk to strangers. What else can you think of?

Gina: Don't go with a stranger if you're asked.

Dad: That's a good part of the plan. What else?

Gina: Yell or go to someone that you know.

Dad: Good. If someone keeps bothering you, you can say really loudly, "Help me! I don't know this person!"

Gina: Okay.

Dad: Good. Now, let's *double-check* our plan. Is any of it hard to do?

Gina: Yeah . . . what if there is no one around I know to yell to?

Dad: What would you do?

Gina: I could yell really loudly and then run.

Dad: Good. I also think that part of our plan should be for you and I to make sure that you are always in a safe place with grown-ups around that you know.

PLANNING HOW TO DEAL WITH BEING LOST

As a child grows into middle and upper elementary grades, he or she increasingly goes on class trips, scout trips, shopping with friends and friends' families, and so on. Again, developing a *plan* about what to do if he or she is lost is another family skill-building activity that can also serve as a model for teaching an important decision-making step. Do you remember how at the zoo, Tommy and his dad worked on a plan for finding the reptiles. If we were to hear Tommy and his dad earlier in the day, they might have had a brief *planning* conversation about what to do if Tommy got lost.

Dad: Tommy, what are some good ideas if you get lost at the zoo?
Tommy: Call out to you? Or try and find you and Mom?
Dad: Those are two ideas. How about another?
Tommy: Tell a park officer?
Dad: Good, maybe we could develop a plan.
Tommy: Well, I remember you told me once to stay right where I am. Maybe I could do that and just wait for a park officer to come along.
Dad: Good job. Is there anything we should check out?
Tommy: Well, what if I don't see a park officer for a really long time?
Dad: What do you think?
Tommy: Just wait and wait? Don't move.
Dad: That's right. Mom and I will find you. Good job, son.

THE BATHROOM BLUES

Young children who are toilet-trained recognize the signs of a full bladder. They know a good solution to the problem of an uncomfortably full bladder is to go to the toilet. However, there are times that preschoolers and kindergartners, and even some older children, feel somewhat awkward about making these needs known. This situation might happen when they are away from their own home. See how this single mother encouraged her daughter to use good planning at her new baby-sitter's house.

Mom: Annette, when you are at Mrs. Flown's house, what's the thing to do when you need to go to the bathroom?
Annette: Tell Mrs. Flown.
Mom: That's right. That's a good *solution*. Sometimes, though, it can be uncomfortable in a new place and with a new baby-sitter, knowing what to do.
Annette: (nodding her head in some relief) Yeah . . . Mrs. Flown is usually really busy taking care of the little kids.
Mom: Well, what kind of *plan* could we come up with that could help you feel more comfortable about talking to Mrs. Flown when you have to go?
Annette: I could go right up to her.
Mom: Good idea. *What if she is busy* talking to someone else?
Annette: I could say, "Excuse me, Mrs. Flown."
Mom: And then what?

Annette: Excuse me, Mrs. Flown. I have to go to the bathroom.
Mom: Good. What kind of a voice should you use?
Annette: Polite?
Mom: That's right, polite and loud enough so that she can hear you.
Annette: Okay, Mom.
Mom: Let me know how your plan works out, okay?

Let's move now to a conversation that might involve a middle or junior high school youngster.

DETENTION DECISION MAKING

All of us make mistakes. Part of growing up, in fact, is to be able to experiment with various kinds of behaviors and reactions. Some of this experimenting may lead even those children whose parents are great teachers of decision making to have troubles at school! In the junior high/middle school a situation might arise where youngsters are being made to stay after school for detention because they violated some school or class rule. Depending upon the particular school, some youngsters can get detention for not doing homework, being disrespectful to a teacher, fighting with another youngster, and so on. A number of students get detention for arriving late to school. Such is the case with the youngster here. Frankie is a seventh grader who is calling his mother (Eileen) at her work to tell her that he has to stay one hour later. He tells her that he is getting detention because he has been late to his first period class too many times. We offer this brief dialogue as an example of how parent-child conversations around real problem areas can also incorporate the teaching of an important decision-making step. In this case, we are emphasizing *planning* and *making a final check*.

Frankie: Hello, Mom? I got detention today so I won't be home until four o'clock.
Mom: What happened, Frankie?
Frankie: I've been late for first period too many times.
Mom: How come?
Frankie: 'Cause I usually stop at the store with Don and the other guys to get some stuff to eat.
Mom: Well, you know what that means?

Frankie: Yeah . . . I know . . . I don't get to use the phone tonight or tomorrow.

Mom: That's right. Frankie, what are you going to do to avoid being late again? You don't want to get detention again, do you?

Frankie: It's hard to do something about it.

Mom: What do you mean?

Frankie: I mean, everybody goes to the store. Don and everyone. Don and the guys are pretty good at talking me into it.

Mom: Well, what can you do about not going along with the other guys?

Frankie: Tell Don I don't want to get detention.

Mom: Good idea. *When's the best time* to tell him?

Frankie: Well, the sooner the better I guess . . . tomorrow.

Mom: How will you do it?

Frankie: I'll catch Don on the way to school. That way he will be alone and I don't have to worry about the other guys too.

Mom: Frank, I don't want you to get detention again. But you did a good job of making some plans to avoid it happening in the future. I'll talk to you about it when I get home.

Let's take a look now at what a conversation might look like between a parent and child when there is a more extended period of time available. Again, we emphasize the new step.

Using the Seventh Decision-Making Step to Handle Everyday Problems

FRANKIE AND ROBBIE: HOW PLANNING AND CHECKING CAN KEEP CONFLICT CONTAINED

Let's stay with Frankie and his mother for a while and meet the rest of his family. Earlier, Frankie had called his mother, Eileen, (age thirty-nine) at the jewelry department which she manages at a large department store. Eileen's husband, Pete, is forty years old. He's an electrician, working days. Because Eileen is in the retail business now, she needs to work a number of late afternoons, evenings, and Saturdays. This schedule has been a big change for the family. Pete now is usually the one to handle the homework and dinner, and all that comes with it with the boys. Decision making has been helpful for Pete since he has taken on additional home responsibilities. Imagine that it is 4:30 P.M. on a Thursday afternoon in spring. Frankie is home with his younger brother, Robbie. Robbie is nine years old and in the fourth grade (see their Family Tree).

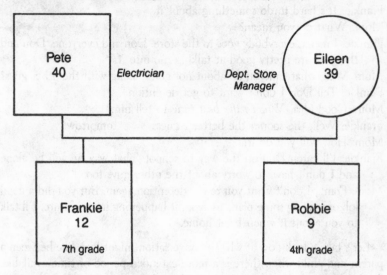

Robbie admires his older brother a great deal. He imitates him a lot. At times this behavior causes some problems. Watch how Dad weaves in some *planning* instruction for his boys. The phrases in italics show how Dad helps Robbie use decision-making thinking. Pete has just arrived home. He enters the living room to hear Robbie yelling.

Robbie: (loudly) Dad! (more loudly) Dad!
Dad: Lower your voice please, I'm right here. What's up?
Robbie: Frankie won't let me use his baseball glove. He never does.
Frankie: That's because you never ask me. You just take it. (irritatedly) Forget all of this junk.
Dad: It's his glove, Robbie.
Robbie: I know . . . I know.
Frankie: I'm going out to play catch with Don . . . he's waiting for me.
Dad: Okay . . . see you at five-thirty for dinner. (Frankie leaves.) Robbie, come in to the kitchen and let's get some juice.

Dad and Robbie go into the kitchen. Dad pours the drink and they sit down for a few moments.

Dad: So, *it really gets you* when your brother won't lend you his glove.

Robbie: Yeah . . . I get so mad at him, Dad. All I want to do is borrow it.

Dad: *What ideas have you had* about how to get a chance to use it.

Robbie: I thought about paying him some money from my allowance or letting him borrow something of mine. But I need my money myself and there is nothing he really wants of mine. The easiest thing would be to ask him but that never seems to work.

Dad: Good job of thinking. Well, *maybe there are different ways of asking him.*

Robbie: What do you mean?

Dad: Well, Rob, it may sound strange, but even the best solution can get messed up if you don't *plan on the best time* and the *best place* and the *best way* to put it to use.

Robbie: You're thinking about when Frankie said that I just *demand* his glove.

Dad: I think that approach is messing you up . . . *how could you change the way you ask it?*

Robbie: By really *asking* him, I guess . . . but I'm afraid to ask . . . I think he won't let me.

Dad: Well, it's not working the other way.

Robbie: No . . . maybe I can ask him when he is in a good mood.

Dad: *When's that?*

Robbie: Maybe after dinner when we're watching TV together.

Dad: I think you're right about that being a good time. Do you want me to be there?

Robbie: Why don't you stay. If you're in the room, he might say yes. If you're gone, he might just do it his same old way.

Dad: Robbie . . . *good job of planning.* I'll check with you later and we'll see how things work out for you.

There were some interesting approaches in Pete's style of guiding Robbie. Note that Pete did not throw himself in the middle of the boys' argument. He listened briefly to them, then Frankie left and that was it. Pete is a believer in natural consequences for children. It was, after all, Frankie's glove. If Pete had demanded that Frankie share with his brother, he may have had more difficulties. First, Frankie would be resentful not only of Robbie, but now of his dad. Second, Robbie would have been rewarded for acting impulsively and unfairly. Rather, Pete let Robbie experience the discomfort that can come with acting impolitely. Without that feeling of discomfort, Robbie might have felt little incentive to try and change.

Also, notice that Pete doesn't jump right in with decision-making talk. Rather, he reduces the tension of the interaction by leaving the scene and going into the kitchen. He further helps by having a snack with his son. Then Robbie was more ready to talk. Notice how Pete was fairly direct and honest with his remarks. He also complimented Robbie's use of decision making.

Let's examine how this is handled when there is much less time to talk.

SHARING THE GLOVE REVISITED: DECISION MAKING ON THE RUN

Imagine that the same problem situation has unfolded. Frankie has just announced that he's going outside to play with Don.

Dad: Okay . . . see you at five-thirty. (Frankie leaves and Robbie comes in to the kitchen.) Let's get a drink of juice. (The scene now changes and there is less time available to talk.)

Robbie: I can't, Dad, I've got to go outside now. The guys are waiting for me. (He walks slowly toward the door.)

Dad: Wait a minute. You really want the glove but I don't think you have a plan.

Robbie: What do you mean?

Dad: Well, you and I know that the best shot you have at getting the glove is to ask. That's not working because you might not be going about it the right way.

Robbie: What do you mean?

Dad: Well, you'd have an even better shot if you'd ask him in a polite way and when he's in a good mood.

Robbie: Like maybe after dinnertime when the three of us are watching TV?

Dad: Yes. That's what I'd call *planning your solution*. See you at supper.

Robbie: Okay, Dad. (He runs out to play.)

Notice that in this shortened example Pete did a little more direct "instructing" in decision making than would be typical for him. Usually it is better to draw decision-making ideas from your children where they can use their own words. But, when under the pressure of time, a better plan for *us* may be to instruct directly. Pete did it and it seems to have worked out.

Let's review now the major themes for this chapter.

Decision-Making Digest

For us, planning a solution translates into being sensitive to the social politics and social graces of the real world. Children need to learn how important it is to be able to put themselves in someone else's shoes and try to imagine how well the planned idea will go over. When the solution involves some kind of person-to-person contact, we emphasize that children should be careful not to be overly intrusive or demanding. For example, we ask that they be sensitive about choosing the best time to talk, or whether something should be said in a one-to-one or a group setting. Often we actually have youngsters rehearse out loud what they will say and how they will say it. Hearing their ideas out loud can change their view and allows for a "final check." It also allows for a child to anticipate what words and what tone of voice to use. This can be especially helpful in real-life situations when they might get slightly anxious. The Decision-Making-Digest chart summarizes all of the major activities of this chapter.

Well, enough on planning. Let's move to a presentation of the last decision-making step: actually implementing the well-planned-out solution and observing how well it works. Onward and upward.

Decision-Making Digest:
Plan It and Make a Final Check

If you'd like your child to

1. See how planning and making a final check can be helpful in everyday situations

2. Become better at developing strategies

3. Value the concept of using planning as a way to prepare

4. Be better able to handle obstacles that are thrown in his or her way

5. Anticipate obstacles on his or her own

6. Experience the usefulness of planning in a more concrete way

7. Use planning to more confidently know his or her way around his or her world

8. Use planning to prevent potentially harmful/embarrassing problems

Then try these activities:

1. Shopping Lists
   Preparing Breakfast for the Family
   Anticipating an Interview
   The First Day of School
   Trying Out for the School Play
   Going out on a First Date
   Planning a Parent Party
   Detention Decision Making

2. Checkers
   Chess
   Tic-Tac-Toe
   Dot-to-Dot

3. Plan and Play

4. Roadblock

5. Double Check

6. Aspiring Architect

7. Mapmaking and Path Planning

8. Planning How to Deal with Strangers
   Planning How to Deal with Being Lost
   The Bathroom Blues

10

Try It and Rethink It

Imagine that you are a high diver, or a ski jumper, or someone about to parachute from an airplane. You *know* what you are supposed to do. You've thought through all the steps in your dive. You've planned carefully so that you have all of your ski jump gear just right. You've made a final check of your parachute. When you stop and think about how it will all go, you can see it going well. If you run into difficulty, you know how to come out of your dive, rotate so that you land feetfirst in the snow, or pull your back-up rip cords. You've used your decision-making skills to the fullest.

Try to picture yourself at the moment before the jump, peering over the edge of the diving board, looking down the ski ramp, or gazing at the ground from the airplane. Perhaps you are experiencing signs of hesitant feelings in your throat, your mouth, the palms of your hands, your stomach. But you also might feel excited and pleased—all your work can now get you to your goal!

You are on the edge of our final decision-making step—the step in which you *act* and *try out your plan*. There is always a mixture of hesitation and positive anticipation as you face the challenge of carrying out your decision or solving your problem. Before we ask you to go ahead and dive or jump, or else get back to safety, just take another look over the edge and notice your feelings. Try to picture what you see clearly, like a photograph from the best camera. You should now have a sense of the importance of the last decision-making step—it's a long way from thinking to doing.

Perhaps one of these situations you have just pictured is familiar to you —perhaps all of them are. Perhaps you become more apprehensive approaching your boss for a raise, telling your mother-in-law why you can't bring the family over for the holidays, or going to a conference with your son's principal. We all differ in what seems easy and what poses a real challenge. The everyday problems that our children bring to us such as, coping with teasing, too much homework, a tough teacher, a pesty sibling, and joining new groups, are often new and challenging. *It is not enough to equip our children with a way to think through problems and make decisions. We must give them the confidence to act and the conviction to learn from their actions.*

"Steptalk": Where We've Been and Where We're Going

Being a decision-making parent and having a problem-solving household takes creativity, patience, and mental energy. You've been working to prepare your children for effective action. They can *look for signs of different feelings* and use their words to *state a problem* and *choose a goal.* At times you can tell they have *selected a best solution* after *considering several alternatives and their consequences.* They've shown signs of *planning* and, at times, of making a *final check* and talking about *possible obstacles.* Perhaps your children are so confident that they've already begun putting their plans into action. We suspect this is true for most families.

If your child tends to be quiet or unassertive, a youngster with good ideas but still hesitant to try them, our final decision-making step will help you draw them out. Let's review *all* of our steps, with a careful eye on our final one:

1. Look for signs of different feelings.
2. Tell yourself what the problem is.
3. Decide on your goal.
4. Stop and think of as many solutions to the problem as you can.
5. For each solution, think of all the things that might happen next.
6. Choose your best solution.
7. Plan it and make a final check.

NEW   8. Try it and rethink it.

Rethinking is, to us, a part of trying. Rethinking means that you ask yourself, "What happened? How well did it work? Did I meet my goal or solve my problem? What obstacles did I meet up with? What can I do differently next time?" By teaching our children to ask themselves these questions, we make it possible for their future plans and actions to work more smoothly and wind up more successfully. We are preparing them for the times when we won't be available to help them plan for the "next time." We are preparing them to learn from the most powerful growth experience—action in the real world. Our task is to send them forward with *thoughtful confidence*. So let's climb up the rung of the last step in our decision-making ladder. Let's *try it*—and *rethink it*.

CASE EXAMPLE: LAUREN TRIES TO MAKE A NEW FRIEND

Lauren is eight years old and she's just moved into a new neighborhood. Her old neighborhood had lots of kids her age. Lauren's on her way to Kim's house. Let's listen to Lauren's thoughts as she walks up the block.

Lauren: These houses are sure big and pretty. But I miss Shelly and Gerry and even Fran. Nobody's ever out around here. Oh, nice butterfly! Kim's the only kid my age on the whole block. I just saw her once for a minute, with her dad. He laughed so loud—he kind of scared me. There's Kim's house! Okay, I'm going to ring the bell and ask if she can come over. But who's going to answer? What if her dad answers?

If you were watching Lauren, you'd see her stop for a moment in front of Kim's house, then turn around and run home. Meanwhile, Lauren's mother, Lucille, had noticed she had signs of nervous feelings. Lauren had seemed so lonely. Lucille was excited that Lauren was finally going to Kim's! When she sees Lauren running home, she feels disappointed. But she is ready to help Lauren get through the problem. "Get calm, Lucille, get calm," she says to herself. Then Lauren enters.

Lucille: Hi, sweetheart. I didn't think you'd be back so soon.
Lauren: Yeah, well, um, nobody was home.
Lucille: Oh, you rang the bell and no one answered?
Lauren: Yeah, well, no, I mean, um, well, I could tell.
Lucille: Really? How?
Lauren: The, uh, lights weren't on and the car was gone and . . .

Lucille: Your eyes are telling me that something else is going on. What really happened?

Lauren: What if Kim's father answers? He'll laugh again and then I'll get so scared.

Lucille: Were you scared when you were at the door?

Lauren: Yeah.

Lucille: So the problem isn't Kim—it's her father?

Lauren: He scares me, Mommy.

Lucille: He scares you . . . well, let's take a look at your plan and think again about how you can ask Kim to come over.

Lauren and her mom generate a lot of alternatives and consequences but really cannot come up with a plan that guarantees Lauren won't meet up with Kim's dad. Lucille uses some *gentle prodding.*

Lucille: It really would be fun to have Kim come over, wouldn't it?

Lauren: Yeah.

Lucille: She's never seen your room or any of your things. She's never seen your hanging balloon or your dollhouse.

Lauren: (a bit sadly) No, she hasn't.

Lucille: Well, it's time for me to make dinner. You can think about your goal—having Kim come over and see your things—and maybe later we can talk more. Can you get Sheila's plate . . .

Two days later:

Lucille: Hi, sweetie, how was your walk . . . who's this?

Lauren: This is Kim. Kim, this is my mom. I was on my walk and said, "Hmm," and I figured that if Kim's father answered the door, I would smile and say, "My name is Lauren. I have to go home right now but, uh, can Kim come over to play?" But Kim answered and she asked him and then we came here!

Lucille: (giving Lauren a hug and a *very* special look) Well, Lauren, I'm glad you brought Kim over and, Kim, it's *so* nice to meet you. Why don't you both go upstairs . . .

Lauren had all the skills she needed to solve her problem, but she had a slight case of "stage fright." Lucille was able to help her. But let's go up the block to Kim's house.

CASE EXAMPLE:
KIM WOULD RATHER KEEP TO HERSELF AND NOT TRY IT

Kim, who just turned nine, does not have many friends. She spends most of her free time reading or drawing or listening to music or watching the world go by from out of her bedroom window. She's a thoughtful girl and a good decision maker. In school when Belinda had a problem with a ripped sneaker lace, Kim quickly figured out two different ways to fix it. But she didn't tell anyone about these ideas. After ten minutes the teacher, Mr. Jones, took care of it. Sometimes Kim just wants to go up to others and say what's on her mind, but something holds her back. Now, her father, Bert, calls her:

Kim: Yes, Daddy.

Bert: I remember you said you wanted to play with that new girl down the street. What's her name, Wendy?

Kim: Her name is Lauren, Daddy. She's not so nice. She walked by and stopped outside yesterday and ran away. And she has all those brothers and sisters—she doesn't need me.

Bert: Kim, if I've said it once, I've said it a hundred times. Don't be so shy. Just go over and ask—it's that easy.

Kim: I'm hungry. When is dinner?

Bert: Kim, we were talking about . . . oh, what's the use? In an hour. Go upstairs until then and . . .

Of course, we know that Kim jumped at the chance to play with Lauren, but it was Lauren's willingness to *try it* that made it happen.

"CASETALK": A CLOSER LOOK AT THE TWO CHILDREN

Even by age nine, a child like Kim can talk herself out of putting her ideas and plans into action. Kim chose to interpret Lauren's running away as a sign that Lauren wasn't nice. She could just as easily have seen Lauren as shy or as answering her mother's call. Lauren's sisters and brothers were another *excuse* to not act. But who is Kim *really* fooling? Who is being hurt in the long run? She is, and so is her *entire family*. The pattern she is starting could become a source of misery for everyone once she enters junior high or middle school. Bert is already showing signs of frustration with her. Kim has the skills. What she needs is confidence and her family's encouragement to meet the challenge of making and keeping friends.

Lauren is not yet fully confident. But her mother has a calm, "You can do it" attitude. Notice that Lucille doesn't *increase* Lauren's stress. Instead, she increases Lauren's desire to *try it* by reminding Lauren of her goal and the fact that she's also losing something by *not* trying it. There were other times when Lucille used the same calm, gentle prodding approach—and Lauren didn't act. But as parents, we sometimes have to lose battles to win the war. Here *the prize is Lauren's self-confidence and self-respect,* her feeling that she *can* do it and she *will* do it and learn from it. Lucille's hug and special glance at Lauren will go a very, very long way toward making it easier for Lauren to *try it* next time.

For some children our last decision-making step is a giant one. Perhaps they are not as good at decision making as Lauren and Kim. But we have worked with many different children, from many different *kinds* of families. And we are convinced that when parents create a *home of encouragement,* their children build confidence and are better off for it. If the kids are already good at steps 1 through 7, or most of them, then they have even more to be confident about, more to *try and learn!* Following are some of the building blocks to a home of encouragement.

How to Teach Your Child to Try It and Rethink It

BE A MODEL

By now you are probably familiar with how to model your own decision making. You know that thinking aloud lets your children learn how you arrive at decisions, choices, and actions. To teach step 8, your task as a model is a bit different because more than thinking is involved. Your child may have a certain step that he or she usually gets stuck on. So often it is *feelings* or *goals.* By modeling only that step, you might unstick things and free up your child for action. But sometimes your child *knows* what to do and just doesn't do it. Or maybe this happens:

Manuel: I figured out how to do it! I can clear the table in one trip! I just
 put this plate over here, stack these cups, and . . .
Father: Watch out! (There is a crash.)
Manuel: (next day) See, I just put this plate on top, put these cups like
 this, and . . .
Father: That's the same thing you did yesterday. (There is another crash.)

He tries it, it doesn't work, and the next time, he tries the same thing.
And you might feel the irritation welling up inside you. Consider being a
model of some alternative ways to *try it* and *rethink it*. *Model how you get
yourself to do a chore or reach a goal.* In many homes taking out the
garbage is a chore—a *real* chore. But it has to be done. To help our
children learn some self-prodding, we'll think aloud:

> "They collect garbage again tomorrow. What a pain. But it's got to
> go out. The garbage can is full, the garbage in the kitchen is starting
> to smell, yecch! Here comes a two-minute commercial—let's see if I
> can do it and not miss any of the program!"

We're sure you can think of other chores, like cleaning up the yard or
washing walls or vacuuming or going out for an "emergency" shopping
trip late at night, that you have to prod yourself to do. Let your children
see how you decide to act and follow through!

A more positive time to *try it* is when there is something you are looking
forward to doing. Say the goal out loud, so that your children can see how
rewarding action can be. Here are some examples:

Do what you're doing	but	*Try to reach a better goal*
I can just sit here and read	but	I'm going to call the travel agent and make that reservation so we can all go and have some fun.
I can watch television	but	there's a great new movie I really want to see, so I'm going to call up and get the times it's playing.
I can eat at home	but	I really want to have pizza and it would be fun for all of us to go out for a change.

The plan is sitting there, ready to move toward a goal—show your children how you confidently take action!

Modeling how you follow up on your plans and rethink them, to help you next time. Sometimes our actions work out and sometimes, we wonder why we bothered! If your children are to become skillful decision makers, they need to learn from their actions: either do it the *same way* next time, *change it* so it will work, or *change it* to try and make it better. Let's see what happened to some of the plans we just talked about—the key words to watch for are "next time," "next week," or the like:

> Be a Positive Model: I made it! The garbage is now out of the way, and I didn't miss any of the program. I'll try it again that way *next week!*
>
> Be a Constructive Model: Oh no! I missed about five minutes of the program. *Next time*, I'm going to *think first* about where we keep the ties to close the garbage bags—they're with the silverware, *not* with the bags. Oh well . . .
>
> Be an Improvement Model: The travel agent said it should all work out fine. But you know, I was just thinking . . . I could have saved money if I waited just ten minutes before I called, because the rates change. *Next time* I'll remember to check the clock!

You can also model how you follow up a plan. You can use important, personal matters, such as asking your boss for a raise:

> "Well, I planned to ask her, I did it, and she said yes. If I didn't try it, who knows when I would have gotten a raise. It really does *pay* to try!"

or

> "Well, I planned to ask her, I did it, and she said she'd think about it. But, you know, I asked her when she was very busy—it's better to wait until someone isn't busy to ask important questions. Next time I'll wait until the right time, then I'll try it."

ENCOURAGE EXPRESSION

Children certainly differ in their willingness or reluctance to put their ideas into practice. But most children—like most adults—do not like to be "pushed" too strongly to do something. We've developed a method for encouraging action that we call Gentle Prodding. Perhaps you are already using it. There are several types of Gentle Prodding:

Remind about the goal:
    What was it you wanted?
    What is it you're trying to do?
    What will happen if your plan works?

Be encouraging and confident:
    I can't wait to hear how it turns out.
    I know you can do it.
    Maybe tomorrow will be a better time.

Get out any fears: (generate consequences)
    What do you think might go wrong?
    What if _____ *does* go wrong? What will happen?
    What's the worst thing that can happen?

Gentle Prodding may help your child to act *or* to express some hesitation or uncertainty. Watch how Gentle Prodding leads into a Role Play—a dress rehearsal—for Vito and his mom.

Mom: Vito! You're still here!
Vito: Yeah, well, it's early.
Mom: What is it that you're going to do tonight?
Vito: I was going to walk over to Theresa's house and see if she wanted to hang out.
Mom: Sounds like fun. I can't wait to hear how it goes!
Vito: Ah, I don't know.
Mom: What do you think could possibly go wrong?
Vito: She may, you know . . . think I'm a jerk.
Mom: Mmm. What was it that you were planning to say to her?
Vito: Ah, um, I'll say, uh, hey, Terri, what's doing?
Mom: Listen, let's have a dress rehearsal to practice. I'll be Terri, you be Vito and come up to me and show me what you'd do . . .

Vito and his mom will *practice* "trying it" to help him get ready. Be encouraging and give some constructive comments. It's also very, very helpful to remind your child to use *Get Calm!*, as we learned in Chapter 3. Sometimes you may also find it useful to switch roles. Vito's mom would pretend she's Vito and *model* one or two ways of carrying out a plan. We've found Role Playing to be one of the best ways to encourage expression of the first part of step 8; try it!

The second part of step 8 is: *rethink it.* If your child learns to review what happened and learns from it for the next time, it can save everyone in your family needless misery. When Sol wants Mac to come over to his house and his plan keeps failing, his father, Dave, helps him *rethink it:*

Sol: He said no again!

Dave: What did you try to do?

Sol: I called and asked him to come to eat and stay afterward, maybe check out my aircraft carrier models.

Dave: You called him yesterday and the day before, right?

Sol: Yeah.

Dave: What did he say?

Sol: He said he was too busy.

Dave: How did you feel about that?

Sol: I was getting angry. I always call him and he always says he can't come over.

Dave: What did you say then?

Sol: I told him if he was too busy, fine. I didn't need to see him.

Dave: What did he say?

Sol: He said he really had to go and he'd call me sometime.

Dave: Maybe it's a good time to rethink calling him so often and asking him to come over. Are you sure you want *him* over?

Sol: I don't know, I'm not so sure now. I'm going to think about it . . .

Sol's dad used something we call The Opening to encourage Sol to talk about his actions. His questions gave Sol an opening to *review what happened* and then prompted Sol to rethink his goal. He also might have had Sol *consider alternatives* to calling Mac or *planning other ways to carry out* the call. But the first thing needed is The Opening, and here are some Opening kinds of questions:

"What did you try to do?"

"What happened?"

"How did it go? . . . I'd like to hear more about it."

"I've been waiting for you to get home . . . you were going to try to _____ today, right?"

ACCEPT AND ACKNOWLEDGE WHAT YOU HEAR

Whether you get to use Gentle Prodding, Role Playing, The Opening, or all three, depends on how comfortable your child feels in approaching you about his or her actions. So many of us are busy parents (or tired when we're not busy!) that our children may hesitate to "bother" us about their plans and attempts to *try it*. Give your child a *clear invitation* to talk with you by saying things like, "Stop by when you get back, no matter what I'm doing," or "Let's talk about this at dinner or before bedtime," or "I really want to hear how it goes—please tell me when you're done." In a *home of encouragement*, children know that parents care.

When your child finally does come up to you, let your child know that you can tell that he or she is *trying it* and *rethinking it*. Sometimes a touch, a nod, a smile, a pat on the back, or a hug will be more than enough to make it more likely that your child will keep coming back to *rethink* things with you. Be on the lookout for times when your child takes action, or seems to make a positive change in some habit or routine. Words of praise or encouragement ("Wow, Ted, that's a whole different way of going about it!" "Cindy, I'm proud of you for telling him he was being unfair" "I see you changed what you are trying to do, Latanya. Good for you! I think this will work out better.") will help you see more of what you're working toward: a decision-making child who can *try it and rethink it*.

Steps 1 through 7 are already pretty familiar to you. Therefore, the family activities we are going to present cover not only step 8, but also include enjoyable and useful ways to combine and review several of the steps at once.

Family Activities You Can Do at Home

CURRENT EVENTS: DOES IT HAVE TO BE THAT WAY?

The news is filled with people's actions. Space missions, trials, politics, legislation, sports—all of these involve actions. So often we read or listen to the news and just shake our heads and say to ourselves, "Does it have to be that way?" Well, Current Events involves taking that question and making it a point for family discussion:

Dad: That new highway is going to create a lot of traffic. Let's rethink that plan. Does it really have to be that way?
Harvey: Hey, maybe we can write them a letter if we have a good idea.

or

Mom: You see, they took that goalie out and the new one gave up two goals already. Did they have to do that? Let's rethink it.
Hal: Yeah, you know, they could have moved their defense back until the first guy warmed up . . .

A FAMILY PLAY

Imagine that it's holiday time or someone's birthday. How wonderful it would be to do something different and special—maybe something that will become a family tradition. In some families a Family Play—following the decision-making way—can be fun and draw everyone together. We've made a chart that outlines the steps to take for your Family Play. Notice that we use a rehearsal to *try it* and then have everyone sit down and *rethink it.*

In one of our families, we used a Family Play to put on productions of *Cinderella* and *The Wizard of Oz* that involved aunts, cousins, grandparents, great aunts, and friends. It took a few hours of planning, but the results were unforgettable. We've also found that just about everyone seems to be familiar with certain children's television characters. There are many, many plays one can do with these versatile creatures. But the most important results will be the warmth of family cooperation and decision making, the fun of *trying it,* and the challenge of *rethinking* and *redoing* it for the delight of others.

TRY IT WITH TOAST

Breakfast. The beginning of the day. In many families the tone for the day seems to be set at breakfast. Of course, there are lots of times when everyone is on such a hectic schedule that no one sits down together for

TABLE 4
A SCRIPT TO PRODUCE A FAMILY PLAY

1. What's the occasion?
2. Who will see the play?
3. What are your family's goals for your play?
4. How will you present the skit? Think of at least *three* different ways to do it (as characters from the present or past; as a musical; as a game show; using a real book or record; using puppets or *Sesame Street* characters).
5. Decide what roles everyone in the family will have.
6. Plan how you will work to make the script, scenery, props, and anything else you might need. Think about when you want to have the play and where it might be.
7. When can you rehearse the play?
8. After you try it, everyone can help rethink it. What would you like to keep the same? What would you like to change?
9. Try it again and rethink it until you're satisfied!

breakfast—everyone takes turns. However, on those occasions when you are sitting at the table with one of your children, we suggest you Try It with Toast. If there are plans to be carried out, some *gentle prodding* can make it more likely that an action takes place. And it's invigorating to leave the house with a sense of confidence! When our children leave for school not worrying about whether or not to carry out their plans, they have more energy left for learning. Here are two families who Try It with Toast. The first is a father with two children, Pat (age sixteen) and Ross (age twelve).

Dad: Where's the jam?

Pat: Right under the newspaper, Dad . . .

Dad: Thanks. Ross, the last few days we've been talking about your progress report and your plan to speak up more in class. How's it going?

Ross: Slow, Dad, real slow.

Pat: Yeah, as in no movement—zip.

Dad: What's the worst thing that can happen if you raise your hand when the homework is reviewed?

Ross: I might be wrong . . . and everyone would laugh at me.

Dad: That happens all the time, huh? You laugh at everyone else who gets a wrong answer?

Ross: No I don't. Only the burnouts do that.

Dad: Oh. So maybe everyone won't laugh, and the kids that do, well, so what?

Ross: Hmm.

Dad: Well, later on I'd like to hear what does happen when you speak up. Who does dishes today . . .

Consider the Galliard family, which includes Carl and Marta and their children Lloyd, (age twelve), Christine, (age six), and Julianne (age four):

Julianne: More milk!

Marta: You mean, "more milk, *please*."

Julianne: More milk please, Mommy.

Lloyd: I don't want to take that bus today. Henry and Calvin are always making trouble, throwing stuff.

Carl: I remember we worked on a plan to do something about it, didn't we?

Christine: Plan, plan, plan. We're always doing plans.

Marta: They help, don't they? Remember when you wanted to do a puppet show and we made a plan and it worked?

Christine: I guess. Well, Henry and Calvin are real pests.

Carl: What if you spoke to the bus driver early by leaving before everyone else gets on the bus?

Lloyd: It might help, I don't know.

Christine: Things wouldn't get thrown around.

Lloyd: I wouldn't have to hold on to all my stuff and argue with Calvin.

Christine: It'd be great.

Marta: After you've spoken to the bus driver, let us know what he does. Then if anything else has to be done, we can help. Julianne! Carl, the paper towels!

RETHINK IT WITH ROAST

Dinnertime is, of course, the occasion when many families are able to sit around a table and review their day. When parents work late shifts, dinner may occur without everyone present. Or perhaps your family gets together before bedtime. Regardless, there is usually some time during the week when you can give your children *the opening* to tell you what they've done. This follow-up lets your children know you are genuinely interested in their problems. It also gives you a chance to help them rethink their plans. Let's look in on how our families' *gentle prodding* worked out:

Dad: Pat, get the phone, please.

Pat: It's for you, Dad. It's Mr. Galliard.

Dad: Hello?

Carl: Hi, Jack. How are you? I just wanted to talk to you about the school bus situation.

Jack: Good. What happened?

Carl: At dinner I asked Lloyd how the bus driver responded to what he had to say. I wanted Lloyd to know that I expected him to follow through. Well, he did talk to the bus driver! He said the bus driver knew about Calvin and Henry but said there wasn't anything he could do about it.

Jack: Well, what do you suppose is the next step?

Carl: Well, we rethought our plan and Lloyd is going to take a note to the principal that we all wrote together and signed.

Jack: Well, I think I'll send in a note with Ross, so they won't think it's just you.

Carl: How did Ross do in class?

Jack: When we were having dessert, I said I'd been waiting all day to find out how things went—that opening usually works well with Ross. He said he raised his hand a few times but didn't get called on. When I asked him, he said he felt disappointed that he didn't get picked. So I think he's going to try again tomorrow. We decided the plan was still okay.

Carl: Terrific! Say, Marta and I and the kids are going to hear the band in the park next weekend. Do you think . . .

These are certainly families who show signs of creating homes of encouragement for their children. Since homework time can put even the most encouraging families to the test, we have a special activity that might help a bit.

BE PROUD OF YOUR WORK

We've noticed that more and more parents and teachers seem to be a bit concerned with the quality of homework children are turning in. The work is sometimes careless or rushed, and often doesn't seem as thoughtful or creative as it could be. One activity we've used successfully with third graders and older children is the Pride Check. It's simple: about an hour before bedtime, explain to your children that you will all do a Pride Check. Every "student" (parent or child!) brings in the work he or she will turn in the next day. Everyone looks it over for neatness and completeness. If there seem to be problems, encourage each other to *rethink* the work and to perhaps fix it up. Make the point that we should be proud of our *effort* and show we tried. The encouragement can be, at times, at least as important as the results. (You can, of course, change the Pride Check to whatever part of the day best suits your family routine.)

Another area in which decision making has been valuable is in helping children prepare reports and presentations for class. The steps are woven into a work sheet that we call "Do Yourself Proud." As you can see, it provides a guideline that is more likely to result in your children making a report or presentation they can be proud of. And it can be used over and over again, for different reports and topics, for years.

TABLE 5
DO YOURSELF PROUD!

Step One: Put your problem and goal into words.
1. What is your topic? _____
2. What are some things you would like to learn or answer about the topic?

Step Two: List some different places you can look for information.
1. Write at least five places you could possibly look for information.
   a. _____
   b. _____
   c. _____
   d. _____
   e. _____
2. Plan which ones you will try first—when, where, how can you do it?

3. If these ideas do not work, who else could you ask for some others?

Step Three: Think of as many different ways to present the topic as you can.
1. Write at least three ways to present your topic. If you are doing a written report, put down *three ways* to write it up.
   a. _____
   b. _____
   c. _____
2. For each of these ways, think of the consequences, choose your best solution, and plan how you will do it.

Step Four: Make a final check!
1. Does your presentation answer the topic and the questions you asked? Is it clear? Is it neat? Is the spelling correct? Will others enjoy it?

FAMILY PROBLEM SOLVING

In a home of encouragement, family members often share their problems and use each other as sources of support or ideas. Family Problem Solving is a way to bring this kind of activity into your home. Pick a time during the week that will be the time for Family Problem Solving. Everyone sits down, and someone starts by saying, "Okay, who has a problem to share—either one *you* have or someone else's you've heard about?" Some families like to put their problems on index cards—then they shuffle the cards and read them in the order they get picked. Other families just have anyone speak who wishes to.

After someone mentions a problem, take your copy of the decision-making steps from the refrigerator (or wherever) and have it handy as you discuss each problem. At first, you should probably start with "easy" problems, like when to call Cousin Helaine, when to get together with the Smither family, when to shop, how to organize a party, and the like. Once your family gets used to meeting and using decision making to solve problems, more difficult and "personal" problems may be mentioned. For your children, this will most often involve problems with friends, teachers, school work, or doubts about themselves or their abilities. As your children move into their teenage years, Family Problem Solving may set the stage for an important activity we'll talk about in Chapter 11: keeping the channels of communication in your family open.

DECISION-MAKING DIARY

Part of *trying it and rethinking it* involves keeping track of our experiences so we can learn from them. And it makes sense that both we and our children should grow up in decision making and not repeat old mistakes too often, not get stuck on problems we've solved before, and not get into a rut using the same plans over and over after conditions have changed. Many families—parents and children—can find it helpful and instructive to have a Decision-Making Diary, a sample page of which is given at the end of this chapter. It takes someone through all of the decision-making steps, which can be especially useful for problems that are too personal to share during Family Problem Solving. You and your children can make diaries any way you'd like to. Make your own binders, recopy our form onto smaller or larger paper, or adapt our form to your requirements. The only thing that matters is that the Diary is used! Later in the chapter we'll show you how a family used the Diary to help solve a problem at home that was affecting everybody.

Family Activities
You Can Do Away from Home

IN SEARCH OF SOFT TOWELS

Many of you have had the experience of doing the family laundry at a laundromat. Getting a good washing is not just a matter of putting the coins in the machine—not by a long shot. Every machine has its own idiosyncracies, its own preferences for certain brands and amounts of powder; and in a dryer certain timing cycles must be respected if towels are not to emerge as melba toast. Bring your child with you to the laundromat to observe an exercise in decision making:

Ellen: Gee, Mom, those machines are big!
Wendy: There we go. Everything is in the first machine. We'll wait and see how it comes out before we do the rest.
Ellen: (a little while later) Mom, I don't think it worked too well. The clothes are still full of soap!
Wendy: So they are. We'd better rethink this. Hmm. I know we need less detergent, but how much less?
Ellen: Let's ask that lady who works here—the sign says her name is Pat, I think.
Wendy: Good idea.

Wendy had a plan and tried it, but she had to rethink it. Her daughter, already introduced to decision making, was able to make a helpful suggestion. Of course, doing a wash is just one place where step 8 can be used. Whenever you find yourself trying something new—you can use the outcome to show your children you *tried it* and how you'll now *rethink it.*

TABLE 6

DECISION-MAKING DIARY

Today's Date: _____

I am feeling _____

_____

because _____

_____.

My goal is that _____

_____.

I am going to *stop and think* of as many solutions as I can, and I am
going to think about their *consequences*.

     Solutions I might try: If I try it, what can happen next?

My best solution is _____

and my plan for solving the problem is that I will _____

_____

_____

_____

After I checked my plan and tried it, I found that it worked _____

_____

_____

Next time, I might _____

_____

_____

_____.

GETTING SOMEONE'S ATTENTION: A FINAL VISIT TO THE DINER

Believe it or not, Shirley, Al, Ilene, and Lou have finally finished eating and they want the check. It's crowded in the diner and they know they must plan a way to get the waitress's attention. Let's listen:

Shirley: Al, go ahead and raise your hand. That's what we decided.

Ilene: Yeah, Dad, it's been ten minutes already.

Al: Do you see this thing at the end of my wrist? Do you know what it is? Hasn't it been up and down like a yo-yo? We need a new plan.

Shirley: Let's stand up and leave. That works when I go shopping with Agnes.

Ilene: Oh, Mom. We can just call out the waitress's name. It was Cynthia.

Lou: I think we should stand up.

Al: Me, too. And if they let us go . . .

Shirley: Al, really.

This family didn't get angry or rude, nor did they passively wait until it was time for the next meal and just order again. *They have become a decision-making family.* When an initial plan doesn't work, the entire family pitches in to rethink it. Here the family went back to step 4—their goal did not change. If we kept listening, we would hear them come up with a new plan and *try it* again. They may not use *all* the steps. After a while decision-making families learn to use the steps *flexibly.* When you want to *get someone's attention* and your first attempt fails, use step 8 and go back to earlier steps as needed.

APPROACHING NEW FRIENDS

At family gatherings or at the houses of your friends, your children will sometimes have the opportunity to meet someone new who is close to their age, or at least is not an adult. Often your child's first strategy, to go up and say hello or to wait until introductions are made, will be enough to get things moving ahead. But what if the first plan doesn't work? Again it may seem a lot like step 7 (plan it and make a final check), except that now, it's a *real* obstacle, and feelings are likely to be hurt. It means you should be extra sensitive to what happened and let your child know that, with a little *rethinking,* a better plan can be made and tried. We suggest you:

1. Acknowledge how your child is feeling.
2. Ask if this has ever happened before and if so, what he or she learned about the situation.
3. According to what is said, help your child think of at least two ways to get to know the other person.
4. Review the plan and encourage your child to try it!

RECALL PAST SUCCESS

Think about this: you are in the car with your child on your way to an important event or gathering. Your child is becoming a little jittery about what is upcoming. This is a perfect time to Recall Past Success. By helping your child rethink similar circumstances in the past that went well, you make it more likely that his or her decision-making powers will not weaken under stress. Here are some situations and some prompts you can use:

Child on the way to	Prompt by saying:
1. a music recital to play for a group	1. Just think about how it was last time, what everybody said.
2. school to take a big exam	2. What were other tests in this class like? Did you prepare enough for them?
3. a friend's for a date	3. You've seen Leslie at other times —where? How did it go?
4. gym to practice some routines	4. How about taking me through the routine, the way you did it last week?
5. school to confront pestering peers	5. How will it be any different today from when you've done this before?

Note that in every instance, the child is being helped to use the past in the present—*rethinking* to gain confidence and commitment to follow through. After all, carrying out decisions and learning from them is the point of step 8, and of the entire decision-making approach.

Using the Eighth Decision-Making Step to Handle Everyday Problems: Terror at 6 P.M.

It's five-thirty in the afternoon. Jane is caught in a bit of traffic on her way home from the graphics company where she works. She had been unwinding, but now she finds herself starting to wind up again. Her Feelings Fingerprint—a knot in her stomach—was giving way to a Feelings Flashback. "I feel this way because I'm heading home . . . home to terror at 6 P.M."

Meanwhile, at home, her husband, Kevin, has just arrived. He was exhausted from his work as an assistant manager of a health club. He had to come home a half hour earlier because their daughter, Katie's, sitter could stay only until five-thirty; additionally, their son, Ted, had to be picked up from school, where he worked on the yearbook staff. So Kevin and Katie got in the car and drove off. As Kevin waited outside the school for Ted, he looked at his watch. Yes, he'd be home at 6 P.M. . . . just in time for the terror.

What *is* the 6 P.M. terror? To put it simply, it's the final exam for you as a decision-making parent. It's that point in the day just before dinner— one or two parents arriving home from a hard day's work, dinner to be prepared, kids tired and hungry, mail waiting to be read, perhaps a phone call to make or receive. You can fill in the rest from your own experience. How this time period is handled influences how the rest of the evening goes. Even more than that, it affects whether you see home as a haven away from the day's stress or a place where triumph gives way to turmoil. It's a test of *anyone's* decision-making mettle.

Ted was packing up his knapsack so he could meet his father on time. He looked at his watch—it would be 6 P.M. soon—terror time. Ted noticed his throat becoming dry just thinking about the terror. He stopped for a moment and had a Feelings Flashback to a few months ago and a then-typical 6 P.M. scene:

Jane: Hi, everyone. I'm home.

Ted: Hi, Mom.

Katie: Mommy, look at my project. The teacher said it was my best ever!

Jane: That's good, Katie, but not just now . . .

Kevin: Hi. How was the drive?

Jane: As usual. Though there was construction on 287—what a . . .

Ted: My turn to set the table. What's everyone drinking?

Katie: Lemonade.

Kevin: Oh, I forgot to make it.

Katie: But you promised!

Jane: Where's the mail?

Ted: What are you drinking, Mom?

Jane: Well, uh, look at this phone bill! Did we make *that* many calls?

Kevin: Let me see . . .

Katie: Daddy, this lemonade is awful.

Kevin: What? Impossible. Let me taste . . . yecch! I must have lost count.

Jane: What's for dinner?

Katie: Yeah, I'm hungry.

Ted: Me, too. I had to skip lunch. The yearbook is shaping up really well, though. Guess who will be on our cover?

Kevin: Chicken with rice.

Ted: Huh?

Kevin: For dinner—chicken with rice.

Ted: Doesn't anybody listen around here?

Katie: I want a cracker—I'm hungry.

Jane: Oh my . . . Aunt Mary is coming to visit.

Kevin: Where's she staying?

Jane: Here, of course.

Kevin: Can we leave town?

Ted: Doesn't anybody around here *listen?*

Jane: I have an awful headache.

Katie: Where's the chicken?

Kevin: ENOUGH! ENOUGH!

If we X-ray the terror, we can get a better idea of just where sound decision making breaks down. What do you notice? Careful listening isn't occurring. No one is asking for help in a way others can really hear. What else? People are not really looking for signs of different feelings, are they?

And . . . goal confusion. This family is trying to do many things at once: greet each other, share events of the day, read the mail, prepare dinner. Of course, there can't be much (if any!) decision making with all this confusion. Yet *each member of the family has a plan that he or she is trying.* No one's just ever taken the time to *rethink* what happens at 6 P.M. What would you do if you were Kevin or Jane? While you are thinking, take a look at their parenting family tree:

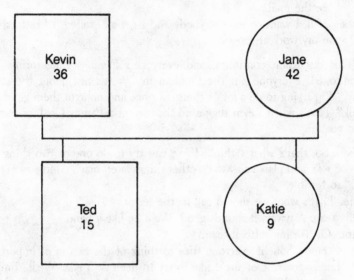

Jane and Kevin began to use the decision-making approach. It's helped in lots of different situations and was especially valuable during the morning routine. Ted, in particular, seemed to respond to it. But they couldn't seem to make it work at 6 P.M. Everyone seemed too tired, and too irritated, to respond. Ted will never forget the first time—and last time—he tried a 6:05 P.M. Goal X Ray on his mom. He never knew she could scream so loud. They talked about it later, but whew! And Kevin found himself saying Get Calm! *Get Calm!* so often, he was getting tense. And it lost something when he would have to shout it to be heard.

Things began to turn around when Ted suggested they talk about the terror at Family Problem Solving time. They took their copy of the decision-making steps off the bulletin board, got a blank Decision-Making Diary sheet, and sat down:

Kevin: This was a good idea, Ted. We weren't getting anywhere the old way.

Ted: Thanks, Dad.

Jane: I'd like to start with my feelings when I come home. I'm looking forward to seeing all of you and hearing about your day. But I'm also worried about getting dinner ready so you can do your homework or whatever before it gets too late. And I kind of feel a little jumpy until I see the mail.

Katie: Well, I want to see everybody and I get all excited. I like to show you my work at school, too.

This discussion continues, and everyone's Feelings Fingerprints are mentioned. Everyone put the problem into words just about the same way: "I'm trying to do a lot of things at once and none of them get done well." That's when Kevin suggested the idea of a Family Goal, or maybe two goals:

Kevin: So, that's what I think. If we can try to do one or two things at 6 P.M. and plan a way to do other things later, maybe things won't be so terrible.

Jane: That's what we should call it: the terror.

Ted: Yeah. Anyway, it sounds good. We'll be like a band.

Katie: Or like my softball team!

Kevin: How about if everyone tries to think of the two most important family goals he or she'd like to try to meet at 6 P.M. We'll "hmm" and not "ho" and write down our goals and tomorrow, we'll check them out. Okay, sweetheart?

Katie: Yes.

Kevin: Ted, Jane?

Both: Sounds good.

We hope you're noticing some good use of decision making. Kevin started by praising Ted's idea, and Ted acknowledged it. Jane labeled the goings-on at 6 P.M. at "the terror"—that somehow makes things seem more contained, manageable, *solvable.* Ted and Katie both took the new idea of family goals and linked them to familiar ideas: a band and a team. Then Kevin suggested they think of *alternative* goals before deciding. You and your family may go about this in a very different way, perhaps less formally, perhaps more so. It depends on the age of your children, what goes on during your "terror," who the members of your household are,

and the like. But in a *home of encouragement,* families can work together
to try different solutions to their common problems. *Try it and rethink it
. . . try it and rethink it . . .* these steps can be used over and over again
until you're all satisfied, or something else comes along to capture the
family's attention. In family living there are rarely perfect solutions. But in
the spirit of decision making, there is at least a way to try to improve
things. Let's look back on our family's progress:

Jane: So our first goal is to talk with each other a bit about our day. And
    since we don't want Katie to faint or Daddy to get a headache from
    hunger, we'll have some salad or some grapefruit or something like
    that to eat while we talk.
Ted: I don't know . . . but it's got to be better than the terror. Let's give
    it a shot.
Kevin: It's getting late, but I'd like to just plan this out a minute more.
    We can take turns getting salad or whatever ready.
Katie: I'm home—I can wash things!
Jane: Wonderful!
Kevin: And when I don't have to pick up Ted, I can get dinner going.
Ted: I'll be home sometimes by three-thirty—I can help set up or some-
    thing.
Kevin: You know, this kind of cooperation tells me one thing: that the
    terror must be pretty bad for *all* of us!
Ted: You're not going to make one of your speeches about togetherness
    are you, Dad? Because I've got a call to make.
Katie: To whom?
Ted: The operator, the weather number, anybody!
Katie: Can I help you?
Jane: All right, all right. Tomorrow, we'll try it and see what happens.

Will it work? It's hard to know. But this family has transformed a
traumatic time into a tolerable time. They have a strategy—a decision-
making approach—to help them handle situations as a unit that can be
overwhelming to them as individuals. And that is the importance of the
final step. To try it and rethink it. To work together to improve *family*
living. To create a *home of encouragement* in which sound decision making can become a habit that children learn and take with them when they
are at school, with friends, and, eventually use when they become parents
themselves.

Decision-Making Digest

You have now completed your journey through the decision-making steps. Of course, it takes a while to get to the point that Kevin, Jane, Ted, and Katie have reached. They worked on each step a bit and gradually got to the point where they used Family Problem Solving as a time to link *all* the steps together, try a plan, and rethink it. They also found it useful to have the steps posted where everyone could see them; Kevin and Jane also used the charts at the end of each chapter in Part Two to point to activities they thought would help Ted and Katie learn particular decision-making skills. To move your household toward becoming a *home of encouragement*, we hope you'll use our chart at the end of this chapter to remind you which activities can teach your children to *try it and rethink it.*

Decision-Making Digest:
Try It and Rethink It

If you'd like your child to	*Then try these activities:*
1. get over his or her reluctance to try out his or her plans	1. Gentle Prodding Role Play Recall Past Success
2. review his or her plans for the day	2. Try It with Toast
3. share with you what happened when a plan was tried	3. The Opening
4. learn to be flexible enough to re-think actions and learn from mistakes	4. Current Events: Does It Have to Be That Way? Rethink It with Roast In Search of Soft Towels
5. learn to check his or her work and be proud of what is prepared for school	5. Pride Check Do Yourself Proud
6. practice using all of the decision-making steps and rethinking the results	6. A Family Play Family Problem Solving Decision-Making Diary Getting Someone's Attention: A Final Visit to the Diner Approaching New Friends

III

Special Applications
of the Decision-Making
Strategy

Chapters 3 through 10 have primed children and parents to be better decision makers. For children, the consolidation of their learning occurs in everyday situations. Part Three presents parents with a variety of examples of how to tailor the decision-making approach to important situations.

Dealing with the "normal" developmental issues that teenagers frequently encounter is the initial focus of this part of the book. With adolescents, strong feelings are the rule, not the exception. Points of conflict can include dating, choice of friends, use of the car, school, and many others. These issues are so important, and feelings on everyone's part so strong, that compromise is often seen as "giving in," and at times may be avoided. Parents are shown how to "keep the channels of communication open"—to listen more, question sensitively, and withhold judgment longer until they know what "channel" their teenager is broadcasting on. Parents are then taught how to encourage their teenager to use the decision-making approach in a constructive, positive way.

The predicament of children needing special long-term care is discussed next. Here, we refer to children who have ailments such as spina bifida, cancer, or diabetes, or those with severe learning impairments. Families in these situations may have to deal with special education placements for their children, become aware of and cope with children's chronic physical limitations, and learn to accept the intense and varied feelings these circumstances inevitably create. The impact of these issues on children and their families cannot be underestimated. The decision-making approach reflects a belief that all children can feel better able to cope with their difficulties. Children with chronic problems can often be involved in making choices and taking responsibility for necessary tasks in a way that increases their own feelings of self-worth and competence.

Decision making as an aid to families during critical points in a child's schooling is discussed next. Vignettes describing these critical points are presented. Some examples include starting a new school, handling parent-teacher conferences, reacting to report cards and progress reports; monitoring studying and homework, and deciding on an academic change. As always, the goal of the decision-making approach is to prepare children to think about their problems, make intelligent choices, and carry them out successfully.

Parents who teach decision making to their children will become better decision makers themselves. The final chapter will highlight how the same principles parents teach their children are applicable to situations parents encounter at work, in household management, in time management, and in their realtionships with other adults. Finally, we take another look at parenting styles to help parents see how they have progressed as teachers of decision making.

11

Keeping the Channels Open: Being a Decision-Making Parent with Your Teenager

Once when we made a presentation to a group of parents of junior high and high school students, the parents seemed a bit nervous. They were very reluctant to share any of their experiences with their children; yet, they had come out on a cold evening to attend the presentation. After a few moments of trying to figure out what the problem was, a question blurted out: "How many of you were ever teenagers—please raise your hands." Amazingly, fewer than half of the parents raised their hands! A follow-up question was asked: "Excuse me, sir. I noticed your hand wasn't up. Were you ever a teenager, even for a short time?" "Well, no, I mean, uh, yes, of course. But it was different. I wasn't, you know, I would, uh, well, uh . . . ."

After this brief exchange, the parents were able to relax a bit. They began to face up to their own embarrassment and uncertainty about the teenage years. We talked about it as a time of transition, as "cute" children gradually turn into "mature" adults. There is no blueprint for how this transition is supposed to occur. And it's natural for parents to want to help their children avoid the "mistakes" or the hurt feelings *they* encountered during *their* teenage years. *How* youngsters come through the transition is very important. Our feeling is that children will be better prepared for the adult world if they learn to use decision making to help them through difficult times. Teenagers especially are often on their own and frequently must make decisions when parents are not around. So we want our teenagers to know *how* to make decisions that will be sound and healthy.

In this chapter we discuss several families with teenage children and show how the parents encourage their children's decision making by focusing on certain key steps. These parents also *keep the channels open* by tuning in to signals their children are sending. Later in the chapter we show how *you* can adjust your own "fine tuner." First, we examine how the Reed family handles a teenage crisis with sixteen-year-old Clifton.

CASE EXAMPLE: CLIFTON WON'T TRY IT AND ASK FOR A DATE

"Clifton! Clifton! Child, what *are* you doing? You've been in a daze. I've asked you four times to pass the potatoes." "Sorry, Mom. Here. I was just thinking." "Well, I have to work tonight, but if there's anything you want to talk about, we can do it when I come back, if you want. Now Elroy and Tasha, finish up and put your plates in the sink."

Linda Reed is thirty-nine years old and was divorced from Melvin eight years ago. Their relationship is "cordial"—not close, but not antagonistic. Mel keeps in close touch with the children, though his traveling often takes him away for weeks at a time. Linda works as a teacher in a private school during the day and does tutoring two nights a week to help pay the bills. Elroy (age eleven) and Tasha (age ten) are both doing well in the local elementary school. Elroy loves photography and nature and Tasha is the hitting star on the girl's softball team.

Clifton is another matter. Always a quiet boy, Clifton had some trouble making the change to high school. He plunged himself into his schoolwork, however, and this seemed to help him manage. Now he was nearing the end of eleventh grade. His friends were having more parties or going for drives, and they'd usually go in couples. Clifton usually went along as the third wheel. This situation was bothering him more and more, especially since his mom started dating, and since Cynthia got switched into four of his classes. Clifton really wanted to ask her to a party or to the mall or—anything! But he just couldn't get himself to do it. Friends offered advice but now started to kid him and call him Ice Cube because he would freeze up around girls.

When Linda comes home, she puts her coat away, checks on sleeping Elroy and Tasha, and then goes over to Clifton. "Well, what's on your mind?" "Oh, it's nothing . . . nothing much." "It's got to be something. Come on, it's late." "It's, uh, Cynthia." "Again? Haven't you asked her out yet? You're just like your cousin James, two left feet and both of them cold. Why don't you just go up and ask her?" "It's not that easy, Mom. She's always got people around her." "If you wait for her to be alone, you'll be like Uncle Willie—single until you're so old it doesn't matter." "Yeah, but she's got so many friends, what would she want with me?" "Child, now *that's* a tough question. And if *you* can't figure out the answer, I doubt that Sally . . ." "Cynthia, Mom!" ". . . Cynthia will, either." "I'm tired now, Mom. I think I'll go to sleep."

Needless to say, Clifton did not get a very good night's sleep. He didn't get much further than he was before the talk, except to find out that he was following in some unpleasant family footsteps. Clifton didn't really even get a chance to say very much, so it's hard to know at exactly which decision-making step Clifton is stuck. Look at how different things might be if Linda would use more of a decision-making approach.

CASE EXAMPLE: CLIFTON IS READY TO TRY IT

Linda: Well, what's on your mind?

Clifton: Oh, it's nothing . . . nothing much.

Linda: Your face has an upset look to it.

Clifton: Yeah, well, it's, uh, Cynthia.

Linda: Go on—I'd like to hear more.

Clifton: I'd, uh, you know, I'd really like to see her outside of school.

Linda: I've never met her, but you've talked about her before. She's in a few of your classes now, right.

Clifton: Yeah, and she's pretty smart—pretty and smart.

Linda: What have you done to try to see her outside?

Clifton: I've thought of a lot of things—writing her a note, stopping her in the hall, talking to her at lunch, calling her on the phone. And I know what'd I'd say—I'd introduce myself and ask her about one of the classes and then I'd say I'd like to do something with her over the weekend, would she like to.

Linda: Well, it sounds like you've got a lot of different ideas. Which have you tried?

Clifton: She really seems to have a lot of friends, so I don't know what she'd want with me.

Linda: Are you saying that in your mind, you have her saying no to you?

Clifton: Well, why wouldn't she?

Linda: How nice is she?

Clifton: Oh, she's terrific.

Linda: And how much fun do you think it would be to spend an afternoon or evening with her?

Clifton: It would be great!

Linda: And if you don't ask her, will it happen?

Clifton: I don't think so.

Linda: And what if she says no? Will lightning strike you where you stand? Will a bubble form around you with a sign that says, "All girls stay away?"

Clifton: No, Mom, of course not. But . . .

Linda: Yes?

Clifton: I'd be so *upset* if she said no.

Linda: Well you're not so happy now, the way things are. You aren't enjoying your food, you aren't even enjoying the music you listen to. And you've missed a few parties, too. Clifton, I'd like to hear how things turn out after you try something. Whichever idea you pick seems much better than not picking any of them.

Clifton certainly has a lot to consider. But Linda's questions have focused on the problem area: step 8, *Try it and rethink it.* Next, take a closer look at what Linda did and where it might lead.

"CASETALK": A CLOSER LOOK AT LINDA AND CLIFTON

Clifton is like a number of other teenagers. Sometimes he does some very good decision making, up to a point. He is not quite ready to *try it,* partly because he cannot stop thinking about possible negative consequences—Cynthia turning him down. Also like many teenagers, Clifton is not always able to easily talk about his problems. Linda was sensitive to his signs of upset feelings. And when he started to talk, Linda *kept the channels open* by saying, "Go on, I'd like to hear more." Next Linda made a statement of fact—not an *evaluative judgment.* This approach also kept the channels open.

Linda's next approach was to *assume the best* about Clifton by asking what he had tried to do. In the first case example, Linda assumed the worst, not only short-circuiting the channels, but also making it more likely that she'll see many reruns of ineffective problem solving by Clifton. Linda keeps probing until Clifton reveals that in his own mind, he's failed. Rather than say, "No, she won't," or "Isn't that ridiculous," or even, as in the first example, agreeing that she probably would turn him down, Linda uses some techniques from Chapter 10. First she helps Clifton think about *how desirable the goal is.* Then she humorously helps Clifton realize that the world will not end if Cynthia does say no. Finally she reflects on the status quo—by reviewing what Clifton is doing to himself by *not* acting, she makes *trying it* seem more attractive.

How is Linda managing to do all this? Some of you, we are sure, would do many, if not all, of what Linda was able to do. There really is no mystery to it. She is familiar with teaching her child decision making. She knows how to *encourage expression* of what her child is thinking and to *accept and acknowledge* what she hears. Her goal is to *keep the channels open*—to create a climate in which Clifton will approach her to talk because he knows she will *listen* and, at times, *help him see things differently.* It's worth a closer look at *keeping the channels open.* It can be an important part of helping your teenager survive and even thrive during some difficult times.

Keeping the Channels Open

PUT AWAY YOUR CRYSTAL BALL

Do you have a crystal ball? Are you sure? Many parents do. If you recall, in Chapter 1 we looked at how our parenting has been influenced by the parenting *we* received. In a similar way, sometimes we use our past history as teenagers to "predict" our child's future. In the first case example, Linda did a good bit of this with Clifton ("You're just like cousin James— two left feet and both of them cold.") Even if you are *sure* you are correct, too much use of your crystal ball can demoralize your teenagers, rob them of confidence and, most importantly, *cut off their room to grow and change.*

There are some signs that can tell you if your crystal ball is working overtime. Watch out for too-frequent statements like these:

"He'll *never* _____."

"You're just feeling _____."

"I know. It happened to me and the same thing will happen to you."

"She's going to _____. How do I know? I just know!"

"It's nothing. In a few days, you'll forget it."

"I knew it. I knew it would happen that way!"

If you are not convinced of the possible harm a crystal ball can have, consider this: your teenager probably has a crystal ball also. And it may work something like this:

"Why tell my father? He just says it's nothing."

"I can't tell my mom. She'll tell me what happened to her, or to Aunt Rosie, or something. She doesn't listen to *me.*"

"She always *tells* me how I'm feeling. I don't need to hear it."

"He always knows what I'm going to do. Well, I'm gonna show him something he'd *never* expect."

The cloudier your crystal ball is, the less you rely on it with your teenager, and the *more* channels you will keep open.

TUNE INTO THE CHANNELS ON WHICH YOUR TEENAGER IS BROADCASTING

In our work with teenagers we have found that they often send signals to their parents. These signals differ, depending on the issue or problem and what the teenagers are looking for from their parents (or other adults they respect and with whom the channels are open). As parents learn what channel their teenager is broadcasting on, reception becomes clearer. There's less static, and the message can be received and responded to accurately. Here's a quick guide to your teenager's broadcast channels.

Channel S: "I need support." For even the most well-adjusted teenager, there will be times when the going gets rough. Perhaps a difficult exam, or a bad game, or an argument with a friend has taken place. If there is a new challenge being faced, you may detect some uncertainty in your adolescent. When your teenager shows signs of being concerned or of being "down" or of being a bit uptight, you are probably receiving broadcasts from Channel S.

Channel H: "I need help." Channel H is usually activated during some very specific task like fixing a bicycle or a car or doing a homework assignment. You will probably notice clear signs of frustration, like the slamming down of a pen or tools, perhaps some groaning, or even, "I give up." While your crystal ball may tell you to say, "I'll help you," or "I didn't think you could do it," refrain from expressing its findings and read below about how to use the decision-making steps to keep the channels *open*.

Channel F: "I need to save face." To be a teenager is, at times, to suffer embarrassment. Sometimes it is caused by peers. But sometimes family members cause feelings of shame or resentment ("He's such a good piano player. Play for Uncle Leo and Aunt Bea. Come on. He'll play—he loves to. Won't you play? Play? PLAY!"). When your teenager needs to save face, to deal with some revelation or incident that exposed an imperfection or two, you may learn about it directly. But you can also tell that Channel F is on if your teenager avoids seeing certain people or rejects certain phone calls. Channel H is more general—it covers lots of situations but most often focuses on your child and some task or object. Channel F is a public channel—it involves other people and is focused around a very limited program content: how to save face.

Channel L: "Please listen to me." Channel L is the most widely broadcast channel. You can tell it's on when your teenager approaches you about talking, or leaves an opening that suggests something is the matter ("Oh, nothing . . . really," "Things went fine. Well, okay," "Yeah, I'm great, I guess"). You'll have to really fine-tune this channel, as Linda Reed did in our second case example. Most often your child will have some confusion or indecision that he or she thinks could benefit from being talked about. Remember, Channel L is not "Please tell me what to do." It's "Please *listen* to me." By listening and eliciting feelings information, you will keep the channel open and perhaps help your teenagers resolve whatever concerns them.

Channel A: "I'm looking for an argument." There are times when your teenager is filled with upset or even just boisterous or contentious feelings; he or she just may be looking for an argument. Signs of Channel A include surly or oppositional behavior, challenges to your authority, and negative statements. Nothing you say is right or even acceptable. Parents whose teenagers are broadcasting on Channel A but *think* their children are broadcasting on Channel S (Support) or L (Listen) are in for a particularly tough time. The longer you tune into A, the more likely it is you will be drawn into a conflict. Sometimes you may be looking for a good argument

—but if you're not, then you'll want to turn off Channel A and open up other channels.

While all of the decision-making steps can be useful for your teenager, we have found that certain steps are of particular benefit. Of course, our first step, *look for signs of different feelings*, serves as *your* guide to which channel is being broadcast by your teenager. But there are three special, "teenager" steps that we will review briefly; then we'll show you how to use them to fine-tune Channels S, H, F, L, and A.

Decide on your goal. Many teenagers, particularly when in a stressful, decision-making situation like dating or joining a club, are like the doubters who believed they would never again see Christopher Columbus after he set sail. No, they aren't boat insurance salespeople. Believe it or not, many teenagers believe the world is flat. More accurately, they believe that if their goal is not met, it is as if they really have sailed off the end of the earth. Here's an example:

Jake: Oh, man, I can't believe it. I just cannot believe it.
Mother: What happened?
Jake: My teacher told me I'm not going to be on the cooking team.
Mother: Cooking team? What's so unbelievable about that? You have
     trouble making toast and buttering it.
Jake: Yeah, but Judy's on the team and I think she's great. Now I've lost
     her forever! That's it. Poof! I can't believe it.

Jake has lost track of his true goal—to spend more time with Judy. He made his solution—join the cooking team—into his goal. So Jake needs to be asked about his *goals* to get him back on the track. But restoring a goal to its proper position may not be enough.

Jake: Oh, oh, oh. You won't believe it. You just will not believe it.
Mother: What happened?
Jake: I was trying to spend more time with Judy, right? So when I got
     turned away by the cooking team, I joined Judy's study hall group.
     But then she started going to Guidance. So remember when I started
     to mumble in the hall so they'd send *me* to Guidance?
Mother: How could I forget?

Jake: Yeah, but they sent me to the school shrink instead. And when I
made it to Guidance, Judy was switched to the Women's Center.
The Women's Center! This school year is a washout, a total washout.

Teenagers like Jake sometimes feel that their present goal is their *only*
goal. Jake has "lost" Judy, and to him that means gloom for the entire
school year. On occasion we can expect teenagers to focus on one aspect
of their personality or talents and forget about the rest. They are trying to
establish a stable sense of who they are, and it is quite important. To help
them keep a healthy perspective, you can help by asking your teenagers to
consider alternative goals. In Jake's case the conversation might continue
like this:

Mother: It does seem frustrating. But, you know, Jake, I was thinking
about that other club you joined two weeks ago.
Jake: You mean the radio broadcast club?
Mother: Yes.
Jake: That's terrific. We get copies of the latest records and special tickets
and we get to do the broadcasts.
Mother: What else looks good this year?
Jake: Ah, nothing.
Mother: C'mon, just stop and think for a minute about something that
you enjoy.
Jake: Hmm. You know, that Mr. Sloane teaches some good stuff in social
studies. He's got us in groups . . .

As you can see, with some gentle prodding Jake was able to focus on
alternative goals—other things he can work for and look forward to when
it's difficult to reach one of his important goals.

Choose your best solution. Teenagers are, as you well know, very concerned about what their peers think of their actions. At times the risk of
making a decision is very high. "What will my friends think of me?"
"What will they say?" "What will they do?" These are the questions that
go through a teenager's mind and create what is commonly called *peer
pressure*. Decision-making step 6 is an important defense against peer
pressure. With teenagers, however, it is important to especially emphasize
two words: choose *your best* solution. The message your teenagers need to
receive is that they should choose an action that is in *their best interest.*
Notice how Geraldine's father helps her with a difficult situation:

Geraldine: It's impossible. They want me to go along and I know what they'll say if I don't.

Father: Are you using your crystal ball again? I thought I was the only one that had one.

Geraldine: No, swami, I guess you're not. But this is serious. Michelle and Janet have been doing some things that have been getting them into trouble at school, and they want me to join in. I really can't tell you much more, Dad, or you'll get angry.

Father: Well, if you don't want to tell me there's not much I can do about it. But I know you've thought about this a lot. What do you think is the best thing for *you* to do?

Geraldine: They may not hang out with me anymore if I say no.

Father: Maybe. But what do you think is the *best* choice for *you?*

Geraldine: Hmm. Well, I think . . .

It's very hard for parents to avoid saying something is "wrong." Often our children *know* that. What we need to do is *show them our confidence* in their decision-making skills. At the same time we can *remind them of their responsibility to make a sound decision.* This extra help, even for an adolescent who seems to know the decision-making steps well, can be a big help during the troublesome teenage years. Eventually your teenager might begin to tell himself or herself the sixth decision-making step and be less likely to give in to peer pressure.

Try it and rethink it. Clifton and Linda provided us with an excellent example of how important it is to encourage shy and anxious teenagers to *try* their well-thought-out decisions. Afterward they can *rethink* what happened to learn for next time. Again, a concern with what peers will think is often an obstacle to what could be a rewarding action.

KEEP THE CHANNELS OPEN

When your child is broadcasting on Channels S, F, H, L, or A, we urge you to put your crystal ball aside and use the three "teenager" steps to *keep the channels open.* There are three rules to follow:

1. Listen more.
2. Withhold judgment longer.
3. Ask questions that stimulate your teenager's decision making.

We have compiled into a chart some questions that we have found useful for encouraging teenagers' decision making. Let's take a look at how some of these questions can be used with your child.

Open Channel S (I need support)

Father: You look a bit down. How was that exam?

Malcom: I've never had a test like that. Those questions on figuring out the taxes were unbelievable. I'll probably get a D if I'm lucky.

Father: That's disappointing, all right. What's your goal for the class? How well would you like to do?

Malcom: I'd like to get at least a B.

Father: Uh-huh.

Malcom: You know, I bet I still can, depending on how the grading is done.

Father: Sounds like the grades were all probably lower than usual.

Malcom: I'm going to check on it tomorrow with Mr. Block.

In this example, Malcom is a good student who had a temporary setback. His father was supportive and helped Malcom see the big picture—beyond the single exam to the overall course. With his goal fine-tuned, Malcom was ready to take an active stance and talk to his teacher. His father opened the Support channel, and Malcom responded.

Open Channel H (I need help)

Nicole: I've had it! That's it! Forget it!

Mother: What's going on?

Nicole: When will I ever need Spanish? I'm going to see my guidance counselor. Mrs. Rosen will switch me to something else, I know she will.

Mother: It seems as if you've been working on the Spanish for a long time.

Nicole: Over an hour!

Mother: What exactly are you doing? I'd like to see.

Nicole: Don't bother—what a waste.

Mother: No, really. I'd like to get a better idea of what they're asking you.

Nicole: All right. Here, see?

Mother: This *does* look hard. How do you try to figure out which tense to use?

Nicole: I just look at these examples.

TABLE 7
QUESTIONS YOU CAN ASK TO
HELP KEEP THE CHANNELS OPEN

To help your child think about these *decision-making steps:*	Consider asking your child questions like these:
1. Look for signs of different feelings.	1. How are you feeling? Am I right in thinking your voice sounds a bit nervous?
2. Tell yourself what the problem is.	2. What would you say is the problem?
3. Decide on your goal.	3. What do you want to have happen? What's your goal in doing that?
4. Stop and think of as many solutions to the problem as you can.	4. What are all the different ways you can think of to reach your goal?
5. For each solution, think of all the things that might happen next.	5. If you _____, what might happen? What do you think might happen if you do that? What else?
6. Choose your best solution.	6. Which of your ideas do you think is best for you? Which idea has the best chance of meeting your goal?
7. Plan it and make a final check.	7. What will have to happen so you can carry out your idea? What do you think could possibly go wrong or block your plan?
8. Try it and rethink it.	8. What happened when you tried out your plan? What did you learn that might help you next time?

Mother: Is there anything else I could try—those examples don't seem too helpful.

Nicole: Yeah, I guess not. I probably should have tried something else, or . . . I know! We have a handout that I bet would help.

Nicole's mom recognized that help was needed. Nicole's initial outburst was one of frustration. Her mom showed she was interested, concerned, and understanding. Notice how she asked how she, the mother, could get help besides using the examples. She was encouraging Nicole to *rethink* her actions and try something else, and Nicole recognized she was stuck on an ineffective approach for too long a time. By keeping the crystal ball in the closet and by not passing judgment, Nicole's mother kept the Help channel open and stimulated her daughter's thinking and problem solving.

Open Channel F (I need to save face)

Grover: I am so embarrassed!

Ernie: What happened?

Grover: I was serving food in the cafeteria and a bug flew right by me and I got scared and dropped my tray.

Mom: Anything break?

Grover: Mom, you don't understand. The food landed right on the principal, Dr. Molloy.

Ernie: Oh, man, really! That's hysterical. Food-face Molloy! And he always wears fancy suits and shirts. What'd you do to him? Did they fire you?

Dad: Ernie, that's enough. What happened next, Grover?

Grover: Everyone laughed at me. And Dr. Molloy wiped off his face . . .

Ernie: His face? All right!

Grover: And asked me to come to his office. He was really mad. He took me back to the kitchen staff and said I couldn't serve for a month. Well, I can't go back there tomorrow. They'll laugh at me and I'll feel terrible.

Mom: I can see that. But what else will happen if you don't go back?

Grover: I would lose my service credits—and I need those to graduate!

Mom: Maybe we can work on ways to handle the teasing you'll get when you go back . . .

Grover showed everyone that he had a weakness. And one of his "victims" was quite unsympathetic. But his mother helped him realize that he couldn't just withdraw—there were negative consequences if he did. So she began to engage him in thinking of some alternative ways to handle the teasing he would almost certainly get. But the Face-saving channel was opened by Grover's mother showing that the consequences of his avoiding or withdrawing from the problem were worse than the costs of coping. Once the channel was open, decision making could begin anew.

Open Channel L (Please listen to me)

Mom: Hi, Peter!

Peter: Hi.

Mom: How was your day at school?

Peter: Oh, it was fine, I guess.

Mom: Mmm. What were some of the good parts?

Peter: Nothing much, really. Gym was okay. Lunch was good—they had pickles and soup.

Mom: Great! Sounds like a regular day.

Peter: Yeah, sort of.

Mom: Was there any part of school that wasn't so good?

Peter: No, not really. Well . . . no, not really.

Mom: It sounds like you're not very sure.

Peter: No, I'm, uh, well . . .

Mom: I think you have to decide whether or not you're going to talk about what happened today. You can talk to me or you can talk to someone else or you can not talk at all. I guess it depends on what the problem is.

Peter: It's, uh, well, I think I'd like to join the Army.

Mom: (struggling to Get Calm!) Well! I'd like to hear what happened today that had something to do with the Army.

Peter: In assembly there were some officers . . .

Peter's mom recognized the signs of a Channel L broadcast. She asked some general questions about his day until he sounded particularly uncertain. Then she commented on his uncertainty without making a judgment or losing patience. Next she encouraged Peter to choose *his best* solution —decision-making step 6. Since only Peter had the facts, it was his decision as to what to do. She simply brought the matter to a *choice*, rather than have the conversation continue in the unproductive way it had been going. Because she had *kept the channels open*, Peter felt comfortable making his revelation. And because his mother's answer was nonjudgmental and calm, he felt comfortable revealing even more. If Channel L was closed, it's very hard to say what might have happened. Clearly, especially with teenagers and all that occurs in their lives and all that goes on in their minds, *open channels give parents a fighting chance to stay connected with their children.*

Open Channel A (I'm looking for an argument)

Sally: What an ugly tie.

Dad: Really? I've worn it before . . .

Sally: What's this?

Dad: Eggs, scrambled the way you like them!

Sally: Are you kidding? Those eggs are runny. I'm gagging just looking at them. You sure don't cook like Mom did.

Dad: Hmm.

Sally: Did you make your mud coffee again? How can anyone drink that slop . . . weird.

Dad: Sally, what is it that you want to have happen?

Sally: What?

Dad: What are you trying to accomplish by talking that way to me?

Sally: I'm not trying to do anything.

Dad: Do you want me to answer to anything you've said?

Sally: No, I don't care. Well, yes. Well . . . uh, I don't know.

Dad: You've got school and I have work. But we'd better talk about this tonight. I don't like what's going on. Something must be bothering you.

Sally: Look, Dad, I gotta go. I'm going to finish getting ready.

Sally was spoiling for an argument. One can detect a hint of resentment about mother's not being in the household anymore. Regardless, her father recognized the messages on Channel A. He did not plunge in by responding to Sally's comments or by becoming insulted and showing anger. Rather, he tried to focus Sally on her *goal* and on exactly what she wanted him to say or do. This strategy broke the cycle of angry comments by Sally because she had to *stop and think.* Then her father followed by stating his intent to talk to her about "real" matters of concern later. He didn't need Sally to say yes. He knew he was successful in *keeping the channels of communication open.*

Keeping the Channels
Open in Handling
Everyday Problems with Your Teenager:
Decisions and Directions About the Future

The teenage years are a transition between childhood and adulthood. In the Miller household, seventeen-year-old Joan is facing many decisions. College? Business? Marriage? Travel? What kind of adult would she be? She has two very different groups of friends. One is "precollege." The other is "noncollege" but also nonfocused. The latter isn't as concerned with grades as the precollege group, and they let Joan know what they think of her studying. Joan's twelve-year-old sister, Diana, is still in middle school. She has her own problems, but they don't seem as serious to Joan as decisions faced by a seventeen year old. Her parents are separated and she lives with her mother now.

Marge Miller is forty-two years old and works as a real estate agent. She feels her parents never really gave her enough direction as a teenager, and so she tries to provide Joan with guidance. We use the word "guidance" because in the past Marge had been more directive with Joan and Joan resisted bitterly. The relationship between Marge and Joan deteriorated quite a bit. Gradually Marge found the decision-making approach useful in giving her another way to relate to Joan. Marge was able to give guidance and be supportive and encouraging. She found that Joan started making some decisions that pleasantly surprised her, and so she continued to *keep the channels open* whenever she could. Her husband, Harold, who is fifty-one, could never support any decision that did not include college and graduate school of some kind. His job, as a service manager in an auto repair store, involved long hours and hard work. He didn't want to see Joan or Diana have to take this kind of a hard road. Now, though, his involvement in the family was cut down a great deal.

Let's take a look at their Parenting Family Tree and then join the Millers for a dinnertime conversation.

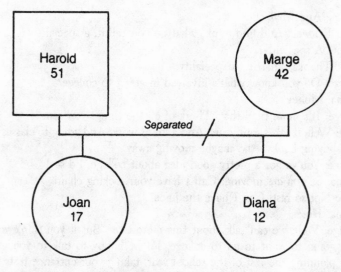

Diana: Can I have some chicken?

Marge: Sure. Joan, I got a letter from your guidance counselor today about college entrance exams.

Joan: Oh. My math teacher mentioned it also.

Marge: What do you think?

Joan: I don't know.

Marge: It's hard to make choices like this. It's not like picking a salad dressing or an ice-cream flavor!

Diana: No way! Are you gonna go away, Joanie?

Joan: I don't know. The more I think about it, the more confused I get.

Marge: If you could be doing anything you want five years from now, what would it be? Try it, picture yourself—how you'd look, where you'd be, how you'd feel.

Marge was trying an interesting way of helping Joan decide on her goal. Picturing the future—and getting the mental picture sharp and detailed—can be very useful for teenagers. As the conversation continued, Joan was able to see herself as a teacher, either in a college or in an elementary school. She described warm feelings being around young children and satisfaction at "seeing" her college students learn.

Marge: To be a teacher, what will you have to do?

Joan: Go to college.

Marge: And what else?

Joan: Do well. And find a, uh, what do you call it, a special topic . . .

Diana: A speciality.

Joan: Thanks, smartie. A speciality.

Marge: Do you know what's involved in going to college?

Diana: Money.

Marge: It's more than that. Think of all the things you can.

Joan: Well, it takes four years. And a lot of work. And going to classes and buying books. And maybe moving away.

Marge: You've got a pretty good idea about college, I'd say!

Diana: So you *are* moving! Can I have your rocking chair?

Joan: Not so fast! Can I have the juice?

Diana: Here.

Marge: Well, we can talk about this more later. But if you think you're going to want to go to college, I'd be happy to talk to you about planning the rest of the school year, taking your entrance tests, and maybe finding out about a college for teachers.

Joan: Yeah. Well, I'd like to keep talking about it. I'm going to try to see what else I can picture in the future for myself, too.

Perhaps a decision has been made, or perhaps not. But we hope you noticed how Marge *acknowledged and accepted* Joan's statements and used the *decision-making steps* and the *keeping the channels open* questions to help Joan feel comfortable talking about her big decision. Marge is *facilitating Joan's careful thinking, building Joan's confidence* in herself, and *building Joan's identity as a decision maker and problem solver.* These are gifts which will last Joan a lifetime. In addition, the decision-making approach can help the Miller family go through the many decisions and changes of the teenage years with less upheaval and with greater cohesion and communication.

Decision-Making Digest

We have taken a brief journey through some issues and problems that face teenagers and their parents. Our decision-making steps can be quite helpful with teenagers. However, we've found that parents can be most successful at encouraging sound decision making by their children if they *keep the channels of communication open.* This involves:

1. putting aside one's crystal ball
2. recognizing certain messages that are most frequently broadcast by adolescents
3. listening carefully
4. withholding judgment
5. asking questions that stimulate decision-making thinking
6. paying special attention to the three decision-making steps that are most useful during the teenage years: 3 (decide on your goal); 6 (choose *your best* solution); and 8 (try it and rethink it).

Throughout this chapter, we've seen the methods used by a number of different families to make decisions and keep the channels open. We hope that some of these examples will be helpful to you as you prepare your child to emerge from the teenage years as a healthy, thoughtful adult decision maker.

12

Decision Making with Children
Needing Special, Long-Term Care

Parenting a "special" child, that is, a child with a disability, is in many ways just like parenting any other child. But it is also a unique experience. Every child and family has general growth and development problems, but these "special" families also face an additional variety of problematic situations, including special education placements, coping with the physical limitations of a child's chronic problem, and learning to accept the varied feelings that being "different" creates. The impact of these issues on children and their families cannot be underestimated. The decision-making process reflects a belief that *all* children can learn to feel that they can actively cope with their difficulties. Children with chronic problems can often be involved in making choices and taking responsibility for necessary tasks in a way that increases their own feelings of self-worth and competence. For example, the child with insulin dependent diabetes mellitus (more commonly known as diabetes) who is encouraged to administer his or her own insulin or plan his or her diet generally feels more control over the situation and feels better about himself or herself. This may result in improvements in physical health as well. The child who experiences repeated hospitalizations can use the decision-making approach to increase coping and to understand as much as possible about the situation.

This chapter begins with an overview of the challenges involved in parenting a special child, with particular attention paid to the readiness skills in Chapter 3 and to steps 1, 3, and 4. First, we discuss ways to read the Feelings Fingerprints of special children and then help them to understand their own feelings. Parents know that children with long-term problems face all of the ups and downs of growing up plus *additional* hurdles.

These children can have many conflicting feelings about themselves and their chronic problem. As they learn to recognize their feelings, they can resolve some of the uncertainties. They can then gain perspective and channel their energy more effectively with the help of readiness and decision-making steps. The next important tasks are to help children keep track of their own behavior and learn that they can have a direct effect on meeting their goals. As children see this connection, they can be encouraged to stay involved with self-care, and to meet the difficulties they face with as much confidence as possible.

This chapter will focus on case examples of three children with long-term health problems. Vanessa, who needs major surgery, Johnny, who has diabetes, and Pete, who has some learning problems. These children and their families have some issues in common—they all must cope with changes in health and daily life, new and difficult tasks that must be mastered, and their many and varied feelings as well as those of other family members and friends. There are also differences among the three cases. Vanessa and Pete's problems developed over time but Johnny's diabetes began suddenly. Johnny will have to constantly monitor his diabetes, Vanessa will have major surgery almost immediately, and then her condition will stabilize. Pete's learning problems may affect his career choices. However, in spite of the differences, these children and their families, as well as children with other chronic problems have something important in common: by using the decision-making steps, children can be helped to see the connection between solving daily problems effectively and long-term medical consequences. The importance of *all* family members considering alternatives in coping with and managing the many troublesome situations that occur is discussed. It is hard to imagine parents providing a more meaningful and lasting contribution to their "special" children's welfare than helping them to recognize and face their feelings, set their own goals, and learn to think about how to meet those goals. The decision-making skills discussed in this book can contribute to a child's sense of well-being, and successful management of difficult tasks.

CASE EXAMPLE: VANESSA'S FAMILY NEEDS A DECISION-MAKING STRATEGY TO COPE WITH HER SURGERY

Vanessa is twelve years old. She and her parents have just been told by a specialist that Vanessa needs to have major surgery. Vanessa's health problem was first detected by the family physician about six months ago. Since then the doctor has been checking her about once a month, as her condition has steadily worsened. Vanessa and her family have just found out that she must have the operation. How will they handle it? This is Vanessa's Parenting Family Tree

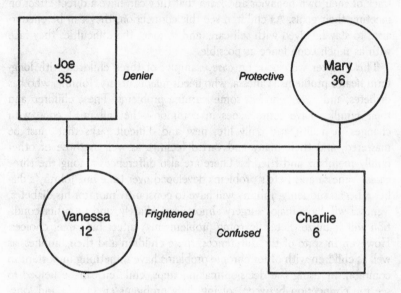

Vanessa doesn't understand what is happening. She knows that her health has been getting worse because she has been feeling tired, having trouble running, and sometimes gets out of breath very quickly. Other children seem to be able to do things that she cannot do. She has tried to talk to her parents but they haven't been able to tell her anything that helps. They seem frightened and their fear makes it harder for Vanessa. Vanessa's mother, trying to protect her, tells her that worrying about surgery and hospitalization is a grown-up problem, that she and Vanessa's dad will handle it, and that Vanessa "should not think about it." Vanessa begins to have nightmares and do badly in school. She picks on her younger brother, Charlie, more and more frequently. She is jealous of him because he is not sick and can run faster than she can even though he's younger. Vanessa's parents fight and she hears her name mentioned in their arguments. As the time for the surgery grows closer, Vanessa's family is increasingly tense and in turmoil.

CASE EXAMPLE:
VANESSA'S FAMILY HAS A WAY TO COPE

Consider an alternative version of the story of Vanessa and her family. Vanessa still has the same health problem, which has been steadily increasing in severity and a specialist has recommended surgery. Vanessa is scared about feeling ill and knowing that she has to go into the hospital. Her parents, although also frightened, discuss Vanessa's fears with her. They explain as much as they can, as honestly as they are able to do, about the surgery which Vanessa will undergo. Certainly these talks do not erase the problem or eliminate the stress. But Vanessa's parents have been able to create an environment of open communication at home, allowing family members to be as supportive of each other as possible considering the difficult situation. Vanessa still may have some nightmares, some difficulties in school, and more problems than usual getting along with her brother. It would be unrealistic to expect this to be an easy time for Vanessa or her family. However, certain decision-making techniques can help Vanessa and her family manage during this time of stress.

One of the first things that happened to Vanessa and her parents was that they became aware of having many difficult feelings. Vanessa's parents' first reaction was *denial:* this couldn't possibly be happening to their daughter! Then they felt *anger* that something like this could happen to Vanessa and their family. After the specialist gave them the news, Vanessa's mother felt her stomach tighten into a knot and she realized that she had been clenching her teeth for the past few mintues. Vanessa's mother and father also felt *fear* because the specialist had explained that the surgical procedures he would follow with Vanessa would be risky. Vanessa's mother also felt *guilt* because other people in her family had the same health problem as Vanessa. Although it didn't really make any sense, she somehow felt as if the problem were her fault. Sometimes at work Vanessa's father felt overcome with *sadness* even when he wasn't thinking about Vanessa.

Vanessa, of course, had a lot of feelings, too. She also felt *fear.* She was afraid of being in the hospital, of being away from her family, of having an operation, and all that comes with not really understanding what was happening to her. She felt *angry* also because this disability had happened to her, and *jealousy* because other children seemed to have life easier than she did. Often Vanessa felt *worried* because it was hard to concentrate on her schoolwork and she had trouble sleeping. Sometimes she just felt *confused* because she had so many feelings, many of which she had never felt before, and also because her parents seemed upset. Vanessa felt *uncertain* about what was happening, and whether or not things would ever be the same again.

What plans can Vanessa's family make in order to deal with this crisis in the best way possible? At first Vanessa's parents were numbed by their *feelings:* they were completely overwhelmed and unable to handle the problem. Then Vanessa's parents began to use their decision-making steps to cope. They talked together and *identified the problem.* They were facing a difficult situation, a major operation on their child, and they began to put their *feelings* into words, look at the many *problems* they faced, and talk about *goals* that had to be identified. Vanessa's parents were able to better understand their own and each other's feelings. They were then able to set the three *goals* they felt were the most critical to help them all cope: (a) accomplishing the necessary tasks for Vanessa's health such as scheduling doctors' appointments and blood tests, (b) keeping the family functioning as smoothly as possible, and (c) keeping channels of communication open. Vanessa's parents, by speaking openly and honestly with each other and Vanessa, were able to work together to make a difficult situation more manageable. Again, no one said that it would be easy or without obstacles. But by identifying feelings and establishing goals, Vanessa's parents were able to keep their actions in focus as well as they possibly could under trying and painful circumstances.

HELPING YOURSELF AND YOUR CHILD COPE WITH SPECIAL NEEDS

Vanessa's story illustrates how complicated the feelings and situations are when a child has special needs. Each special situation brings with it unique problems that must be solved. However, there are some elements that are similar in each of the cases discussed and that may be similar to what you and your family experience. One common element is that using decision-making skills can help to reduce some of the stress, conflict, and uncertainty as you try to meet your child's special needs. Let's take a look now at an illness that affects 1.0–2.0 out of each 1,000 children—insulin dependent diabetes mellitus.

**DECISION MAKING
AND DIABETES**

Insulin dependent diabetes mellitus is the medical term for the metabolic disorder where the pancreas stops making insulin with the result that the glucose (blood sugar) the body needs for energy cannot go into the cells and be used. Thus there is too much sugar in the bloodstream and not enough in the cells. Shots of insulin and a careful diet help the body regain balance. Sometimes the balance is not exactly right, and the child may need a change in insulin dosage, a change in diet or exercise. In such a family, children and their parents must constantly make decisions about *things* such as blood and urine tests, dosage levels, and diet, and this situation affects daily living.

Getting any child ready for school in the morning takes a combination of patience and energy, and sometimes a bit of luck! But when your child has regular special needs that must be taken care of, this task becomes more demanding both in terms of the energy and the time required. As children get older they increasingly learn to manage more of their health care themselves, but they still may need a certain amount of help from parents.

What kinds of decisions must a child with diabetes make before beginning the day? Along the lines of our Children's Choices Chart in Chapter 8, here's a sample.

Should I get up and test my blood	or	stay in bed until Dad calls me?
Do I need to change my insulin dosage	or	does my blood test tell me that the dosage is okay?
Am I feeling a little shaky	or	am I feeling okay?
If my insulin needs changing do I change the Regular	or	the NPH (intermediate acting)?
How many units to my dosage do I add	or	by how many units do I lessen it?
Did I measure the insulin correctly	or	should I check it?
When will breakfast be ready so I know when to take my insulin—now	or	in half an hour?

Did I record my glucose level and dosage	or	did I forget?

At which site should I inject my insulin—

arms	or	legs?
left arm (or leg)	or	right arm (or leg)
stomach	or	buttocks?

For breakfast do I have my fruit, grain, and protein balanced in a way that I like	or	can I exchange this banana for some orange juice?
Do I want to follow my diet	or	am I going to "cheat" on my diet?
Have I been "cheating" on my diet a lot lately	or	have I been so careful that I deserve a "treat"?

These are the kinds of questions that a child with diabetes and his or her parents must address each morning and then again two or three times during the day. And these questions come up in addition to other problems:

> Why am I (is my child) urinating too often?
> Why am I (is my child) losing weight?
> Why do I (does my child) seem so lethargic?
> What is diabetes?
> How will we learn everything we need to know about diabetes?
> Will I (my child) die?
> How do we choose a physician?
> Will we ever learn to manage?
> How do we adjust the insulin?
> Why is the diet so complicated?
> How much exercise is optimal for good control?
> What are potential complications of diabetes?
> Since I have (my child has) diabetes will my child (my grandchild) have diabetes too?

These questions and problems in the case of a child with diabetes are different from many of those discussed earlier in the book because they are *nonnegotiable.* That is, more than one with a definite positive consequence is generally *not* available: the insulin must be taken; a diet must be strictly followed; the threat of complications must be addressed. *But* using a problem-solving approach can help your child learn to cope with these issues and questions and deal with implementing a treatment routine. Our eight decision-making steps, beginning with identifying your feelings and the problem and ending with selecting your best solution, trying it and rethinking it, can be comforting allies to help a parent and child get through a morning routine.

HANDLING DIABETES AND RELATIONSHIPS WITH OTHER CHILDREN

Issues such as resolving conflicts with friends and sharing family chores may seem overwhelming when they are combined with the additional pressures of special needs. For example, a child with diabetes must follow a diet that includes a balance of protein, starch, milk, fruit, vegetables, and fats. Many times one or two daily snacks are also included in the diet as a necessary part of control. This diet is one that would be healthy for everyone, but the child with diabetes *must* follow it in order to maintain diabetic control. Managing this and convincing your child to follow such a specific diet are complicated tasks.

Consider the case of ten-year-old Johnny playing at his friend Mike's one afternoon. Johnny has had diabetes for only about a year and has about completed his "honeymoon" period, meaning that his pancreas is no longer producing any insulin *at all*. His glucose level is erratic and his insulin level fluctuates quite a bit. Johnny and Mike have been playing baseball for most of the afternoon and have both used up a lot of energy. Johnny has forgotten his snack.

What are two possible scenes that could take place? In the first one Johnny has not really told his friend Mike very much about his diabetes. Johnny is not yet comfortable with a lot of the physical aspects of his diabetes and he feels a mixture of sadness, anger, and embarrassment about suddenly having all of these special needs. "Why can't I just be like everybody else?" he often asks himself. "Anyway," he says to himself, "I feel okay, so why do I need the snack?" Later he begins to feel shaky, and he knows that this means that he needs to eat something. Then he realizes "Oh no, I left my snack at home on the kitchen table!" He begins to feel really dizzy now and has to sit down. Johnny is really scared! Mike and the other boys rush over but they don't know what to do to help Johnny, and Johnny has begun to feel so irritable and shaky that he has trouble telling them. In this case Mike and the boys do not know what to do to help Johnny; a bad situation because Johnny *does* need help!

How could this scene have happened differently? If Johnny had been able to explain to Mike about his diabetes at an earlier time, Mike could have helped him.

Mike: (worried) Johnny what's wrong?

Johnny: (irritated) I'm just hungry and I have a headache. I feel dizzy.

Mike: (considering the alternatives) Well, Johnny's just exercised a lot, he didn't eat his snack, and lunch was a long time ago. I don't think that he has a cold or the flu or anything. He must be having an *insulin reaction.*

Johnny: (eating Mike's left-over peanut butter sandwich) Thanks, Mike. I'm feeling better.

Johnny and Mike were able to talk this way because their parents had practiced the problem-solving steps with them. Johnny had identified his *feelings* of sadness, anger, and embarrassment and *told himself what the problem was.* His *goal* was to feel comfortable enough to discuss his diabetes with Mike and then do it. The *solution* was to practice until he felt ready to discuss it with Mike. When Johnny tried his plan he found that it was effective. It also made him *feel* more comfortable, and less different from the other kids when they understood his diabetes and were able to help him.

One of the reasons having a child with special needs can be so complicated is the impact this situation has on the whole family. The new routines demand flexibility from everyone. Each family member must learn to adjust to the stress. Since each family member is a separate individual with his or her own unique needs and desires, and his or her own strengths and weaknesses, this adjustment process can be complicated (see Johnny's Parenting Family Tree).

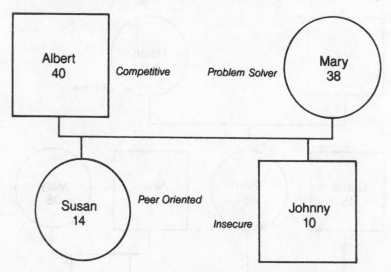

Albert, Johnny's father, is a very competitive, work-oriented business-man. His wife, Mary, is an artist. She typically takes the lead in resolving family problems. Susan, Johnny's sister, is an eighth grader who spends a lot of time with her friends, listening to music, talking on the phone, and less time with her family than she used to. Since his diagnosis of diabetes, Johnny has become much more insecure than he used to be. They all bring such individual characteristics to their family relationships. For example, Albert tends to be pushy when trying to encourage Johnny to administer his own insulin, whereas Mary's natural tendency is to go through her own version of the eight decision-making steps.

In the case of diabetes and other health problems that may appear in the family, we have to consider another kind of family tree besides the usual Parenting Family Tree. Everyone in the family has his or her own personality determining the way in which he or she handles a health problem. The situation is further complicated by whether or not each has the problem himself or herself. Take a look at Johnny's Diabetes Family Tree.

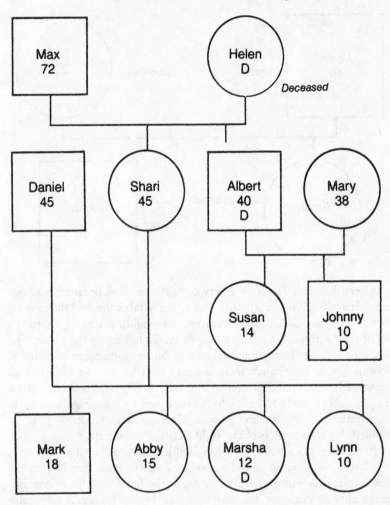

Each family member has his or her own feelings profile, and it affects how each copes with a family member who has diabetes. For example, Albert, Johnny's father, has diabetes and so did Helen, Albert's mother. Albert watched Helen deteriorate over a long, painful period of time—because not much was known about diabetes then. Albert has always kept up on the latest developments and has encouraged Johnny to do the same, a positive point, since Albert tries to be a constructive role model for

Johnny. However, at times he tries too hard. We know from his feelings profile that he tends to be a bit pushy—and Johnny often perceives his "help" as more of a "hassle." Mary tends to take a problem-solving approach toward helping Johnny with his diabetes. This is helpful, but sometimes it's hard for her to fully understand because she doesn't have diabetes and so has not experienced the feelings and physical problems herself.

Susan worries about her brother and tries to help him, but she is absorbed in being a teenager and doesn't always have the time. Johnny seems to be able to talk with his cousin Marsha, who is close to him in age and who also has diabetes. This is helpful since they have had many of the same diabetes-related feelings and experiences. Mary is also able to get some help and support from her sister-in-law, Shari, who is Marsha's mother. Thus, problem solving with diabetes involves feelings, situations, and whether or not a person has diabetes. Each person in the family has strengths and weaknesses that sometimes clash and sometimes work together.

SCOLIOSIS: VANESSA'S FAMILY GETS BAD NEWS

Vanessa has scoliosis, or curvature of the spine. As she was growing and getting taller, her spinal column began to curve into an S shape. When you look at her you can see that her shoulders are a little uneven, and one of her shoulder blades sticks out a little. Some children have a slight curve in their back which doesn't require treatment, or they may have trouble with their backs later on as adults. Other people have such a large curve that it must be corrected so they don't become "hunchbacked," and so their internal organs (lungs, stomach, and so on) don't become too cramped. This is the case with Vanessa. She and her parents have just been told that Vanessa's curvature of the spine is too pronounced to go untreated. What kind of decisions have been made up until now and what must be decided for the future?

Is Vanessa's complaint of shortness of breath a health problem	or	because she has been playing hard or is tired?
Should she be checked immediately	or	in a few months at her regular checkup?
Do we go ahead with what the pediatrician suggests	or	get a second opinion?

Should we see a specialist	and	if so, who?
When can the specialist see Vanessa	and	can we both get off work that day?
Should we go ahead with the surgery	or	not?
Do we want that specialist to do the surgery	or	someone closer to home?
Have we made the best decision	or	have we forgotten to consider something important?
Should we register Vanessa for the preoperative program	or	handle it ourselves?
Is there a support group where we can meet other families in a similar situation to ours	and	would this be helpful?
What are the tasks that must be accomplished (X rays, blood tests, office visits) before	and	what is the best way to get them accomplished?

VANESSA'S SURGERY

Helping Vanessa face surgery is different from helping Johnny learn to handle his diabetes. Johnny's diabetes is *chronic*—it is a lifelong condition. He must learn concrete skills such as insulin injection, blood testing, and dietary planning. His diabetes may be adversely affected at times throughout his life by illness or psychological stress. He may make some trips to the hospital; his health will always have to be carefully monitored. Vanessa's physical condition is *acute*—it requires onetime corrective surgery. Although her symptoms have steadily worsened, the surgery should end this deterioration of her health. She will have some discomfort or limitations afterward, but her condition will be known almost immediately and may not change much over time. Both children will have some feelings about their conditions that they may need time to understand, depending on their particular health needs, and individual personalities. Each child's condition includes a variety of problems, some of which the children have in common, and some of which differ. Using the problem-solving steps can help the two families deal more effectively with their own situations.

The eight problem-solving steps can be useful to Vanessa's family as they begin work through all of these questions. Each of these *problems* involves many *feelings*. The *goal* is for Vanessa's family to choose from the many possible *solutions* and select the ones with which they feel the most comfortable. The problems that have been already outlined are critical for Vanessa's parents to resolve since they involve Vanessa's life, and her feelings and suggestions should be an integral part of the decision-making process. Earlier in this chapter we saw how the way Vanessa handles the situation is affected by how much of a partner Vanessa is in the decision-making process. Research has shown that people are much more positive about their lives when they are given an understanding of their situation and some control over the decisions affecting them. For example, given information and choices, Vanessa may feel less fearful before surgery, be more cooperative while in the hospital, and recover more quickly after surgery.

Here is an excerpt of what the conversation with Vanessa and her parents could be like:

Mom: Vanessa, your dad and I would like to discuss what the specialist said this morning. How do you feel about what he said?

Vanessa: (crying) I don't want to do it.

Dad: Well, honey, we don't want you to have to do it either, but let's go over the different options he explained and discuss each one.

Mom: Let's see, he mentioned a brace.

Dad: But that might work only temporarily.

Vanessa: Well, I don't want to do that because I might end up having to get the operation anyway.

Dad: He also said that we could wait and see if your spine became more curved, and we could reconsider this again in six months.

Vanessa: Or the other choice was to do it sooner.

Dad: Right, he said that since he felt the surgery really would need to be performed, we could do it now, get it over with, and get you back on your feet.

Mom: What do you think about each of these possible solutions?

This is an oversimplification of an extremely complex situation. However, it serves as an example of how an honest and complete presentation of a problem permits a child to feel like an equal partner in a decision concerning her life.

Vanessa's parents can also help her by keeping the channels of communication open, and by being as approachable as possible to Vanessa so she feels she can come to them with questions. Helping Vanessa get ready for surgery involves helping her understand as much as she is able to about the procedure itself, how she will feel physically, what limitations or restrictions she will have to live with, if any, and how to cope with all of the fear, anxiety, or depression which she may feel.

Vanessa will be out of school for brief periods to have lab tests run and to see physicians before her surgery, and again when she is in the hospital. So she will need to get caught up on the work that she misses. She won't be feeling well for a while after her surgery, but when she begins to feel better she will need a tutor. She will be in a body brace for six to ten months after her surgery and will need to be careful not to overexert herself or trip and fall. When she is able to go back to school she will need to be excused from physical education classes, may need special transportation arrangements for getting back and forth to school, and may need to have a classmate accompany her when she changes classes to avoid being jostled in the hall.

HANDLING INTERACTIONS WITH OTHERS

Clearly, Vanessa and her parents will be doing some negotiating with many different people. For example, Vanessa's school system needs to be notified that she will need to have special arrangements made to be out of school and to be tutored for a while. Since children are often sensitive to being treated differently, these contacts will have to be planned carefully. Vanessa and her parents can use the decision-making steps to handle this situation. A sample conversation follows:

Dad: Vanessa, how would you like to handle notifying your school that you are going to be out for a while because of your surgery?

Vanessa: I don't know.

Dad: Well, let's think about what the options are. Your mom and I could call your teacher.

Vanessa: Or maybe you could just write a letter.

Dad: Let's think about that and see if it would be a good decision.

Vanessa: That wouldn't be too good. It would seem like it wasn't too important and she might not understand all of the details.

Dad: So, what do you suggest?

Vanessa: Let's all go in together and I'll explain the operation to the teacher.

In this way Vanessa's parents have made her a competent partner in decisions that affect her life. They have begun the decision-making process as a family unit, and Vanessa has taken the lead in saying that she will explain the surgical procedure to her teacher. The family will face many more decision points like this, using the problem-solving approach to find solutions that will make Vanessa feel more confident in her ability to face the difficult days ahead.

LEARNING DIFFICULTIES

Everyone wants his or her child to do well in school. Many children will have times when schoolwork seems more difficult and they perform less well. For other children school is difficult right from the beginning. Some of these children may have shown signs of problems before they begin school. At ages when their peers are quite comfortable with these skills, some children may seem physically awkward—have trouble riding a bike; not be able to draw, hold a pencil, or say the alphabet; have difficulty following directions; seem not to hear when spoken to; have speech or other related problems. For a child with these learning difficulties, this new experience of school may be overwhelming. These children may not be able to read, spell, write, copy from the blackboard, add, remember facts, understand directions or may have other similar difficulties. Upsetting to a child, these problems may lead to behavior problems at home or school.

At first it may seem as if a child with learning problems is merely immature, or growing a little too slowly. It is common to hope that the child will "grow out of it." A number of children do indeed have slight lags in their development which even out over time. Some other children, however, may never catch up to their classmates. These children may have more and more trouble with school. As a result of this trouble, the child may feel unhappy, frustrated, angry, bewildered, or some combination of these feelings. It may become uncomfortable for the child to sit in the classroom because he or she is unable to work well; teasing from peers can become an issue; and nervous habits such as nightmares, bed-wetting, and nail-biting may occur.

RESPONDING TO THE NEWS:
WHAT DOES IT ALL MEAN?

Eventually it becomes apparent that a child may have a difficulty that does not seem to go away and appears to be growing more and more unmanageable. If this situation emerges in your family, you may feel very frightened. Your child's teacher or school may suggest that you have him or her evaluated by the specialists in the school or at a nearby medical or testing center.

As you may already know, an evaluation involves a series of tests and interviews with a number of new professionals (learning consultant, audiologist, psychologist) who use unfamiliar concepts (neurologically impaired, perceptual deficit, speech impediment, verbal performance, motor skills).

You will be asked to think about a lot of new (and possibly overwhelming) information that has been gathered about your child. Important decisions may be necessary concerning your child's future. Although there are professionals to assist you in the decision-making process, parents often feel alone as they are confronted with a lot of "facts" such as test scores and recommendations used as the basis for these decisions. *Using the decision-making approach can help to isolate the important issues.* The steps can help parents decide how to use the available information to make the best choice possible for their child. Let's see how this can occur.

Specialist: Yes, Mrs. O'Garr, it looks as if we will have to recommend a special class placement for Michael.

Mrs. O'Garr: Special class? What did his tests show?

Specialist: He manifested the behavioral and neurological signs of a child with some minor cerebral dysfunction. This affects his visual motor integration and the way he processes information, resulting in his current difficulties in learning to read.

Mrs. O'Garr now feels her hands trembling and she notices that her palms are moist. These are *signs of stressful, frightened feelings.* While she does not know exactly what these details mean, she does know that this situation is one in which she can turn to her decision-making steps. First she starts to breathe slowly and steadily while she prepares to consider the alternatives with the specialist and plan a strategy for reaching a final goal.

Mrs. O'Garr: Are you telling me that my son has a reading problem because there's something wrong with his brain?

Specialist: No, it's not quite like that. It's more like a gap in communication between his brain and the rest of his body.

Mrs. O'Garr: I'm still not sure I understand. Tell me more about it.

Mrs. O'Garr used a valuable skill—she identified her most confusing feelings and set about defining the problem so the specialist could explain everything clearly. After all, a *major goal* is to make a clear decision about the question: *"What does it mean for my child?"* Another *goal* is to gather information that relates to this question: *"What can be done about this?"* Listen to how Mrs. O'Garr and the specialist *consider different alternatives:*

Mrs. O'Garr: What options do I have for helping Michael reach his fullest potential?

Specialist: One option would be to have him repeat the grade he's in so that it may be easier for him to catch up.

Mrs. O'Garr: This might be difficult for him since all of his friends will be moving on to the next grade.

Specialist: We may want to consider having him spend part of the day in a special classroom where he can receive more individualized attention.

Mrs. O'Garr: What sorts of possibilities for that would there be in his school?

In this way the specialist and Mrs. O'Garr explore the various options for her son in order to help him cope with his difficulties.

HANDLING INTERACTIONS WITH OTHER CHILDREN

One of the most difficult situations a child can face is that of feeling different from the other children. When a child has problems in school it becomes public—other children in the classroom see what is happening and can talk among themselves, adding to the child's trouble. A child who is already having school problems must also cope with not having much privacy—"everybody" knows what's going on. Other children often tease or ridicule a child who is different.

These situations are a real threat to a child's self-concept or self-esteem —the way a child feels about himself or herself. We know that how a person feels about himself or herself comes through in just about everything that person does. So if a child is already having school problems, these problems can affect the child's self-concept and, eventually, his or her motivation to work toward the goal of reaching his or her potential. Research has shown that when children receive emotional support from parents, teachers, and peers, some of these negative feelings can be overcome. Having support from friends can be particularly important; but sometimes, this is not easy to achieve.

How can parents help their child with learning problems find a way to deal effectively with the reactions of peers? Imagine that Pete (age eight) is a youngster in your neighborhood who has to repeat the second grade because he has been having difficulty with most of his subjects. He has been tested by the school specialists, and they found that Pete has some areas of weakness. But he also has the ability to overcome most of these lags in the best way possible for him if he gets some extra help.

Pete's parents are happy that the test results show that Pete has some abilities that can be developed. But they are also distressed that his school problems have become serious, and he has been teased terribly by a child in his class, Joe.

Pete has finally told his parents that Joe has been picking on him at school. They have helped him *find the signs of all of his feelings* of distress, fear, sadness, and apprehension. The problem has been identified as Pete's being teased by Joe, and the *goal* is to put an end to it. *Several possible solutions* were written down by Pete and his parents when they talked about it: to call Joe names too, to beat him up, to ignore him, or to try to talk with him.

Pete and his parents have carefully thought about the alternatives and decided on the best one: they enlisted the help of Pete's best friend, Mark. Pete and Mark are going to approach Joe to speak with him. They are going to tell Joe that Pete is having a few problems with school, but that he does some things really well also. They are going to remind Joe about the time that Joe himself failed a math test, but did well in spelling. How would Joe have felt if he had been teased about the math test and the fact that he cried on the way home? They plan to explain to him that just as this would have made Joe feel bad, it makes Pete feel bad. Perhaps with the help of the problem-solving steps, Mark and Pete can help work out this problem with Joe.

As Pete changes classes and makes progress in school he can use his decision-making skills again and again. Each time he is confronted with a difficulty in school or with his various teachers and classes, Pete can choose to focus on his goals and resolve his problems by using the decision-making process. As he grows older, he will become better and better at problem solving.

Decision-Making Digest

We all want to have happy, healthy, successful children. We all look forward to having children who will meet life's challenges head on and come up as winners. Many times we hope that the difficulties and problems we have faced in our own childhood will not trouble our children.

In addition we are constantly bombarded by the media with images of the "perfect" or "ideal" American family, influencing us into actually believing at times that there really is some "perfect" family ideal. Our idealized notion of what our families "should" be like gets especially threatened when we learn that our child has a need, condition, or disease that makes him or her "special" and different. It's helpful to remember that *all* families are confronted with problems. The key, we feel, is to develop a thinking strategy that will help all of our loved ones confidently and successfully negotiate life's challenges.

Being a parent of a child with special long-term needs requires adjustment. It is a big responsibility. The child needs his or her parents to help him or her adjust to school problems, peer difficulties, having a chronic physical condition, needing surgery, or any other problem. But parents have feelings about their child's difficulties and they need time, energy, and their own problem-solving skills to work this out for themselves. The way a parent comes to terms with his or her own feelings about the child greatly influences the way the child handles the situation.

It is easy to say "accept your family as it is," but it is not so easily done. Research has shown that the process of acceptance follows a pattern of stages. During the process of acceptance our feelings change, and we often have the perception that the world changes as well. Our goal and the plans we make to reach these goals generally change as the process of adjustment continues.

We have found in our work with families and children that using the decision-making approach we have discussed throughout the book can be helpful during the process of adjustment. In this chapter, three different long-term conditions have been considered—diabetes, scoliosis, and learning problems. These and other long-term health conditions all require an adjustment and acceptance period for the child and parents. They all require the family to carry out certain activities that may be difficult and new to them, and to cope with changing routines, changing relationships with friends, and with working with many different professionals. Parents of children who have health problems not specifically mentioned in this chapter can, we are certain, see similarities to the case examples discussed. While the details of each particular situation may change, what we feel will *not* change is that the problem-solving approach can be a tool you can rely on as you and your family cope. We have seen it help with many families, including our own.

13

Decision Making and Your Child's Education

Sometimes we can get passive and think that once our children enter school, decision making about their education is mostly out of our hands. Certainly that isn't so. Schools and teachers have the responsibility to teach many children simultaneously. Moreover, they work with each child for a limited period of time. Parents, however, have a long-term contract with their children. A major part of the contract involves taking care of them so they can get the most out of school and learn the skills they will need to effectively deal with a computerized, high-technology age. Complex technologies may require new teaching approaches, such as learning from computers. But learning itself is still a very individual and human event. And although computers can be added to classrooms, and curricula —the learning plans and materials that teachers use—can be updated, learning to cope depends on *human* interactions. *How* our children learn in school is as important as what they learn, and parents are key participants in the process.

For the purpose of this chapter, think of yourself as a *collaborator*, someone who works together with other teaching adults to enhance what your child learns. You can assist your child's learning efforts in two ways: within the home and going to school. In the home you can care for your children's basic human needs, show them you care about them, and provide a place for them to do their homework. By going to your child's school you can exchange information, ask questions and cooperatively work with teachers to help your child do the best at learning. You support your learner by being attuned to daily successes and tough times, by preparing for challenges in periods of transition from one age and grade to the next, and by collaborating with teachers and school resource people. Collaborators are people who can mesh their own goals with the goals of others. Your goals as a parent will not always be the same as a teacher's goals and a teacher's goals won't always perfectly match your child's goals. But collaborators can work as a team and also independently to promote successful learning for students. Once educational collaborators have a strategy for getting started on, noticing, and sorting out goals, they can create opportunities for children to do their best at learning. This chapter illustrates ways that a decision-making approach can help you to enhance your child's education.

Case Example: Steve and His Family Need a Strategy for Starting School

Beginning a new school can provide a challenge to a student at any age. Children will send out signs of different feelings that parents can tune into and use to help prepare the student. The problem may be knowing how to get started, and this is where the decision-making steps can help.

Picture two families with young sons ready to enter kindergarten. It is the end of the summer. The boys are friends and went to the same neighborhood nursery school. Both sets of moms and dads attended parent meetings to try to learn about the new school. But there was uncertainty at the school about who would teach kindergarten and there was no opportunity for the children to visit the class ahead of time. The boys' names are Joshua and Steve. They happen to live on different floors of the same three-story apartment house. Joshua has a younger sister, Robin, and Steve is an only child. Use your imagination to help fill in the details— perhaps you can picture some family you have known in a situation like this.

A predicament surfaced the night before school was to open. Steve's family had kept busy throughout the weekend, with little mention of the upcoming opening of school. When bedtime approached, there was an unusual outburst of crying and flailing on the floor from the usually quiet son, Steve, as he sobbed about the new school and not wanting to go. "What's going on with Steve?" "I don't know—I've never seen anything like this. My head is pounding and my mouth is so dry—what's happening here?"

The outburst had surprised Steve's mother and made her even more

anxious. Her own feelings were confusing her. She felt that she was supposed to feel happy that her son was going off to kindergarten, but she also
felt she didn't know enough about the new school. Now her son was
crying that he didn't want to go—and she was really worried. The school
building looked like a fortress to her. There was a high brick wall all
around the asphalt yard and the school itself sat on the corner of a busy,
noisy city street. She wondered what would happen once Steve got inside
—he's only five, after all. All these thoughts and feelings washed over her
like a giant ocean wave.

Then Steve's dad moved into action. Although he looked puzzled by
Steve's crying and flailing, he announced that it was time for bed and
scooped his son off the floor and into his bed. The rest of the night was
mostly sleepless for everyone. But finally morning came. As you can imagine, the opening day of school was fairly tense for Steve and his family.
And the tension didn't lift, even after a few weeks.

Case Example: Joshua and His Family Are Ready for School

The weekend before the opening of kindergarten, Joshua's parents had
been talking with him about the new school so he would feel more confident.

Joshua's parents had noticed that as the summer ended, *they were feeling a little anxious and excited* about their son going off to kindergarten.
They used the decision-making steps to *tell themselves what the problem
was.* Here's a sample of one of their family conversations:

Mother: I've been thinking about your new school.
Joshua: (Looks at his mom and smiles broadly.)
Mother: I know you've been thinking about school too.
Joshua: When do I go?
Mother: Monday—in four days. We'll all walk you there, Robin too.

Joshua's parents had talked over the situation and used the decision-
making approach to *consider alternatives* for *choosing the best way* to help
Joshua feel prepared for the opening day of kindergarten. They knew that
Joshua had his own feelings about the situation and they paid attention to
the signals he was sending. His mom and dad also decided that in order to
remain calm for the event, they needed to keep the weekend activities

manageable, to take time to talk with Joshua and show him their confidence that he could handle the opening day at kindergarten.

"CASETALK": A CLOSER LOOK AT THE TWO FAMILIES

When the opening morning of kindergarten came, Steve and Joshua walked off to school with their dads and moms alongside. Joshua's little sister, Robin, tagged close behind the boys as Joshua smiled broadly. Steve still looked unsure of himself. Both boys entered the classroom and made it through the opening day.

What you may have noticed was that Joshua's family read their Feelings Fingerprints and knew they were a little anxious about the school situation. They sorted out their feelings and used a strategy to choose the best alternative for starting school on a positive note.

Steve's family also felt tension about the first day of kindergarten, building up to Steve's Sunday night crying episode, which left them more worried than relieved. They were stuck—victims of goal paralysis. It was hard for them to determine how they could best help their son prepare for the opening of kindergarten. Noticing feelings and putting what is happening into words can help parents make the most of educational experiences for their children. This is part of Sorting It Out, a technique we introduce next.

SORTING IT OUT: BEING CLEAR ABOUT GOALS

What do you want to accomplish as an educational collaborator? Your goals are likely to shift and change as your child grows. Sometimes you take your cues about the progress of your youngster's growth by observing your child, listening to what he or she has to say, and noticing how things are going. Occasionally you will have to sort out information from other sources such as teachers, neighbors, or books or magazines as well. You may need to stop and think in order to put your own goals into words. Of course most parents have a goal to help their child grow up into a happy, healthy adult. But educational situations require more specific goals: for instance, I want my child to experience success in learning to read; or I want my daughter to be confident about speaking up when she doesn't understand the assignment. But your goal of wanting your daughter to speak up may not be shared by your daughter. She may be more concerned about what her friends think of her. By being specific about your goals in school situations, you can better guide your child regarding her own goals. When you help your child to think about how to handle school situations, knowing your own goals can assist you as you listen and ask your questions.

Remember to be aware of the fact that several goals can coexist in a situation. In Joshua's family the parents noticed their Feelings Fingerprints and realized that their feelings could lead their actions into several possible goal directions. They wanted to enjoy the last weekend of the summer and could have considered celebrating, but they also were excited about their son going off to school and were worried about what opening day could be like. They wanted to help Joshua feel confident about going to school. The goal they focused on was to help Joshua feel confident about the beginning of school. As a result of their planning, Joshua was really curious about the new school. His goal was to go to school so he could learn more things. Of course, Joshua's family hadn't met the new teacher yet but she also had a goal of teaching the children routines for school and getting them started off comfortably right at the beginning of the year. When Joshua and his family arrived at the school that first day, there were at least three goals existing: one for Joshua's parents, one for Joshua, and at least one for Joshua's teacher. By noticing feelings and sorting them out, Joshua's parents were able to focus on helping Joshua feel confident about going to school.

Sorting It Out is a way of focusing on the best alternatives in a given situation. Sorting out starts with *noticing feelings* and *putting the situation into words* in order to clarify *what you want to have happen*, so that you can *make the best possible plans* to reach a goal. Sorting it out is a way that a parent can move through the set of decision-making steps to decide which action has the best possible chance of reaching the goal. The situations that require sorting out can be large or small, limited to a predicament with your child or involve other children and adults as well. Getting comfortable with the decision-making strategy as a *sorting out tool* can help when your child is young and you are the only teacher and caretaker. The strategy can also help when your child enters a preschool, or child care situation, as well as throughout the rest of his or her school experiences. You can plan to collaborate as soon as you begin sharing the responsibility for your child with adults outside the family. Whether you are cooperating with a classroom teacher, a guidance counselor, a physical therapist, or a high school adviser, you can use the decision-making strategy to help you sort out school situations.

With each succeeding year of schooling, you can keep in touch with your own goals, notice your child's growth and needs, and get acquainted with your child's teachers to learn what they are trying to accomplish. You already know that one of your goals is to support your youngster as a successful learner, and you can plan to do that at home and at school. Parent-teacher conferences will be a staple in the diet of school experiences you will have as parents. Teachers of children at any age can benefit from information you share about your child. You could also use information you gain from teachers to help plan for additional learning activities at home. Following are some typical school situations. See how parents of children at several different ages try to sort out what is happening by using the decision-making approach.

A Decision-Making Approach to Parent-Teacher Conferences

BENJAMIN: A PRESCHOOLER WITH ENERGY AND ENTHUSIASM TO SPARE

Natalie and Doug Hodge are parents of Benjamin who is three years old. Mrs. Faulkner is the preschool teacher. She has asked the Hodges to come for a conference. Mrs. Faulkner greets the Hodges as they arrive and invites them into the office.

Natalie Hodge: Hello. Benjamin certainly likes to come to school here.
Mrs. Faulkner: I'm glad to hear that.
Doug Hodge: What does Benjamin do when he is here?
Mrs. Faulkner: He likes to build with blocks and he loves wearing the fireman's hat from the dress-up clothes. He looks happy. I am really glad that we could get together to talk about how things are going for Benjamin.

Sometimes there is a little small talk at the beginning of a conference to get everyone feeling comfortable. The Hodges were feeling anxious to get to the bottom of whatever the reason was that Mrs. Faulkner had called them for the meeting—so they started right in.

Natalie Hodge: Oh, is there a problem with Benjamin?

Mrs. Faulkner: I wouldn't say there is a problem, but I did feel that we should be in touch with each other and see if we could learn more about Ben. Tell me what he likes to do at home and how it has been since he started school.

Let's stop here and take a look inside the collaborators at what they might be thinking.

Look for Signs of Different Feelings

Parent	Teacher
Mrs. Faulkner sounds concerned about something. But she is friendly and smiling.	Benjamin's parents sound interested, curious, maybe a little anxious.

Tell Yourself What the Problem Is

Parent	Teacher
Mrs. Faulkner is saying there isn't a problem. But it sounds like something is happening in school.	Benjamin's parents wonder why I called them. I think they are wondering if there is a problem.

Decide on Your Goal

Parent	Teacher
Mrs. Faulkner's goal must be to learn more about Ben. We think things are going fine with him at home.	Ben's parents seem motivated about Benjamin's schooling. My goal is to enlist them to help figure out ways to reduce Ben's overpowering play behavior.

Doug Hodge: Ben likes to go to the park in the afternoon. He seems more tired since he started coming to school. He really takes long naps!

Mrs. Faulkner: He uses a lot of energy when he is here. We go outside every day, too. He never seems to run out of steam! A few times he has moved fast and knocked down another child. He can be overpowering.

Natalie Hodge: What do you mean—overpowering?

Mrs. Faulkner: Well, sometimes when he is interested in playing with another child, he gives a great big hug that once or twice has been too much for the other child to handle. A few of the children are frightened of him—but he really just wants to play.

Natalie Hodge: Oh, I see.

Mrs. Faulkner: Does Ben play with other children at home in the neighborhood?

Natalie Hodge: No. Sometimes other children are at the park the same time we are, but Ben doesn't really play with them.

Mrs. Faulkner: Sounds as if Benjamin is just beginning to experience what playing with other children is like. Maybe he needs a little help in learning how to play with other children gently. How can we make it easier for him?

STOP AND THINK OF AS MANY SOLUTIONS TO THE PROBLEM AS YOU CAN

Parents think of alternatives	*Teacher thinks of alternatives*
1. We could invite children from school to play with Ben.	1. I could help Ben notice when his actions frighten another child.
2. We could wait—maybe this overpowering is not a problem.	2. I could assist in play situations when Ben is with other children.
3. We could observe Ben at school to see what is happening.	3. Ben could play alongside another child for a while.
4. We could wait to see what Mrs. Faulkner says—maybe she wants to handle it just at school.	4. There is a book about Bear Hugs—we could read the book and practice gentle hugging.

These parents are using the decision-making approach to keep on track. They thought of several ways that they could help with the situation Mrs. Faulkner mentioned. Now they can focus on the possible consequences of these alternative solutions and select the one that will work the best for Benjamin. They are concerned about their son—this overpowering situation may or may not be a problem.

As the Hodges discussed Benjamin more with Mrs. Faulkner, they decided that they would invite one child from school to play with him. They would also guide those play situations at home and Mrs. Faulkner would keep them informed of how his playing progressed at school. For now the situation is on its way to being solved. Parents who are familiar with the decision-making strategy can feel confident during parent-teacher conferences. They could ask for more information. They could also say that they want to consider what the teacher has said and plan to meet again. They also might know already what they think is happening with their child and be able to explain it to the teacher so she can guide their child more effectively in the school situation.

Teachers usually start conferences with a goal in mind. Sometimes the goal is a routine one of getting acquainted with the child's family. Sometimes there may be a specific matter of concern to discuss. Parents can think ahead about any goal they might have too. Conferences can be more comfortable if both teachers and parents keep calm, on track, and focused on assisting the child.

ROSA: WHEN SERIOUS PROBLEMS AT HOME INTERFERE WITH SCHOOLWORK

We offer another scenario of a routine parent-teacher conference. Sometimes parents in a difficult situation want to be supportive of their child but may also need support themselves. Rosa is in the second grade. She has an older sister and brother but they are both away at college. She is the youngest and only child at home now. Her mother is seriously ill and recently entered the hospital. Her father wants to keep supporting Rosa in school. The teacher is Mrs. Barton.

Mrs. Barton: Hello, Mr. Garcia. I'm concerned about Rosa—she seems so preoccupied here at school. She doesn't seem to be her usual self.

Mr. Garcia: Rosa is really sad now because her mother is very ill and will be in the hospital for a couple of weeks.

Mrs. Barton: Oh, Mr. Garcia, I'm sorry. Considering all that Rosa has on her mind now, I understand how it can be difficult for her to concentrate. Thank you for letting us know. How can we help?

Mr. Garcia: Things are hard for all of us now, but we are concerned about Rosa's schoolwork. How is she doing?

Mrs. Barton: Here is her progress report. She is improving in reading. Here is the book she is reading in now. In math, she is beginning to learn subtraction with borrowing. It is hard for her—but she just got started and it takes a while to fully master this material. I certainly won't pressure her to try too many new things right now.

Mr. Garcia: You said a little while ago—how could you help. Could we stop and think about some ways to help Rosa right now?

Mrs. Barton: Coming today and letting me know about this situation has been a big help already. But I'm sure we could think of more ways to support her through this difficult time.

Mr. Garcia: Let's discuss some ways and then together we can decide which ones would be best to carry out.

Mrs. Barton: If it's okay with you, I would also like to talk to someone on the school guidance staff—this seems like a situation where that department could be helpful too . . .

This routine parent-teacher conference turned out to have a not-so-routine concern raised by the parent, Mr. Garcia. But the teacher was grateful to know what might be bothering Rosa's concentration and was willing to help think about ways to help Rosa through this difficult time. And Mr. Garcia *kept his goal in mind* and used the decision-making steps with Mrs. Barton to make sure ideas were made *concrete* before he left.

As Rosa's situation reminds us, school situations can be affected by something that is going on in the child's life at home or in the neighborhood. Parents and teachers can be collaborators and sort out alternative approaches for supporting the child. Parents can also talk with school nurses, guidance counselors, and usually the principal if they have a concern and are seeking information. Sometimes it will be necessary to contact the school because of a need that arises when there is no routine conference coming up soon. It's possible that calling the school might feel like "intruding" but if that happens consider it a Feelings Fingerprint and don't let it get in the way of reaching the goal that will assist your child. Some times will be better than other times for reaching a teacher or school staff person who is in the best position to talk with you—you can leave a message and ask to have the person return your call, or ask the person who answers the telephone to suggest when the best time to call back would be.

Parents who are tuned into what is happening with their child will hear about situations at school and may want to think about the best way to support their student in handling these situations. Of course, hearing about what's happening at school may become more difficult for parents of children as they reach middle or junior high school, because students want more privacy as they grow older. Certainly we know that staying supportive is also important as children grow to adolescence! Parents can respect their children's privacy but still keep the channels open for communication.

Keeping in touch with teachers and school resource staff can be more challenging for parents of children in middle or junior high school. Your child has so many more teachers to deal with now! But the basics of being a successful collaborator (noticing signs of feelings, sorting out goals, and handling situations before they become major problems) don't really change. Since there are now several teachers helping your child learn, you will have to find the collaborating approach that works best for you. You could talk to each of the teachers at conference time, communicate with the guidance counselor who is in contact with all of the teachers, or select a subset of your child's teachers with whom you want to share information and collaborate. Enhancing your child's education can be even more rewarding at this age as you see him taking on more responsibility for learning. Although schools vary as to their practices for parent-teacher conferences and handling communication to parents, teachers usually still want to know that parents are involved in helping their youngsters stay on track with learning responsibilities. Certainly, knowing the daily routines of the school and what is expected of your child can help you to guide and enhance learning. You'll need to keep up your confidence as a collaborator with other teaching adults, especially if the ranks of parents coming to school have thinned out around you!

ROGER: NOT WORKING UP TO POTENTIAL IN SEVENTH GRADE ENGLISH CLASS

Below is a parent-teacher conference regarding Roger, a seventh grade student. Roger's parents attended the open house at the beginning of school and met each of his teachers. Mr. and Mrs. Brown want Roger to feel encouraged and motivated by the expectations they have of him to succeed in school. Roger now has six different teachers and brings home his own report card. Conferences are optional, unless someone at school marks on the report card that there is trouble—then a conference is required. A bad report card is one sign of a problem but there are other signs too. Some of the teachers are surprised when the Browns appear for a brief conference during the scheduled time because none of them had marked that a conference was needed. But the Browns had noticed signs from Roger that indicated he was more at ease about assignments in some classes than others. Every time the Browns tried to discuss the English assignments that Roger had completed at home, he got frustrated and quickly closed the conversation. There hadn't been the usual collection of papers that Roger was proud of and showed his parents. These were signs that Roger's parents started to pay attention to so they could assist him. The Browns had a conference with Miss Ardsley, the English teacher.

Mrs. Brown: We're Roger Brown's parents, and we're interested to know how things are going in his English class.

Miss Ardsley: Roger is doing all right. But I don't think he is working up to potential. He daydreams a lot.

Mr. Brown: Oh . . . does he participate in class and complete his assignments?

Miss Ardsley: Well, yes. He does the work, I just think he could do much better because he seems like such a bright boy.

Mrs. Brown: Well, we all certainly want the same thing for Roger: for him *to do his best in school.* Even though it is really up to Roger to get more involved . . . maybe we could think of a few *alternative* ways to spark his interest in English.

Miss Ardsley: That's a great idea. I'll take notes.

Together they think of some ideas for sparking Roger:

Mr. Brown: All right, so far we know that Roger is interested in bicycle racing, dogs, camping, and fishing.

Mrs. Brown: And eating—and let's face it, daydreaming.

Miss Ardsley: Maybe I could use one of the things you mentioned he is interested in for a writing assignment. That might spark some enthusiasm.

Mr. Brown: We could plan for a weekend outing—maybe Roger has some ideas.

Miss Ardsley: Maybe we should have a chat with Roger and see what he is thinking. It's just possible that he doesn't realize how relevant what he is learning in English will be to his job skills and future learning.

Mr. Brown: That's a good idea. And I think I'm going to let him know how pleased we are that he is taking responsibility for the work and find out what he's thinking he might like to do in the future.

Miss Ardsley: Let's see. We came up with a few ideas. And you know, I feel more hopeful about Roger's interest in English—I'll see what I can do.

You don't have to wait until you hear there is a major problem to contact a teacher. Parents can help teachers and their students even when the situation seems minor. Never underestimate the power of thinking through situations to find solutions!

Decision-Making Conversations with Your Child Around Academic Performance

MEGAN:
WHEN A FIRST GRADER'S EXPECTATIONS AREN'T MET

Megan has just started first grade. She comes home at the end of the school day during the first week of school.

Mom: Hi! How was your day today, Megan?

Megan: Awful. All we did was sit around and play games. I thought we were going to learn how to read!

Mom: Oh, sounds like you are a little disappointed. Is that how you feel?

Megan: (smiling broadly) Well—I'm mostly tired. I did like playing some of the games but I hope we don't do that all the time! I did get a chance to sit next to Jayne. What a day of sitting on hard chairs!

Mom: Mr. Barker told us at the open house that learning to read is a big part of the work you will do this year. So every day won't be spent on those hard chairs, playing games. Come on, let's have a snack and I'll read with you now if you'd like.

Megan was starting to settle into the school routine and she probably did find sitting on school chairs for a whole day to be a challenge! She wasn't sure she was learning much. She seemed glad when her Mom *noticed her feelings* and acted to reassure her. In this situation Megan's parents noticed different goals. Megan wanted to learn to read soon, Mr. Barker wanted to settle the class into routines for sitting in their chairs and doing work. Megan's mom wanted Megan to feel good about school. Although there are usually several goals, at least one for every person in a school situation, the adults can observe the child's feelings and focus on supporting her, without necessarily compromising their own or the teacher's goals.

Megan's mom had attended the open house and remembered that Mr.

Barker, the first grade teacher, said that they do a lot of learning activities that are fun and seem like games to the children. He said that first graders learn at different rates of speed but that by the middle of the year there should be a lot of progress for children in the class. Thus Megan's mom had some information about what to expect. She surely wanted Megan to learn to read, too. But in this situation she quickly decided that she first wanted Megan to adjust to the routine at school comfortably, so she reassured her. Knowing what was expected by the teacher helped Megan's mom guide Megan in her thinking about this new school experience.

Teachers and parents usually do their best for a child and children start out in school trying their best, too. But sometimes situations arise that seem complicated and possibly even confusing. The adults involved need to stop and sort out the situation with a goal in mind of clearing signals so they can support the child as a learner.

MELISSA: A FOURTH GRADER WHO SAYS, "I CAN'T DO THIS HOMEWORK!"

Here is another common, elementary school situation. For many children, doing homework on time and well can be challenging. Guiding your child to think about and successfully take responsibility for homework becomes a similar challenge for parents.

Melissa is in fourth grade and lives alone with her mother. She was attending an after-school program but now she is on her own for about two hours after school while her mom works. When Mrs. Brack arrives home, she begins to prepare supper and usually they talk about what has happened during the day. The day this scene takes place, Melissa says she can't possibly finish her homework.

Mom: (Wondering what to say—her daughter sounds panicky—but she notices her own feelings too—impatient and edgy.)

Melissa: I have to write a paragraph about nature for English. Then I have to read a whole chapter for reading and there's a spelling test tomorrow!

Mom: Sounds like you have enough work to keep you very busy. Is that all of the homework you have?

Melissa: The worst part is these math problems that I don't understand.

Mom: (taking a deep breath to relax) Let's think through this situation together. You say you have so much homework. Just what is it that you are feeling?

Melissa: I feel like giving up!

Mom: What would happen if you didn't have your homework completed tomorrow?

Melissa: Oh, I'd get into trouble or Mrs. Smith'd get mad at me.

Mom: Sounds like right now you are feeling overwhelmed but you really want to get your homework finished. Is that how you feel?

Melissa: Well, I hate it when I get stuck on part of my homework and when that happens I don't feel like trying to finish the rest. I guess you're right. I really do want to get it all finished.

Mom: Where did you get stuck?

Melissa: The math problems are too tough—I'm not sure how to do them.

Mom: Are they review problems? Usually homework is something you have already learned and you are just practicing.

Melissa: Yes—we did some like this in class yesterday.

Mom: Maybe if you can Get Calm, you will be able to think of how you did problems like these in class.

Melissa: Get Calm? That will just take more time.

Mom: Well, sometimes when I have to do things after work and I am tired, I have to stop and relax so I can concentrate on what I'm doing. You've seen me do that, right?

Melissa: I *have* seen you do that. And Get Calm worked when you showed it to me when I had that fight with Trudy.

Mom: Okay, so let's try it together. By taking time to Get Calm, you'll save time later on.

Melissa and her mom take a few moments to sit down and Get Calm, by taking a deep breath, looking around and saying what they see, and then taking another deep breath.

Melissa: That wasn't so bad! Now I'd better get back to my homework. I'll try to do that math again after I write my paragraph.

Mom: When you get up to it, you can show me your math problems— maybe I can help you remember how to do them . . .

Sometimes our children just need to have a little help in organizing their thoughts in a situation where they feel stuck. And homework can be a very sticky place! If you keep the steps in mind, you can use them to guide your child. The steps will also help you to focus your own thinking and keep you on track of accomplishing what you want to accomplish.

JASON: WHEN A MIDDLE SCHOOL "LACK OF PROGRESS" REPORT COMES HOME

The following is another distressing school situation: an eighth grade student has received a progress report that says he is failing in social studies as of the middle of the marking period. The student is Jason and his parents are Mr. and Mrs. Wentz. This is the first time he has ever had a failing report.

Jason: (waiting until supper before he tells his parents about the progress report) Mom and Dad, there is something you have to sign.

Mrs. Wentz: Yes, Jason, what is it?

Jason: Oh, it's just a progress report from school.

Mr. Wentz: That sounds interesting. What is the progress about?

Jason: Well, a . . . a . . . here. (Jason bends down his head and hands the paper to his dad).

Mr. Wentz: (looking at the report and then frowning) Progress—how can they call this a progress report—sounds like no progress to me! Well, son, what about this?

Mrs. Wentz: Yes, Jason. Did you know that you were failing in social studies?

Jason: Well, sorta. There was this big test and I got a sixty-five. That really messed up my grade. I have thought about what I can do. I'm going to study very hard for the next test.

Mr. Wentz: (smiles) I'm glad to hear that you are thinking about what you can do to improve your grade. What other things are you graded on in social studies?

Jason: Oh, we have group projects and the teacher grades us on class participation . . .

Mr. Wentz: It sounds like you know what areas to work on to bring up your grade. Would you like some help in reviewing the material before your next test?

Jason: Thanks, Dad. But I think I can do it. I thought you would be angry.

Mr. Wentz: Well, I was a little angry and surprised. You were probably thinking that way too. I feel a little better now because you say you're planning on working harder. Besides, you are doing well in everything else!

This situation appears to have worked out comfortably—Jason had put the problem into words and thought about what he could do to solve it. His parents were surprised by receiving the progress report but were able to focus on supporting Jason. His parents could choose to have a conference with the social studies teacher to find out more about expectations for classroom participation and the material that is being covered. Perhaps Jason is having a difficult time with other areas in social studies assignments but reluctant to admit to difficulty or ask for assistance. It is also possible that the teacher has a grading procedure that is tougher than previous classes have offered. Parents need to keep tuned through difficult situations as well as through comfortable ones. Handling academic failure can be tough for students, teachers, and parents as well. But by using the decision-making strategy to keep on track, parents can help their child focus on what the problem is and look for the best alternative solution. Paying attention to and solving difficult situations *as they arise* will help your young student handle difficulties before they turn into overwhelming failures.

Other Aids to Collaborating for Improved Education

An important part of decision making for our children's education is finding information when we need it. Parents can learn much from reading materials available in school newsletters, public libraries, magazines, newspapers, and from talking with other parents. Recall Steve and Joshua, who were getting ready for kindergarten at the beginning of this chapter. Joshua was looking forward to the opening of school and Steve wasn't feeling prepared. Let's change the scenario a bit and look at what can occur when parents collaborate and help each other out. Remember, Joshua seemed to be looking forward to school and Steve had an outburst of crying.

Joshua's mom meets Steve's mom on the way to the supermarket the Friday afternoon before that big last weekend of the summer.

Joshua's mom: Hi, do you have plans for the weekend?
Steve's mom: Well—plans . . . no. There is just so much left to do. There's always something going on that seems to keep us busy.

Joshua's mom: We've been thinking about Joshua's first day of kindergarten on Monday. It's exciting—but to tell you the truth—I am a little worried, too.

Steve's mom: Oh . . .

Joshua's mom: I know he'll like it. But, at the same time, I cross my fingers and hope the class won't be too large and that his teacher will be great. We've been talking to Joshua about school. You know, letting him know that we think it will be fun for him to go and he'll be able to handle whatever comes up.

Steve's mom: I've been trying not to think about opening day. I feel a little sad—I guess I'm not so sure that it's going to work out well. It's a hard situation for a five year old.

Joshua's mom: Well—maybe if you notice your feelings and make a plan, you'll feel better and you'll be able to encourage Steve about school. Sometimes feelings get in the way of my thinking about what would be the way to help Joshua. (By now they are at the supermarket door.)

Joshua's mom: Why don't you come over for some iced tea after you get those groceries put away. I've been using some decision-making steps that have helped me. I can show you what I mean.

Steve's mom: What do you mean by decision-making steps?

Joshua's mom: The first step is to look for signs of feelings, to help move from feelings to thinking. The next step is to put into words what the problem is, to help think about how to solve it.

Steve's mom: That sounds like just what I need!

Joshua's mom: Why not bring Steve and his dad. The boys can play and we can talk about getting ourselves ready for the big opening day and all that follows!

Joshua's parents had gotten started and clarified their goal for this school situation. They also might be able to guide Steve's parents to think through their goal. Often we genuinely know difficulties that our children will face in school. That's all the more reason to get an early start at collaborating with other people who are also concerned about children as learners. Friends, neighbors, community resource people and, above all, teachers and school staff can join you in assisting your child.

There are a surprisingly large number of routine opportunities for communication with teachers and school resource staff. Here are some points of contact we've found helpful:

**OPEN-HOUSE—ORIENTATION
—BACK-TO-SCHOOL NIGHTS**

Generally all of the teachers are present at these meetings to meet parents and explain the expectations for students during the coming year. Usually the principal speaks briefly, then introduces key staff people. Sometimes this brief program is followed by parents meeting in classrooms with individual teachers. In middle school and high school, parents would probably go to each of the classes that their student is assigned to attend by actually following the student's schedule in shortened periods.

PARENT-TEACHER CONFERENCES

Schools handle this differently, but often in elementary schools, parents visit teachers in the child's classroom by appointment. Teachers give the parents the child's report card and information about what the teacher expects and how the child is doing. Conferences are usually scheduled at least twice a year but parents can request them at any time. In middle and junior high schools, conferences are usually held during a specified time, such as twice a year when parents can drop in and talk briefly with each of the teachers or ones they choose. If there isn't enough time or privacy, ask for an appointment to talk more at a later date. Parents can contact the school guidance counselor for a conference or to request communication with teachers.

PARENT-TEACHER ORGANIZATIONS AND ASSOCIATIONS

Parent meetings provide an opportunity to meet other parents and to learn about school programs. Generally only designated teachers and administrators attend these meetings. The content of meetings will vary according to the purpose of the parent organization. Here are some examples of organization purposes: building common purpose around school programs, advising school administration, fund raising, educating parents about school programs, planning and evaluating programs, supporting parents in new or challenging situations.

PROGRESS REPORTS

Report cards, notes from teachers, phone calls from teachers or other school staff, and disciplinary actions are all forms of progress reports in which the school contacts the parents either in person or in writing.

SCHOOL HANDBOOKS

School publications, available at the school principal's or superintendent's office, can explain policies and procedures ranging from grading system to disciplinary action. Student handbooks are usually distributed to each student at the beginning of the school year. Procedures for conferences and schedules are often explained in such handbooks.

CALENDARS, ANNOUNCEMENTS, AND NEWSLETTERS

Each school develops its own timetable of events and usually notifies parents of upcoming activities via announcements attached to the school calendar or separate newsletters. The materials most times originate from the principal's office.

INDIVIDUALIZED EDUCATIONAL PLANNING MEETINGS—SPECIAL EDUCATION STUDENTS

The purpose of these meetings is to plan goals for learning according to the child's special needs. Parents, along with such specialists as a school psychologist, social worker, and learning disabilities consultant, participate as collaborators in this process that occurs when a child is identified with special learning needs. The meeting is repeated for a review of progress for as long as special help is necessary.

TELEPHONE CALLS, NOTES, AND INFORMAL CONVERSATIONS

As we have mentioned, parents can always call the school and request a return call from a specific teacher or resource person. Usually the school secretary takes a message or can suggest a good time for the parent to call back. Notes to a teacher can be sent in an envelope with your child. Sometimes an informal conversation with a teacher can be very productive, especially if it can be arranged at a mutually convenient time.

Each school has its own set of practices for communicating with parents and sending out information about educational happenings. If you want to know something that isn't covered in the routine publications, use the decision-making strategy to specify what it is that you want to know and how to start to find out. You can contact people at school and ask for information once you have clarified what you want to know. Using the decision-making strategy, you can help focus on and keep track of your goals. Your goal might be to learn about what is expected of students in a specific grade, or what are some of the usual predicaments that children have as they grow up. Reading about children and education in books, pamphlets, newspapers, and magazines can add to your understanding of what is happening with your child. But even when you read information, you will need to pay attention to Feelings Fingerprints and decide for yourself how the suggestions in the written material match your own goals for helping to enhance your child's learning. Whether it is responding to a crisis situation, sharing excitement over learning successes, or simply clearing signals, the opportunities for staying informed about school expectations can occur routinely.

Decision-Making Digest

In this chapter we've talked about the value of using a decision-making approach to collaborate regarding your child's education. Sorting out school situations is a way of making sure that your goals are clear. Many people are involved—including your child—and they all have goals. Being clear about your goals, the goals of your child, and your child's teacher will help you to pick the best alternative approach to guide your child to academic success.

Remember how sorting out school situations starts with *noticing feelings*. Then the job is to put *what is happening* into words, clarify *what you want to have happen* (your goal), and *make the best possible plans*. In this chapter you've read about several school situations and examples of parents sorting them out. For other examples of how to focus your own and your child's goals, reread Chapter 6. Remember, by being able to focus on your own, your child's, and your teacher's goals, you can work as an educational collaborator to help your child achieve academic success and not get overwhelmed by academic failures.

A decision-making approach to parent-teacher conferences can keep you confident as a collaborator, able to focus on the goals, and able to act on the best alternative. Talks with teachers can be comfortable when you are clear about your goal and can keep on track. Whether there is a difficult situation at school or at home, or no problem at all, conferences with teachers can help all the people involved.

Now that you know about the decision-making strategy, you can use it as a tool to handle your conversations with your children around academic situations. School situations can be complicated, but parents can assist their children to do the best possible. Decision-making conversations will help your children put what is happening into words, so that they can plan the best approach to achieve what they want. Conversations will also help you to put your concern for your children's well-being into concrete terms.

Finally, as we mentioned, there are other sources of help available for educational collaborators. Reading materials, resource information from school publications and school personnel can provide answers to questions. And routine opportunities for contact with teachers and other parents can assist in clarifying some of the questions. The human resourcefulness that exists within students, teachers, and parents can solve difficult and not-so-difficult problems. By using the decision-making strategy parents can collaborate to enhance their children's educational experiences—at home and at school!

14

Not for Children's Problems Only: Practicing What You Teach

Whether you've read straight through this book or sampled some of the chapters here and there, you've opened your eyes to a variety of ideas and techniques. Some of the ideas you were familiar with. Others are newer. When you're used to parenting in a certain way, it's not always easy to suspend your judgment and hear what others have to say. You've considered our ideas and allowed them to stimulate your own thinking. Now you can selectively use these techniques to prepare your child for the real world.

After years of teaching decision-making to children, parents, and teachers in our own work, we've developed better decision-making skills ourselves. We use decision making in our adult lives as consumers, organizers of households, friends, voters, and in countless other ways. *You can too* by using the steps to get through tough situations: shopping, paying bills, managing your time, dealing with difficult neighbors, and handling your relatives. If you do use a decision-making *strategy*, we think you avoid a good deal of stress and hassle. If you're coping better, you can set a happier tone in your family, which can be contagious! As you become better able to sort out your own adult decisions, you'll be more relaxed and more calm. In fact, you'll be in a better frame of mind to teach decision making to your child.

First, though, a review of the key points in learning about decision making. Then consider completing our second Parenting Styles Activity (PSA). This work sheet can serve as another measure of your parenting thinking.

Where We've Been

From the beginning you already possess important parenting skills. This book stimulated you to widen your already workable array of parenting skills and consider yet one more: teaching decision making to your child. Why? Because we won't always be able to be with our children when they're confronted with difficulties. As the years go by, our youngsters spend less time with us at home. They spend more time at school and with friends in various activities. That's how it should be, developmentally. They need to feel confident when they're on their own. We need to feel confident in them as we let them go. How can we be assured they'll do fine, be able to handle the inevitable negative peer pressures, dares, and embarrassing moments that will confront them? If they've developed a decision-making ability to fall back on, our research indicates that they'll be able to cope with a wide range of different situations.

In thinking through the decision-making process, you know how important it is for children to be "ready" for decision making. You know the value of encouraging your children to be attentive to the goings-on around them. You've also been emphasizing the importance of developing children's interpersonal skills, such as giving and receiving praise, so they can more comfortably be a part of the many groups they will encounter as they grow up.

We then began to look at the decision-making steps. Your children's ability to recognize and understand their own and others' *feelings* was the first skill. Then if they could literally *put the problem into words,* they made difficulties somehow more manageable. The third step was for your youngsters to try to focus on one *goal* at a time: what do they really want to have happen? You then learned some fun ways to help your children see that they never had to feel stuck: there is always *more than one solution* to a problem that they can think of. That is a powerful skill to have.

We next started helping our children to try to *anticipate the consequences* of their ideas. How often do we all need to slow down from trying out an idea so we could back step in order to consider what would happen next? The next skills were inevitable: *choose a solution, plan it out, make a final check,* and *try it and think about how it worked.* One of the most significant points raised was the importance of helping your child anticipate obstacles. It's inevitable that even with the best-thought-out solutions your child might run into difficulties. Helping your child become prepared for difficulties eases the impact of such experiences and minimizes his or her feeling discouraged. The second major theme was the importance of your youngster carefully planning when, where, and how he or she could carry out a solution. Should your child talk to the teacher after school, alone, or write a note? Planning is of critical importance when a child puts ideas into practice.

When you think about all that is involved in decision making, it seems like a real workout. But decision making is a skill that you will be teaching your child in a gradual way over some time. Your six year old may need some help now in learning how to set goals and may also need similar help or reminders in being able to set goals when he or she is ten years old. We encourage you to consider being flexible in how you teach decision making, so you and your child don't feel overwhelmed. For example, your child may be terrific at thinking about several different solutions for a problem, but he or she may be less skilled in verbalizing feelings. If that is the case, you will probably be taking a look at Chapter 4 for ideas and reminders. Your child may be able to discuss solutions with you, get really excited about a good idea, and quickly want to try it out. For that youngster, you may find yourself needing to skim through Chapter 9. You are the best person to decide how to use the ideas that we have presented in a way that will comfortably fit in with your own family situation.

We have included some new Parenting Styles Activity situations to give you another opportunity to look at your parenting styles. The goal here is to get you thinking about how you would respond *now* after reading the previous chapters. You may be responding in a similar way to how you felt in Chapter 1, which is fine. Or you may find yourself entertaining other options. That's fine too, because you probably now know your parenting style better and are more alert to some possible changes in yourself. If your child is with you now, observe him or her for a moment. If your youngster is not around, try to picture him or her in your mind. Think about how your youngster is with you and others. Think about yourself as a parent and consider the approaches that you have used and have learned about. As before, we have provided a minimum of detail with each situation presented, so you can fill in with family details on your own. Put a circle around the letter that identifies the decision you would make.

Parenting Styles Activity
(PSA)

1. It's 7 P.M. on a Saturday evening. You'll be leaving in a while to go out to dinner with some friends. Your six-year-old child is in the living room with your baby-sitter. As you brush your hair in the other room, you overhear your child sadly say to the baby-sitter, "I don't want Mommy to go out. I don't like it."

    A. You put the brush down and walk over to your child and say, "It looks like you're unhappy about Mommy going out. You know, I'm going to miss you too, but before you know it . . . it will be breakfast time and we'll be together again."

    B. You decide that talking to your child about the situation will make it worse. You don't want to make it more of an issue than it already is, so you decide to let the matter rest. You allow your child and the baby-sitter to handle it themselves.

    C. You approach your child and say, "You know when Mommy's gone, you might feel better if you watch a little TV and have a snack."

    D. You call your child into your room and supportively suggest, "When I'm out, I wonder what we could do to help you feel less sad?"

2. You're sitting down reading a book on parenting. In the next room your kindergarten-aged youngster is playing trucks with his friend. They are talking excitedly. With some difficulty, your child, on his own, is trying to construct a bridge out of some blocks. The other youngster is moving some cars a few feet away. As your youngster puts the last block on the bridge it collapses. Your child turns to the other youngster and says, "Look what you made me do!" The other child looks at your child angrily and is about to say something.

    A. You put your book down, approach the children, and say to your youngster, "It's hard when something you're working on falls apart. It can make you angry at everyone."

    B. You decide to let them handle it themselves. You figure that the other child, because of the age, probably has done the same thing to your youngster. The best move is not to interfere.

    C. You walk over to your child and say, "I'm sorry that your blocks fell, but you shouldn't blame it on others and hurt their feelings too."

D. With the book put to the side, you leave your chair, step between the children, and say, "It looks like you two might be having a disagreement. How do you think we should handle it?"

3. It's a family reunion weekend. You are at the home of a relative whom you haven't seen in a number of years. You notice that your seven-year-old child has been shyly sticking close to you, not saying much to anyone and not participating in the activities with the other children.

A. When your conversation ends, you sit down with your youngster and comment, "I know it's hard to be in a new place. You can feel kind of shy at first."

B. You decide that this type of shyness in new places is not unusual at all for a seven year old. Rather than saying much, you let your child stay with you, thinking that a feeling of security will provide the base from which your child will eventually go off to be with the others.

C. When things quiet down, you suggest, "Maybe I could help by going with you to see the other children and staying a while."

D. At a quiet private moment you observe, "What do you think we could do to help you feel more comfortable here?"

4. It's the end of another busy day. It's past bedtime for your seven-year-old son. Tired, you gratefully sit down to relax for the first time today, and you hear him rummaging around in his room. The next thing you know, your son enters the room and says impatiently, "Mom, have you seen my new jeans? I can't find them and I want to wear them tomorrow!"

A. You turn toward him and say, "You know, son, I'm really feeling tired tonight. You look upset, it's a pain when you can't find something that you want. I just don't know where you put your jeans."

B. You say, "I don't know where your jeans are either. I guess if you don't find them you won't be able to wear them tomorrow."

C. You say to your son, "I don't know where they are. Whenever I lose something, I always stop for a moment and try to imagine where the last place was that I saw it. Maybe you could try that."

D. You ask your son to come in and say to him, "Well, I wonder what ideas you have about how to handle this?"

5. You are in the kitchen getting yourself a drink of water. School is just over and your eight-year-old son comes in the door. You ask him how school was today. He responds, "Okay, I guess." But then he adds in an irritated way, "But I never ever get to be the first person in line coming back from recess. I am always either in the middle or last."

A. You look at him sympathetically and say, "When you really want something to happen and it doesn't, you can get really unhappy. It's happened to me, too."

B. You say, "Gee, that's too bad. You know, tough as it is to hear it, it's really true that these things have a way of working themselves out."

C. Finishing your drink, you turn toward your child and say, "You know, maybe you can use your watch to help out. Why don't you walk over to the line a few minutes before the end of recess. Maybe if you get over there earlier you'll get a shot at being first in line for a change."

D. You swallow the last of your water, look at your son, and inquire, "Well, I'd be interested in hearing about any of your ideas about how to get to be first in line."

6. Your eight-year-old daughter has been increasingly frank about her ideas and her feelings lately. You're at a family gathering where a number of friends and relatives have gotten together. You are talking to one of your aunts. Your daughter is on the other side of the room. You overhear her observe to your uncle, "Gee, Uncle Ed, how come you are so bald?" You watch as Uncle Ed grows uncomfortable and moves away. Your daughter now also looks uncomfortable and a bit puzzled.

A. You approach your daughter and privately remark, "It looks like you and Uncle Ed feel a little uncomfortable. You know, a lot of men who don't have too much hair feel embarrassed when someone talks about their being bald."

B. You decide from the look on her face that your daughter will soon realize what has happened. You figure at this time her own discomfort at losing the conversation with her Uncle Ed will be the best way for her to learn from this situation.

C. You approach her and quietly confide, "You know, it would probably be a good idea to not talk out loud about how someone looks, sometimes it can cause problems, like with Uncle Ed."

D. In a few moments you quietly approach her and suggest, "Looks like you had a tough time with your uncle Ed. What do you think would make things better?"

7. Your son is now nine years old. He has been working all Sunday afternoon on a science project for school. He's in his room and you can hear him getting irritated and frustrated with what he is doing.

A. When the noises have died down a bit, you go to his room and offer, "You have been working really hard on that project all day. That's great. Are you getting frustrated about anything in particular?"

B. You decide that he is probably learning a lot by working things out with this project on his own. You figure if he wanted my help he knows enough to come out and ask for it. So you let events unfold in his room in a natural course.

C. At a time when things are quiet, you go to his room and suggest, "Would you like to take a break for a while? After your break I can help you if you'd like."

D. When the goings-on in his room quiet down, you go to his room, say hello, and tell him, "It's great that you've been working so hard. When you get stuck and upset, I wonder what ideas you have about getting unstuck."

8. Your daughter, Kathy, is twelve years old. Like most of her classmates, she has been more and more attached to a particular clique of friends who share secrets, plans, and activities together. From the kitchen you overhear her getting pressured by one of the members of the clique. This friend is trying to get her to go skating with the group on Saturday. Your daughter is undecided because she has been thinking of using this Saturday to go shopping for a new pair of shoes for herself.

A. When the conversation is over, you comment to her alone, "Making decisions isn't easy. In fact, I'll tell you, I usually feel tense when I'm in a situation like that. I feel like I am in the middle."

B. Either buying the shoes or going skating is a fine solution. You decide therefore, to let Kathy handle this one on her own. You feel that this is a terrific and safe chance for her to again practice thinking on her own.

C. When her friend has left, you approach your daughter and say, "Well, what do you think about going for shoes on Saturday morning. Then, if you like, you might still have enough time to go skating with your friends."

D. You mention to her, "I couldn't help hearing your conversation. What are some of your choices again?"

9. It is a Wednesday evening and it is 8:30 P.M. You are relaxing and watching television. Gradually you hear a conversation between your sixteen-year-old son and your thirteen-year-old daughter grow into an argument. Your daughter is on the telephone and your son is complaining loudly to her that she seems to stay on the phone for an hour at a time (which, in your view, is accurate). Your son is yelling at her that his friends can never get through on the phone to him because the line is always busy.

A. When the conversation is somewhat calmer, you go in and comment, "Look, both of you. I know it is frustrating, but we have only one phone in the house. I know you are angry and now *I* am getting angry with all of this. You're big kids so you'd better straighten this whole situation out right now."

B. You decide to stay right where you are, watching television. You feel that this is something that the two of them should continue to try to work out on their own.

C. When your daughter is off of the phone, you suggest to both of them that your daughter might have the phone from eight o'clock until nine o'clock and your son can have the phone from nine o'clock to ten o'clock, or some other similar arrangement.

D. At the next meal, you ask for their suggestions about how to work out a more fair use of the phone.

10. Your neighbor has stopped over for a short visit. She is pregnant and you gather that she has been having a difficult pregnancy. As you are conversing she seems to look particularly pale and sad today.

A. You comment, "How is it going? You look a little down today."

B. You remember your own pregnancy and decide that it is better to let her tell you in her own time how she is feeling rather than ask her questions. You feel that you might be intruding a bit on her privacy.

C. You comment, "Having a baby can be rough sometimes. I used to try to take a short nap and put my feet up for a little while when I was pregnant."

D. You observe, "You hear so many ideas about how to feel more comfortable during pregnancy, what have people been telling you?"

Let's take a look again at your parenting styles. As in Chapter 1, categorize your responses, by putting the number of each letter answers in the blank space next to the corresponding letter.

A. *Verbalizer of Feelings*
B. *Real-Life Consequences*
C. *Giver of Advice*
D. *Elicitor of Ideas*

Take a look at your pattern for a moment. Is there one style that is strongly preferred by you over another? We would like you to consider turning back to page 10 and making a comparison of your responses. How many different categories did you use in the first chapter? And most important, how did you arrive at your choices *this* time? We'd like to think that you are now a bit more comfortable with a wider range of responses than when you began this book. We hope you've found you used our decision-making strategy to help you decide how to respond. Perhaps, as is often the case, you've used decision making without even realizing it! The best way to tell is to compare your answers now and in Chapter 1 and think about *your goal* as you responded to each problem situation.

In keeping with one of our major decision-making themes, there are always more alternative choices than the ones we have provided for you in the Parenting Styles Activity. As you were reading the situations, you may have come up with your own unique alternative approaches frequently, perhaps even more frequently than you did in Chapter 1. If so, good for you! Just remember that *how you think through a problem* situation— whether with your child, your spouse, your relatives, friends, or others—is the important thing to keep in mind. At these times, remember you are making choices and decisions. You don't have to react out of habit, or always do things because your parents did or didn't do them that way. You can choose, based on your goals and your family's goals, what to do. In the end, decision making is not only for your children—*it's also for you.*

What may be helpful for you, and for your family, is to consider applying decision making to your own life outside of parenting. You will be amazed at the number of opportunities that adults have to apply decision making as a conscious help. Just as with the children, there are different problems that can emerge for adults at different stages of life.

Growing Older Is Not Easy: The Big Decisions

There are a number of writers who have examined the process of how adults develop over time. Basically adults encounter a series of problems, decisions, and choices, much as children do. Here are some different problems and issues that arise at different ages.

FROM EIGHTEEN TO TWENTY-EIGHT: BECOMING A RESPONSIBLE ADULT

Between the ages of eighteen and twenty-two, there are a number of decisions that confront young adults: what to do about further training and education, considering whether college would be appropriate, and if so, what college? Young adults think about such issues as "should I live away from home or not?" It's the first fling at being an adult.

From ages twenty-two to twenty-eight, the choices could be deciding to commit yourself in marriage and considering when or whether to have a child, and for college graduates the decision to secure that first job. It may also be a time of trying to develop a commitment to a career and to another person: forming one's own family and work life.

FROM TWENTY-NINE TO THIRTY-FOUR: MAKING OUR CHOICES WORK

Between the ages of twenty-nine and thirty-four, many have worked for a number of years, either at home or away from home. It is a time for questioning the family and career choices that have been made. New decision-making opportunities include thinking about a geographic move, purchasing a house, deciding how many children to have, and so on. For those of you who already have been parents by this time, consideration may turn toward schooling and getting comfortable as the parent of a preschooler or elementary school child. It is a time period when it is normal to question and even feel a bit dissatisfied.

FROM THIRTY-FIVE TO FORTY-THREE:
RETHINKING OUR PLANS
AND GOALS

At about ages thirty-five to forty-three, we can be caught up with an intense rush to reach all of the dreams that we had for ourselves when we were young. There is a feeling of racing against time to get the house that we always wanted, the number and kind of children we had planned on, the kind of work or income that we had fantasized about, and so on. It can also be a time of reflection on the accomplishments and desires of youth that have finally been reached. Our children are also growing more adult-like and nearing the time to make life decisions about how and when to leave home and operate independently. If we are successful in working through this period, it is a time when we can take a realistic view of ourselves and what we have accomplished. A successful resolution here would mean coming to some kind of compromise between our youthful dreams and the realities of adult life.

FROM FORTY-THREE TO SIXTY:
NEW DECISIONS TO BE CARRIED OUT
. . . AND SOME NEW ROLES

From ages forty-three to sixty, there can be a period of settling down and acceptance of ourselves. For many of us, our children will be either teenagers and out of the house a good deal of time, or older and out altogether. We will be adjusting to not being with them on a day-to-day basis. For women who had recently taken on a full-time career outside of the home, it can be a time of significant career advancement and change. For others among us, it may be time to *begin* a career for the first time. For men and women who have been working outside of the home for many years, it may be a period of less interest in career advancement.

Between the ages of fifty-three and sixty, we may be experimenting with our new roles as grandparents. The scope of our goals changes. We may feel rejuvenated by having some more young lives to help mold and shape. We may even want to redo the Parenting Styles Activity as if we were grandparents, either handling the problems or watching *our* children use A, B, C, or D. Regardless, being grandparents signals an important shift in family relationships, one which can be aided by a decision-making strategy.

FROM SIXTY AND BEYOND: MORE RETHINKING AND LOTS TO COPE WITH

We think about our own parents in this regard. If they are doing well, they have developed more tolerance, are less bitter, and in general are calming down a bit. At this period we may be anticipating the time we may be able to retire and make decisions about where and how to live. Accepting the physical changes that accompany the aging process is also a task. Adjusting flexibly to losses such as those of our own parents is also a part of the job during this period.

Age sixty and beyond usually includes the time of retirement from a career. Decisions about our own health and that of our partners are made. Adjustment to living alone and to new financial realities are also a part of this time period.

The issues you face with your child at certain ages are always superimposed upon *your* own issues at certain ages. We have chosen to highlight general developmental changes. Other important factors certainly include where you live, the quality of your family relationships, your income, and the kind of work you do. It is our feeling that using decision making yourself, in your own adult life, will help out. As we suggested before, you will then become more receptive to helping your child with his or her difficulties. Once a parent, always a parent . . . we will be able to use decision making to guide ourselves whether our children are forty-three or three!

Decision Making for Me?

In Chapter 2 we asked you to imagine being invited by your mother and your mother-in-law for Thanksgiving dinner at their respective houses. The decision-making process seemed to help out. Here are some more opportunities where you can put your steps to work. As you grow more comfortable with the process, you will think of situations where decision-making strategies might help for you or for your family.

SITUATION 1:
DEALING WITH YOUR SISTER AS A GROWN-UP

Picture this: you have decided to have Thanksgiving dinner at your house. Your mother-in-law and father-in-law are there. Your parents are there too. You also have at your house your sister, Lynne, with her husband, Jim, and their eight-year-old daughter, Katie. You, your husband, Bob, and your two boys, Andrew (age seven), and Patrick (age four), have been socializing the whole day with the group.

Look at this Parenting Family Tree.

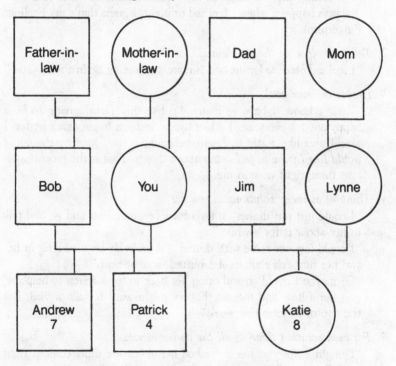

You are in the kitchen getting some of the food ready. Lynne and her husband are having an intense disagreement about how to handle Katie, who has been rather loud and at times rude. In a few moments Lynne joins you in the kitchen. You talk about how you are preparing the food.

As Lynne is fixing the salad, you notice out of the corner of your eye that she has been crying. In fact, her eyes are filling up with tears now. She quietly excuses herself and leaves the kitchen to go into one of the other rooms.

Imagine how you would deal with these circumstances. You say to yourself, "I've never really done it, but why don't I think through this situation in the same way that I have been trying to get the kids to solve their own problems." In a few moments, as you finish fixing the salad, you go through the steps.

1. *Look for signs of different feelings.*

"I'm feeling that tightness in my stomach again. It never fails . . . it always happens when I feel sad or upset. I guess that's my Feelings Fingerprint."

2. *Tell yourself what the problem is.*

"I feel sad *because* Lynne and Jim are disagreeing again about Katie."

3. *Decide on your goal.*

"I don't know. I have so many. I'd like this Thanksgiving to be a happy one for everyone. I'd like Lynne and Jim to get along better. I would also like Katie to begin behaving better. Mostly, though, *I would like Lynne to feel better* about things. That is the most important thing right now to me."

4. *Think of as many solutions as you can.*

"I could just put dinner on hold for a few moments and go and talk to her about it for a while."

"I could just continue with dinner. I'd probably be meddling in her and her husband's affairs if I butted in right now."

"Or maybe I could go and bring her back to the kitchen to help me, give her a hug, and suggest that we might want to talk or visit, just the two of us later this week."

5. *For each solution think of all the consequences.*

"I might embarrass her if I asked her about her disagreement right now. Besides, dinner would be late."

"I don't really think I'd be meddling. After all, she is my sister. Maybe she is not really ready to talk to me yet though."

"She will feel better if she is doing something like helping with dinner. If I get her to come back in here and give her a hug at the very least she will know that I care. She might like the idea of meeting with me next week."

6. *Choose your best solution.*
"I think I'll try to coax her back into the kitchen. I know that she probably wants to help. Just a sign that I care is enough for her now. There's really no time to talk today anyway. We can just save it until next week when this holiday rush is over."

7. *Plan it and make a final check.*
"I better go now before she gets settled in with the others. I'll serve some of these potato chips to everyone and then I'll just take her hand and tell her that I need her help in the kitchen. Maybe I'll lighten it up a bit by joking around with her."

8. *Try it and rethink it.*
"I'm glad I got her back in the kitchen, and she liked the idea of talking next week. I don't know if I'd hug her like I did, though, we both seemed to feel a little bit awkward with it. All in all, she seemed happier because I think that she knows that I care."

Sounds like a thoughtful person doesn't it? Again, in real-life situations you may need to think through circumstances like this rather quickly, and it won't be quite this easy. What you need to consider, however, is the use of the decision-making steps as a reminder for yourself that you have a strategy you can fall back on. The more you teach it to your child or children, the more automatic it will become for you in your own life.

Let's take a look at a more rapid use of decision making.

SITUATION 2:
DECISION MAKING TO SORT OUT ADULT RELATIONSHIPS

Imagine that you have just had a disagreement with your spouse or a close friend. You both are suffering through another of many periods of not talking to one another. You are beginning to feel more and more stuck in this conflict and you want to do something about it. As you are in the car, picking up your child from school, you get a chance to think about how decision making is shaping your child to be more and more capable at generating various alternative solutions. At this point you decide to do the same thing in your situation, that is, to use problem solving. You think to yourself:

1. Look for signs of different feelings.

2. Tell yourself what the problem is.

3. Decide on your goal.

   You think to yourself:

   Boy, do I have those first three steps down pat. I feel *hurt because* we're not talking and *I want* us to be close again.

4. Think of as many solutions as you can.

   Well, I could break the ice by kidding around.
   I could come right to the point and say that not talking is just not good for either of us and that we should start communicating better.
   I could bring up again the whole reason why we are disagreeing: my wanting to buy a new car.

Somewhere along the line, you are beginning to feel less sad about the "not talking" problem because you have started doing something constructive about the difficulty. *Decision making has helped you start resolving the situation.* We know it as a strategy that can have the effect of freeing you to take control of your problem. And being freed is a good feeling to have.

Decision Making For Me

We like having that feeling of being "unstuck" so much, that we truly practice what we preach. We've put the decision-making steps into a self-questioning format and we'd like to share that with you now. We call this work sheet, "Decision Making for Me." You might want to put a copy on your dresser at home, in your pocketbook, wallet, or glove compartment. The whole point is when you're confused or upset, referring to a concrete guide like Decision Making for Me can help.

Let's move to an example of how one parent used Decision Making for Me.

DECISION MAKING FOR ME

1. WHAT PART OF ME *FEELS* UNCOMFORTABLE?

   HOW AM I FEELING ABOUT WHAT'S HAPPENING?

2. WHAT *SPECIFICALLY* HAS BEEN OCCURRING THAT MAKES ME FEEL UNCOMFORTABLE?

3. BEING AS CLEAR AS I CAN BE, WHAT IS MY *GOAL?*

4. WHAT *SOLUTIONS* CAN I COME UP WITH THAT WILL HELP ME REACH MY GOAL?

5. WHAT MIGHT HAPPEN IF I _____ OR IF I _____?

6. WHICH SOLUTION SEEMS TO BE THE BEST ONE FOR ME?

7. I NEED A PLAN. HOW AND WHEN SHOULD I PUT MY SOLUTION INTO ACTION?

   WHAT POSSIBLE OBSTACLES ARE OUT THERE?

   HOW COULD I DEAL WITH THEM?

8. OKAY. TIME TO TRY OUT MY SOLUTION. I'LL SEE HOW IT GOES.

TIME MANAGEMENT:
GAIL REDUCES HER STRESS

It's another busy Saturday in Gail's thirty-five-year-old life. It's 1 P.M. and she's at home with her third grader Wendy. Her husband, Howard, is outside putting a quart of oil in the car. In her head Gail starts to consider the long list of chores that she's assigned to herself this afternoon. This includes:

> You must return those books to the library!
> You have to go to the supermarket for milk, meat, and eggs!
> You have to get a gift for Mom's birthday party tonight.
> You really should help Wendy with her science project too.

As Gail goes to the refrigerator to get Wendy a glass of juice, unpleasant feelings bubble up in her. They begin to intensify and Gail experiences it now as a mild headache. She decides to use the same steps she's been teaching Wendy on and off for the last few months. Gail decides to slow down a moment to practice what she's been teaching.

Decision Making for Me (Gail)

1. WHAT PART OF ME FEELS UNCOMFORTABLE?
   My forehead. I've got the start of a headache.
   HOW AM I FEELING ABOUT WHAT'S HAPPENING?
   I feel overwhelmed . . . rushed too. I'm beginning to not like Saturday and I don't like that feeling.

2. WHAT SPECIFICALLY HAS BEEN OCCURRING THAT MAKES ME FEEL UNCOMFORTABLE?
   I feel pressured because I've been giving myself too many things to do.

3. BEING AS CLEAR AS I CAN, WHAT IS MY GOAL?
   You know, that is my real difficulty. I have too many *goals*. I don't *have* to do any of those things, really. The only one that's really important to me is getting a gift for Mom. The library and science project will just have to wait. If I have enough time I'll pick up some food on the way home. I am not a superhero!

4. WHAT SOLUTIONS CAN I COME UP WITH THAT WILL HELP ME REACH MY GOAL?

   Why complicate things, why don't I just go and buy Mom the vase and pick up a few things at the supermarket on the way home?

   Howard and I saw a blue vase last Saturday at that new store that just opened. Mom'd love it. Howard could buy the vase and I'll do some food shopping.

   I could ask Howard to do the food shopping and I'll go buy the vase.

5. WHAT MIGHT HAPPEN IF I _____ OR IF I _____?

   Why should I rush around so much? I'd like to take my time and either shop for Mom *or* shop for food . . . not both!

   The blue vase might be sold. If it is, I'd rather be the person to buy the gift for Mom, not have Howard do it.

   It'll be easier if Howard shops for the food and I go for the vase. I'll have both jobs done then.

6. WHICH SOLUTION SEEMS TO BE THE BEST ONE FOR ME?

   The last one I just thought of.

7. I NEED A PLAN. HOW AND WHEN SHOULD I PUT MY SOLUTION INTO ACTION?

   While Wendy's finishing her juice I'll go outside and ask Howard to go to the food store. I'll make a quick list of just a few items. I'll offer to take Wendy with me if that'd be easier for him.

   WHAT POSSIBLE OBSTACLES ARE OUT THERE?

   Howard may not be able to go food shopping. He may have some work he needs to do here.

   HOW COULD I DEAL WITH THEM?

   Well, just like I thought in the beginning. Getting the food can wait until tomorrow. We have enough for dinner and breakfast.

8. OKAY. TIME TO TRY OUT MY SOLUTION. I'LL SEE HOW IT GOES.

Because we know about this situation, we can tell you. Howard agreed to go food shopping. But . . . he wanted to take Wendy because she knew where everything was. Gail centered on one of the key problems that many of us busy adults have: narrowing down our goals. It's not easy because it means that we have to let go of some of the things that we really want to have happen. But to be able to handle the stresses of our busy lives as parents, workers, sons, daughters, and friends, we have to be reasonable and kind to ourselves. In the kind of situation Gail was in, narrowing down her goals may have sufficed as far as deliberate decision making was concerned. The rest of the day's and evening's activities looked more reasonable to Gail without her needing to operate in a rush, getting in and out of the car several times, and so on.

Decision-Making Digest

In keeping with the theme of the final chapter, we need to look at goals one more time. You've been preparing your child to act with confidence and skill. Your youngster now has some thinking techniques that we feel can serve him or her well when he or she is under stress. Just as you gradually and supportively let go of your child so your child can practice what's been learned, *you* need to do the same. Feelings, problems, goals, solutions, consequences, choices, plans, and action are ideas you are comfortable with now. They are ideas that can easily reside with one another in your way of approaching difficulties.

Selecting a gift and then happily giving it, as it sounds as if Gail was doing for her mother, is a sign of real caring. Decision making is also a gift that you have been giving your child and will continue to give. It has taken time to read about decision making and to do some of the problem-solving exercises with your child that were suggested, time that you have taken away from other activities. But you set your priorities and made that decision. You have grown as a parent. You have acted on your realization that one of your jobs is to prepare your child for the real world, when he or she will be wanting to operate successfully on his or her own. You can feel more comfortable if your child practices some of the skills you have been teaching, because he or she will be much less likely to feel helpless when confronted by problems or decisions. You have done a lot to teach your child decision making.

Index

A

Academic performance, 134–38, 303–7

See also Education; School

Acceptance and acknowledgment, 73–74, 99–100, 126–27, 147–48, 171–72, 199–200

Action. *See* Trying and rethinking

Activities. *See* Family activities

Ad Attack, 128–29, 140

Adolescents, 27, 95, 127, 249, 251–55

communication with, 255–69

and decisions about the future, 266–68

and the parental crystal ball, 255–56, 260, 263, 269

privacy needs of, 300–1

rules for dealing with, 260–65

signals sent by, 256–68

Adult decision making, 312–22

Advice

giver of, 10, 321

premature, 42

See also Suggestions

Age, 153, 182–83

early elementary school years, 27–29

and emotions, 95

later elementary school years, 29–31

and life issues, 322–24

and planning skills, 204–5

and problems faced, 26–43

and readiness for decision making, 47–48

and sibling conflicts, 161–65

See also Adolescents

Alcohol or drug use, 5

Alternative Alternatives, 153–54, 167

Anger. *See* Argument, looking for; Get Calm!

Approaching new friends, 239–40, 247

Approval or praise: accepting, 50, 59–60, 66

Argument: looking for, 257–58, 265

Asking. *See* Questions

Aspiring Architect, 207, 218

At the Barbershop, 132–33, 140

B

Back at the Diner, 131–32, 140

Barbershop, 132–33

Bathroom Blues, 211–12, 218

Beamers, 59

Be Proud of Your Work, 234–35

Body postures, 79

Books and stories: signs of feelings in, 75, 90

Breakfast: family
    activity with, 230, 232–33
    preparing, 198, 218
Breathing, 57, 58

C

Calendars, announcements, and
    newsletters, 310
Calming down. *See* Get Calm!
Car trips: family activities for
    Decisions Decisions, 182–83
    Driving in the Car, 180–81, 191
    Feelings on the Road, 81–82, 90
    Mapmaking and Path Planning,
        207–9, 218
    Predicting Peer Problems, 183–86,
        191
    Problems in the Car, 104–5, 115
    Route Planning, 206–7
    What If, 158–61, 167
Cereal Progression, 54–55, 66
Checkers, 201, 218
Checking. *See* Planning and checking
Chess, 201, 218
Children needing special long-term
    care, 270–90
Children's Choices Chart, 174–76,
    191, 275
Choosing. *See* Solution, choosing the
    best
Cigarette Smoking, 184–87, 191
Cliques, 30
Collaborators: parents as, 291–96,
    307–12
Communication, 274
    with adolescents, 255–69
    encouraging, 73, 97–99, 124–25,
        147–48, 170–71, 199–200
    and problem-solving atmosphere,
        39–43

and questions, 41–42
Concentration, 50
    and calming down, 57–59
Confidence, 47, 121, 180, 220, 232,
    314
    and age, 27, 28
    building, 224, 227
    and goals, 133
    rethinking to gain, 240–41
    thoughtful, 221
Consequences, 10, 321
    See also Solutions and
        consequences: thinking of
Costumes! Costumes!, 79, 90
Crystal ball, 255–56, 260, 263, 269
Current Events, 229–30, 247

D

Dares, 30
Date: first, 200–1, 218
Decision making
    with children needing special care,
        270–90
    and children's problems, 26–43
    and education, 291–312
    eight-step approach to: summarized,
        31–38
    for oneself, 312–22
    and parenting styles, 5–25, 250
    and problem-solving atmosphere,
        39–43
    readiness for, 47–66
    with teenagers, 251–69
    See also Feelings: signs of different;
        Goals: deciding on; Planning and
        checking; Problems: verbalizing;
        Solution: choosing the best;
        Solutions and consequences:
        thinking of; Trying and
        rethinking

Decision-Making Diary, 236–37, 238, 243, 247
Decisions Decisions, 182–83
Delinquency, 5
Detention Decision Making, 212–13, 218
Dewey, John, 91, 143
Diabetes, 270, 271, 274, 282, 289
and decision making, 275–77
and relationships with other children, 277–81
Diary for decision making, 236–37, 238
Different People Make Different Decisions, 177–78, 191
Dinnertime
family activity for, 233–34
stress preceding, 241–45
See also Restaurant meals: family activities for
Direction Following, 55–57, 62, 66
Disabilities: children with, 270–90
Dot-to-Dot, 201, 218
Double Check, 205–6, 218
Do Yourself Proud, 234–35, 247
Dreamers, 59
Driving in the Car, 180–81, 191
Drug or alcohol abuse, 5

E

Ears Ready!, 52–53, 62, 66
Eating out. *See* Restaurant meals: family activities for
Education, 250
academic performance issues in, 134–38, 303–7
and goal clarification, 294–96
and goal decisions, 134–38
parents as collaborators in, 291–96, 307–12

parent-teacher conferences, 296–303, 309
See also Homework; School
Eight-step decision-making approach
application of, 33–38
summary of, 31–33
See also Feelings: signs of different; Goals: deciding on; Planning and checking; Problems: verbalizing; Solution: choosing the best; Solutions and consequences: thinking of; Trying and rethinking
Elementary school. *See* School
Elicitor of Ideas, 10–11, 321
Embarrassment, 257, 263–64
Emotions
controlling, 57–59
noticing other children's, 51
and putting problems into words, 93–115
verbalizer of, 10, 13, 19, 321
See also Feelings: signs of different
Encouragement: home of, 224–29, 245
See also Communication: encouraging
Ending visits, 108–9
Exit Only, 108–9, 115
Eye contact, 39

F

Face saving, 257, 263–64
Facial expressions, 79
Family activities
for choosing the best solution, 174–86
for deciding on goals, 127–34
for planning and checking, 201–13
for readiness skills, 51–62

for recognizing signs of feelings,
74–82
for thinking of solutions and
consequences, 148–61
for trying and rethinking, 229–41
for verbalizing problems, 100–9
Family Goal, 243
Family Play, 230, 231, 247
Family Problem Solving, 236, 243,
246, 247
Family trips. *See* Car trips: family
activities for; Travel: family
activities for
Feelings: signs of different, 31, 32, 91,
92, 112, 117, 142, 170, 193, 220,
242, 258, 262, 286, 288, 326,
328
and everyday problems, 82–88
family activities to develop
recognition of, 74–82
helping children recognize, 72–74
importance of, 67–72, 88–89, 90
willingness to look for, 71
Feelings Detective, 77, 78, 89, 90
Feelings Fingerprints, 45, 72–73, 74,
82, 138, 241, 270, 294, 295, 300
Feelings Flashbacks, 76–77, 81, 82,
89, 90, 138, 241, 245
Feelings Footlights, 77, 79, 82, 89, 90
Feelings on the Road, 81–82, 90
Feelings Word List, 74–75, 82, 89, 90
Final check. *See* Planning and
checking
First date, 200–1, 218
First day of school, 198–99, 218
Following directions, 50, 55–57
Friends
approaching new, 239–40
choosing, 186–89
ending visits with, 108–9
inviting, 178–79

G

Generating alternative solutions, 141–
42
See also Solutions and
consequences: thinking of
Gentle Prodding, 222, 224, 226, 229,
232, 233, 247
types of, 227
Get Calm!, 57–59, 85, 119, 133, 138,
227, 243, 264
applications of, 62, 64, 66
description of, 57–59
Getting Someone's Attention, 239,
247
Giver of Advice, 10, 321
Goal
alternative, 141–42, 259
clarifying, 294–96
group, 133–34
reminding about, 227
visualizing, 176–77
See also Goals: deciding on
Goal analogies, 127, 140
Goal confusion, 120–21, 134, 138,
243
Goal Drill, 129, 140
Goals: deciding on, 31, 32, 117, 142,
193, 220, 258, 262, 326, 328
in everyday situations, 134–38
family activities to encourage, 127–
34
helping children with, 122–27
importance of, 116–21, 138–39
Goal X Ray, 128, 133–34, 138, 140,
243
Going to a Restaurant, 181–82, 191
Grandparents, 323–24
Group goals, 133–34

H

Haircut, 132–33
Health problems: children with, 270–90
Help: asking for
 and adolescent signals, 256–57, 261
 and readiness skills, 47–48, 50–51, 60–62
Helping Exchange, 61, 66
Helping Hand, 61–62, 66
Helping in the Media, 60, 66
Hesitation, 227
Hobby Probes, 101–2, 115
Home of encouragement, 224–29, 245
 See also Communication: encouraging
Homework, 304–6
 family activities to encourage, 103–4, 106, 115, 234–35
 and family goals, 134
 pride in, 234–35
Homework Time, 103–4, 106, 115
Humor, 126, 128

I

Improving Social Awareness-Social Problem Solving Project (ISA-SPS), 4
Impulsive acts, 141
 avoiding, 193
 consequences of, 192–93
Independence, 11, 19
Individualized educational planning meetings-special education students, 310
In Search of Soft Towels, 237, 247
Instant Replay, 53–54, 66

Insulin dependent diabetes mellitus. *See* Diabetes
Interview: anticipating, 198, 218
In the Spotlight, 77, 90
Inviting Friends Over, 178–79, 191

J

Jigsaw Puzzles, 129–30, 140
Junior high/senior high system, 30

L

Labels, 62, 71, 73, 85, 201–2
 Feelings Word List, 74–75
Laundromat, 237
Learning problems, 271, 285–90
Listening, 39–40, 242
 family activities to develop, 52–55
 as readiness skill, 50, 52–55
 to teenagers, 255, 257, 264–65, 269
List the Goods, 130, 140
Lost: planning how to deal with being, 210–11

M

Mall Detector, 80, 90
Mapmaking and Path Planning, 207–9, 218
Meals. *See* Breakfast: family; Dinnertime; Restaurant meals: family activities for
Media: activities using
 Ad Attack, 128–29, 140
 Current Events, 229–30
 Different People Make Different Decisions, 177–78
 Helping in the Media, 60, 66

Media Characters Make Choices
Too, 177, 191
Movie and TV Consequences, 158
Problems in the News, 100–1, 115
SHAVEing in the Movies, 80, 90
Weatherperson, 157–58, 167
Media Characters Make Choices Too,
177, 191
Menstruation, 30
Mirror, Mirror, 81, 90
Modeling, 130, 227
choosing the best solution, 171–72
deciding on goals, 122–23
generating alternatives and
consequences, 146–47, 148
in a Helping Exchange, 61
planning and checking, 198–99
putting problems into words, 96–97
sensitivity to feelings, 72–73
trying and rethinking, 224–26
Movie and TV Consequences, 158
Movies, SHAVEing in the, 80, 90

N

Nature Challenge, 107–8, 115
New experiences, 30, 132–33

O

Obstacles, 201
anticipating, 197, 203, 205–6, 220,
314–15
as normal occurrences, 200
Open-house—Orientation—Back-to-
school nights, 309
Opening, The, 228, 229, 233, 247
Other children's feelings: noticing, 51

P

Parenting Family Tree, 5, 11, 19–22,
25
form for, 23–24
Parenting style, 250
identifying one's own, 5–11
roots of, 11–25
Parenting Styles Activity (PSA), 6–11,
25, 313, 315, 316–21, 323
Parents
as collaborators in education
process, 291–96, 307–12
decision making for, 312–22
as stressors, 30
and teenagers, 251–69
See also Modeling
Parent-teacher conferences, 296–303,
309
Parent-teacher organizations and
associations, 309
Party Planning, 204–5, 218
Peer pressure, 30, 180, 259, 266
anticipating, 183–86
Piaget, Jean, 91
Pictures used to teach alternatives,
148–51, 167
Plan and Play, 202–3, 218
Planning and checking, 32, 33, 220,
262, 327
with everyday problems, 213–17
family activities to encourage, 201–
13
helping children with, 198–201
importance of, 192–98, 217, 218
Planning How to Deal with Being
Lost, 210–11, 218
Planning How to Deal with Strangers,
209–10, 218
Praise, 100, 199, 200

accepting, 50, 59–60, 66
Predicting Peer Problems, 183–86, 191
Predictive thinking, 142
Present: selecting, 130
Pride Check, 234–35, 247
Privacy, 39, 300–1
Problem Finding, 102–3, 115, 138
Problems: verbalizing, 31, 32, 117, 142, 170, 193, 220, 262, 274, 278, 326, 328
  in everyday situations, 110–13
  family activities to encourage, 100–9, 115
  helping children with, 96–100
  importance of, 91–96, 114
Problems at the Diner, 105, 107, 115
Problems in the Car, 104–5, 115
Problems in the News, 100–1, 115
Problem-solving atmosphere: creation of, 39–43
Prodding. *See* Gentle Prodding
Progress reports, 310
Psychological problems, 5
Puberty, 27
  See also Adolescents

Q

Questions, 130, 143, 147
  choices expressed with, 172
  communication aided by, 41–42
  expression of feelings encouraged by, 73
  expression of goals encouraged by, 124–25
  and independent thinking, 11
  overuse of, 40–41
  planning encouraged with, 199–200
  rephrased as statements, 41
  teenagers' decision making stimulated by, 260–65, 269
  verbalization of problems encouraged by, 97–99, 100
Quiet on the Set!, 77, 79, 90

R

Readiness, 47–50, 65–66
  evaluating, 50–51
  family activities to develop, 51–62
  used in everyday problems, 62–65
Real-Life Consequences, 10, 321
Recall Past Success, 240–41, 247
Recreation with the Family, 179–80, 191
Relative Enthusiasm, 81, 90
Relatives and friends: leaving from visits with, 108–9
Respect, 123, 174
Restaurant meals: family activities for
  Back at the Diner, 131–32
  Getting Someone's Attention, 239
  Going to a Restaurant, 181–82, 191
  Problems at the Diner, 105, 107, 115
  What If, 158–61
Rethinking. *See* Trying and rethinking
Rethink It with Roast, 233–34, 247
Road Block, 203–4, 218
Role Playing, 227, 229, 247
Route Planning, 206–7
Routine: changes in, 73
Run Through the Script, 79, 90

S

School
  early elementary years, 27–29
  first day of, 198–99, 218

and growing up, 26–31
later elementary years, 29–31
starting new, 292–96
See also Education; Homework
School handbooks, 310
School play, 200, 218
Scoliosis, 281–85, 289
Self-concept, 287–88
Self-confidence. *See* Confidence
Self-control. *See* Get Calm!
Sexual thoughts and feelings, 30
SHAVE, 79–80, 82, 89, 90
   at the mall, 80
   at the movies, 80
   with relatives, 81
Shopping, 181
Shopping lists, 198, 218
Sibling conflicts, 161–65
Signs of different feelings. *See*
   Feelings: signs of different
Simon Says, 56
Smiling Faces, 81, 90
Social awareness, 142
Social problems, 30
Socrates, 143
Solution: choosing the best, 32, 33,
   193, 220, 259, 262, 327
   for everyday problems, 186–89
   family activities to encourage, 174–
   86
   helping children with, 171–74
   importance of, 168–71, 190, 191
Solution review, 170, 172–73, 183,
   191
Solutions and consequences: thinking
   of, 31, 32, 170, 193, 220, 262,
   288, 298–99, 326–27, 328
   in everyday situations, 161–65
   family activities to encourage, 148–
   61
   helping children with, 145–48
   importance of, 141–45, 165–67

Sorting It Out, 294–96
Sound Detector, 54, 66
Special education students, 310
Special needs, 270–90
Steamers, 59
"Steptalk," 68–72, 92–96, 117–21,
   142–45, 168–71, 192–98, 220–24
Stories and books: signs of feelings in,
   75, 90
Story Stems, 151–53, 167
Strangers: planning how to deal with,
   209–10
Suggestions, 97–99, 124, 130, 147
Supermarket Scribe, 131, 140
Support: communicating need for,
   256, 261
Surgery, 271–74, 282–85

T

Team Goals, 133–34
Teasing, 183–84
Teenagers. *See* Adolescents
Television. *See* Media: activities using
Thinking, 123
   independent, 11
   predictive, 142
   and putting problems into words,
   91
   See also Solutions and
   consequences: thinking of; Trying
   and rethinking
Tic-Tac-Toe, 201, 218
Transitions, 37
Travel: family activities for
   Feelings on the Road, 81–82, 90
   Mapmaking and Path Planning,
   207–9, 218
   Planning How to Deal with Being
   Lost, 210–11

Planning How to Deal with
Strangers, 209–10, 218
Route Planning, 206–7
See also Car trips: family activities
for; Restaurant meals: family
activities for
Trips. *See* Car trips: family activities
for; Travel: family activities for
Trying and rethinking, 32, 33, 254,
260, 262, 327
with everyday problems, 241–45
family activities to encourage, 229–
41
helping children with, 224–29
importance of, 219–24, 246, 247
Try It with Toast, 230, 232–33, 247
TV and Movie Consequences, 158

U

Uncertainty, 227
See also Confidence
Using Pictures to Teach Alternatives,
148–51, 167

V

Vacations. *See* Car trips: family
activities for; Travel: family
activities for
Verbalizer of feelings, 10, 13, 19, 321
Verbalizing problems. *See* Problems:
verbalizing
Visits: ending, 108–9
Visualizing Your Goal, 176–77, 191
Vocabulary. *See* Labels

W

Walks: activities for
Decisions Decisions, 182–83
Nature Challenge, 107–8
Predicting Peer Problems, 183–86
Warm Up, 77
Weatherperson, 157–58, 167
What If, 158–61, 167

LIBRARY.
ST. LOUIS COMMUNITY COLLEGE
AT FLORISSANT VALLEY